# Virtual and Mobile Learning Activities in Higher Education

Lisbeth Amhag
*Malmö University, Sweden*

A volume in the Advances in Educational Technologies and Instructional Design (AETID) Book Series

IGI Global
PUBLISHER of TIMELY KNOWLEDGE

Published in the United States of America by
IGI Global
Information Science Reference (an imprint of IGI Global)
701 E. Chocolate Avenue
Hershey PA, USA 17033
Tel: 717-533-8845
Fax: 717-533-8661
E-mail: cust@igi-global.com
Web site: http://www.igi-global.com



Library of Congress Cataloging-in-Publication Data

Names: Amhag, Lisbeth, 1950- author.
Title: Virtual and mobile learning activities in higher education / by Lisbeth Amhag.
Description: Hershey, PA : Information Science Reference, 2020. | Includes bibliographical references and index. | Summary: "This book focuses on virtual and mobile learning activities in higher education for student-centered learning and in what way teachers can design and use different learning activities, both blended and mobile, for self-directed and motivated 'smart' education"-- Provided by publisher.
Identifiers: LCCN 2020001185 (print) | LCCN 2020001186 (ebook) | ISBN 9781799841838 (hardcover) | ISBN 9781799852872 (paperback) | ISBN 9781799841845 (ebook)
Subjects: LCSH: Education, Higher--Effect of technological innovations on. | Virtual reality in education. | Mobile communication systems in education.
Classification: LCC LB2395.7 .A627 2020 (print) | LCC LB2395.7 (ebook) | DDC 371.33--dc23
LC record available at https://lccn.loc.gov/2020001185
LC ebook record available at https://lccn.loc.gov/2020001186

This book is published in the IGI Global book series Advances in Educational Technologies and Instructional Design (AETID) (ISSN: 2326-8905; eISSN: 2326-8913)

British Cataloguing in Publication Data
A Cataloguing in Publication record for this book is available from the British Library.



For electronic access to this publication, please contact: eresources@igi-global.com.

# Advances in Educational Technologies and Instructional Design (AETID) Book Series

ISSN:2326-8905
EISSN:2326-8913

Editor-in-Chief: Lawrence A. Tomei, Robert Morris University, USA

## MISSION

Education has undergone, and continues to undergo, immense changes in the way it is enacted and distributed to both child and adult learners. In modern education, the traditional classroom learning experience has evolved to include technological resources and to provide online classroom opportunities to students of all ages regardless of their geographical locations. From distance education, Massive-Open-Online-Courses (MOOCs), and electronic tablets in the classroom, technology is now an integral part of learning and is also affecting the way educators communicate information to students.

The **Advances in Educational Technologies & Instructional Design (AETID) Book Series** explores new research and theories for facilitating learning and improving educational performance utilizing technological processes and resources. The series examines technologies that can be integrated into K-12 classrooms to improve skills and learning abilities in all subjects including STEM education and language learning. Additionally, it studies the emergence of fully online classrooms for young and adult learners alike, and the communication and accountability challenges that can arise. Trending topics that are covered include adaptive learning, game-based learning, virtual school environments, and social media effects. School administrators, educators, academicians, researchers, and students will find this series to be an excellent resource for the effective design and implementation of learning technologies in their classes.

## COVERAGE

- Instructional Design
- Classroom Response Systems
- Curriculum Development
- Social Media Effects on Education
- Educational Telecommunications
- Online Media in Classrooms
- Web 2.0 and Education
- Collaboration Tools
- Instructional Design Models
- Adaptive Learning

IGI Global is currently accepting manuscripts for publication within this series. To submit a proposal for a volume in this series, please contact our Acquisition Editors at Acquisitions@igi-global.com or visit: http://www.igi-global.com/publish/.

The Advances in Educational Technologies and Instructional Design (AETID) Book Series (ISSN 2326-8905) is published by IGI Global, 701 E. Chocolate Avenue, Hershey, PA 17033-1240, USA, www.igi-global.com. This series is composed of titles available for purchase individually; each title is edited to be contextually exclusive from any other title within the series. For pricing and ordering information please visit http://www.igi-global.com/book-series/advances-educational-technologies-instructional-design/73678. Postmaster: Send all address changes to above address. 

## Titles in this Series

*For a list of additional titles in this series, please visit:*
http://www.igi-global.com/book-series/advances-educational-technologies-instructional-design/73678

***Cognitive and Affective Perspectives on Immersive Technology in Education***
Robert Z. Zheng (The University of Utah, USA)
Information Science Reference • © 2020 • 337pp • H/C (ISBN: 9781799832508) • US $195.00

***Using Literature to Teach English as a Second Language***
Veronica Membrive (University of Almeria, Spain) and Madalina Armie (University of Almeria, Spain)
Information Science Reference • © 2020 • 267pp • H/C (ISBN: 9781799846703) • US $175.00

***Textbook Theory and Invariant Approaches to Language Learning Emerging Research and Opportunities***
Elena Orlova (Lobachevsky State University of Nizhny Novgorod, Russia)
Information Science Reference • © 2020 • 150pp • H/C (ISBN: 9781799826729) • US $145.00

***Examining Content and Language Integrated Learning (CLIL) Theories and Practices***
Liudmila Khalyapina (Peter the Great St. Petersburg Polytechnic University, Russia)
Information Science Reference • © 2020 • 325pp • H/C (ISBN: 9781799832669) • US $195.00

***Teaching Practices and Language Ideologies for Multilingual Classrooms***
Ashok Bhusal (The University of Texas at El Paso, USA)
Information Science Reference • © 2020 • 290pp • H/C (ISBN: 9781799833390) • US $195.00

***Handbook of Research on Online Discussion-Based Teaching Methods***
Lesley Wilton (University of Toronto, Canada) and Clare Brett (University of Toronto, Canada)
Information Science Reference • © 2020 • 536pp • H/C (ISBN: 9781799832928) • US $265.00

*For an entire list of titles in this series, please visit:*
http://www.igi-global.com/book-series/advances-educational-technologies-instructional-design/73678

IGI Global
PUBLISHER of TIMELY KNOWLEDGE

701 East Chocolate Avenue, Hershey, PA 17033, USA
Tel: 717-533-8845 x100 • Fax: 717-533-8661
E-Mail: cust@igi-global.com • www.igi-global.com

# Table of Contents

# Preface

In my research and review of several peer reviewed articles in these book, show that higher education faces major challenges both pedagogically and technically (Amhag, 2011; 2012; 2013a; 2013b; 2016a; 2016b; 2017; 2020; Amhag, Hellström & Stigmar, 2019; Amhag & Jakobsson, 2009). In the articles provides several opportunities to design and teach for self-directed and motivated higher education with smart pedagogy in a resource-enriched virtual learning environment, VLE through technology-embedded blended prerequisite and activities across various dimensions, including the notion that students can learn self-directed at anywhere and anytime, and easily switch learning contexts to another or a variety of scenarios. These blended learning activities combines both in- and out-off the university and during practical training in the profession by using face-to-face, F2F classroom lessons, teacher-recorded flipped lesson videos and mobile online webinars F2F with chat communications that contribute to increase internationalization, globalization and digitization of higher education.

An important factor for successful integration of virtual and mobile learning activities in higher education is, above all, that teachers can identify the pedagogical and the technological benefits in their teaching and learning contexts with wearable tools to enhance student-centered learning and active participation at anytime and anywhere. Therefore, the perception of teachers in higher education are of great significance because they have a fundamental role in teaching and serve as role models for virtual and mobile learning activities among students with different wearable tools, lecture material, lecture recordings, online face-to-face webinars, F2F, chat, discussion forums, and other online resources i.e. interactive white-board (Amhag, 2016a; 2016b; 2017; 2020). The following questions would be answered in each chapter:

- In what way can teachers a) design and b) use different virtual and mobile learning activities and wearable tools that are appropriate for student-centered learning and active participation?
- How do the students experience the virtual and mobile activities and the wearable tools for their learning?
- In what way can the virtual and mobile activities and tools be analyzed comparing to the students' performance?

In Chapter 1, focus is on Smart Mobile Learning Activities in higher education. There is no existing tool that evaluates teachers' perceptions of mobile learning (m-learning), therefore innovative solutions are needed of using wearable tools for student-centered learning and active participation. Important is the use of smart education and smart technology to develop professionally the courses in higher education about underlying pedagogical perspectives and didactic strategies (Amhag, 2016a; 206b; Baran, 2014). Methodically, illustrates two frameworks, one with three distinctive features of m-learning (Kearney, Schuck, Burden & Aubusson, 2012) and one with dialogic levels, to highlight and explore the experiences of mobile learning. Theoretically, the analysis of 40 students' contributions (N=919) (Amhag, 2011; 2012; Amhag & Jakobsson, 2009) is based on Bakhtin's (1981; 1986/2004) specific approach to understand dialogues and Toulmin's argument pattern, TAP (1958). The results show that teachers' digital competence consists of, among other things, dealing with different digital devices and its software to use wearable technology for pedagogical purposes and to enhance student-centred learning. Central is to enhance understanding of the skills, dispositions, assignments, tutoring and examinations with focus on knowledge for teaching-learning contexts where students' communication and active participation with resource-enriched and technology-embedded activities is increasingly pivotal.

In Chapter 2 focus is on Smart Mobile Learning Environment in higher education to promote academic studies and professional training in higher education, both blended prerequisite and activities across various dimensions (Amhag & Jakobsson, 2009; Chen et al., 2016; Couros, 2006; Gros, 2016). The design of a smart mobile learning hub, MLH goes beyond simply adding new teaching, learning, and assessment strategies to an existing course. Instead, it is shown as a portfolio for smart learning and how it can be organized through a smart mobile learning environment (Hwang, 2014; Hwang, Lai & Wang, 2015; Spector, 2014). Methodically, it illustrates and analyses a smart mobile learning hub, MLH for student-centered learning both in- and out-off the university and during practical training in the profession by using smart devices such as mobile laptop, tablet or smartphone (Amhag, 2016a; 2016b). Theoretically, the analysis joins the research tradition of Computer Supported Collaborative Learning (Wenger, 1998), complemented with Computer Self-Efficacy (Bandura, 1977; 1982; 1984; 2002; Compeau & Higgins, 1995). The excerpts demonstrate that is it highly important for the design of a smart learning environment to motivate different students, recognising their competencies, learning styles and interests for academic studies, both theoretically and practically for the future profession.

In Chapter 3 focus is on Smart Learning With Seamless Activities in higher education and the design of smart education both in and out of classroom in online webinars with verbal face-to-face, F2F communications and parallel textual chat exchanges with other students and teachers for their seamless flipped learning and teaching (Amhag, 2016a; 2016b; 2017; 2020; Chen, Cheng & Chew, 2016). The chapter demonstrates in representative excerpts seamless activities and how they can increase student-centered learning and bridge between smart pedagogy and intelligent technologies in different professional teaching practices. Methodically these conditions are compared by using wireless technologies such as laptops, tablets, and smartphones accessible from different locations at anytime and anywhere (Hwang, 2014; Zhu, Yu & Riezebos, 2016). Theoretically, the analysis is based on the concept of mobile-assisted seamless learning activities, MSL based on six dimensions of actual learning (Wong, Chai, Aw & King, 2015; Wong & Looi, 2011). The results are raising some challenges and implications presented by using smart learning environment to expand smart learning, active participation and collaboration across different contexts for creation of smart education.

In Chapter 4 focus is on Peer Learning Activities in Smart Education and in what ways various peer learning methods can be a tool for students learning and development in a formative and creative way in smart higher education. The chapter describes various peer methods and peer learning activities (Amhag, 2013b; Boud, Cohen & Sampson, 2001a; 2001b; 2001c; Topping, 2005) and the way peer activities can contribute to complex types of academic works, which heavily relies on the active role of teachers when the nature of online settings promotes self-directed and self-regulated learning. Methodically, there is a comparative design of various peer learning strategies and activities and how they can contribute to student-centered learning for self-directed and motivated smart higher education. Theoretically, the comparative analysis is based on socio-cultural theory by using dimensions of community of practice (Wenger, 1998) and the zone of the proximal development (Vygotsky, 1978;

Del Rio and Alvarez, 2007) for student-centered learning to address the course content itself, i.e. what the student know, what they can do, and where they are aiming to be. The results demonstrate that the approach of peer learning activities is a key factor to consider and adapt the courses special features, its learning goals and learning outcomes, and the educational environment in which the peer learning activities will takes place, and in- and out of the university or both. Positively correlated with academic learning, the outcomes in a mobile setting have teachers' strategies of time and place.

In Chapter 5 focus is on Peer Feedback Activities in Smart Education and how peer feedback processes can support student-centered learning toward higher-order thinking and critical ability (Evans, 2013; Topping, Smith, Swanson & Elliot, 2000; Wiliam, 2011; 2013). Important benefits of implementing peer feedback between students is that the feedback becomes available faster during the course, and that more analysis, strengths and weaknesses, or alternative strategies for improvement are available earlier than the teachers could ever provide, as well as an intermediate step for self-assessment is organized when they evaluate their own work. Methodically, various types of feedback are given, based on review of selected articles from previous research. The qualitative empirical data of feedback processes (N=155) among 22 students was grounded on criteria and guidance on feedback for collaborative learning (Amhag, 2013b). Methodically, the feedback design was grounded on criteria based on Dysthe, Hertzberg and Løkensgard Hoel (2011) and Sadlers (1998) three components of self-assessment. Theoretically, the two-phase analysis is grounded on the assessment cycle with six activities by Reinholz (2016) and the model of feedback by Hattie and Timperley (2007) with four levels of feedback to reduce the gap between where the students are, and where they are aiming to be. The results demonstrate that the power of the social value and development of peer feedback are one of the most critical and self-directed impacts on student-centered learning and higher-order thinking and critical ability in smart higher education.

In Chapter 6 focus is on Reflection and Self-Assessment in Smart Education to motivate reflection and self-assessment as a further integral part of the professional educational training with critical incidents about a situation, incident, or issue for encouraging the students to find their own ways of learning and to act and think critically and professionally (Amhag, 2020). The concept of reflection is common to a number of learning theories, but they have different meanings and implications and reflective methods are not often used (Dewey 1938/1997; Jordi, 2011; McIntosh, 2010; Schön, 1987). Methodically, selected reviewed articles show a number of different focus and common terms of reflection and related ideas from theories by associated authors. Theoretically, the analysis of six students' digital log journals during their school, created on practical training courses, is based on Bain, Ballantyne, Mills and Lesters (2002) five 'R's' major levels of reflection: *reporting, responding, relating, reasoning* and *reconstructing* and Tomkins (2009) steps: *noticing, making sense*, and *making meaning*, as well as *working with meaning*. The qualitative data from the log journals demonstrate the importance of letting students have agency and mediate their subjective knowledge experiences in progression, in a resource-enriched learning environment with technology-embedded tools, to understand and make sense of experience in relation to self, others, and contextual conditions for personal and professional learning.

In Chapter 7 focus is on Virtual Learning in Smart Education to expand the knowledge about virtual learning environment, VLE and virtual reality, VR and how the learning processes can be a tool for motivated and student-centered learning in a resource-enriched environment with technology-embedded tools. Virtual reality, VR can be defined as a computer-generated simulation of a three-dimensional image or virtual learning environment, VLE with which a person can interact with different tools (Kennedy & Dunn, 2018). Methodologically, selected reviewed articles show that VLE and VR are a relatively broad concept and are often used in the areas of education, special education and motivation (Ott & Freina, 2015). Theoretically, the analysis of the answers of an open question (N=57) among teacher educators (N=105) about what kind of education they need for using a virtual learning environment with different tools (Amhag, Hellström, & Stigmar, 2019) is based on the TPACK model by Koehler, Mishra and Cain (2013) with a focus on the technological, pedagogical and content knowledge, as well as complemented with Gees (2007) five learning principles. The findings highlight that higher education and academic researchers have much to learn about teaching and learning in a virtual learning environment and in virtual reality that can enhance student-centered learning and discover the pedagogical surplus value in their own teaching and learning context through the use of technology in an educational purpose.

## REFERENCES

Amhag, L. (2011). *Students' Argument Patterns in Asynchronous Dialogues for Learning. In Research Highlights in Technology and Teacher Education 2011*. Society for Information Technology & Teacher Education.

Amhag, L. (2012). High school students' argument patterns in online peer feedback. Handbook of Research on Didactic Strategies and Technologies for Education: Incorporating Advancements, 2, 711-723.

Amhag, L. (2013a). High school students' argument patterns in online peer feedback. *K-12 Education. Concepts, Methodologies, Tools, andApplications*, *1*, 209–221.

Amhag, L. (2013b). *Creativity in and between Collaborative Peer Assessment Processes in Higher Distance Education. Creative Education, 4(7A2),* 94–104. doi:10.4236/ce.2013.47A2011

Amhag, L. (2016a). Mobile technologies for student centered learning in a distance higher education program. In *Wearable Technology and Mobile Innovations for Next-Generation Education,* (pp. 184-199). IGI Global. https://www.igi-global.com/book/wearable-technology-mobile-innovations-next/142108

Amhag, L. (2016b). Mobile technologies for student centered learning in a distance higher education program. *Blended Learning: Concepts, Methodologies, Tools, and Applications*, *4*, 802–817. doi:10.4018/978-1-5225-0069-8.ch010

Amhag, L. (2017). Mobile-Assisted Seamless Learning Activities in Higher Distance Education. *International Journal of Higher Education*, *6*(3), 2017. doi:10.5430/ijhe.v6n3p70

Amhag, L. (2020). Student Reflections and Self-Assessments in Vocational Training Supported by a Mobile Learning Hub. *International Journal of Mobile and Blended Learning*, *12*(1), 1–16. doi:10.4018/IJMBL.2020010101

Amhag, L., Hellström, L., & Stigmar, M. (2019). Teacher Educators' Use of Digital Tools and Needs for Digital Competence in Higher Education. *Journal of Digital Learning in Teacher Education*, *35*(4), 203–220. doi:10.1080/21532974.2019.1646169

Amhag, L., & Jakobsson, A. (2009). Collaborative Learning as a Collective Competence when Students Use the Potential of Meaning in Asynchronous Dialogues. *Computers & Education*, *52*(3), 656–667. doi:10.1016/j.compedu.2008.11.012

Bain, J.D., Ballantyne, R., Mills, C. & Lester, N.C. (2002). *Reflecting on practice: Student teachers' perspectives*. Flaxton: Post Pressed.

Bakhtin, M. M. (1981). *The Dialogic Imagination: Four Essays by M. M. Bakhtin* (C. Emerson & M. Holquist, Trans.). Austin: University of Texas Press.

Bakhtin, M. M. (1986/2004). Speech Genres & Other Late Essays (V. W. McGee, Trans.; Vol. 9). Austin: University of Texas Press.

Bandura, A. (1977). Self-efficacy: Toward a unifying theory of behavioral change. *Psychological Review*, *84*(2), 191–215. doi:10.1037/0033-295X.84.2.191 PMID:847061

Bandura, A. (1982). Self-efficacy mechanism in human agency. *The American Psychologist*, *37*(2), 122–147. doi:10.1037/0003-066X.37.2.122

Bandura, A. (1984). Recycling Misconceptions of Perceived Self-efficacy. *Cognitive Therapy and Research*, *8*(3), 231–255. doi:10.1007/BF01172995

Bandura, A. (2002). Growing primacy of human agency in adaption and change in the electronic era. *European Psychologist*, *7*(1), 2–16. doi:10.1027//1016-9040.7.1.2

Baran, E. (2014). A review of research on mobile learning in teacher education. *Journal of Educational Technology & Society*, *17*(4), 17.

Boud, D., Cohen, R., & Sampson, J. (2001a). Peer learning in higher education: Learning from and with each other. In Introduction: Making the move to peer learning. Routledge.

Boud, D., Cohen, R., & Sampson, J. (2001b). Peer learning in higher education: Learning from and with each other. In Designing peer learning. Routledge.

Boud, D., Cohen, R., & Sampson, J. (2001c). Peer learning in higher education: Learning from and with each other. In Strategies for peer learning: some examples. Routledge.

Chatti, M. A., Agustiawan, M. R., Jarke, M., & Specht, M. (2010). Toward a personal learning environment framework. *International Journal of Virtual and Personal Learning Environments*, *1*(4), 66–85. doi:10.4018/jvple.2010100105

Chen, N. S., Cheng, I. L., & Chew, S. W. (2016). Evolution is not enough: Revolutionizing current learning environments to smart learning environments. *International Journal of Artificial Intelligence in Education*, *26*(2), 561–581. doi:10.100740593-016-0108-x

Compeau, D. R., & Higgins, C. A. (1995). Computer self-efficacy: Development of measure and initial test. *Management Information Systems Quarterly*, *19*(2), 189–211. doi:10.2307/249688

Couros, A. V. (2006). *Examining the open movement: Possibilities and implications for education* (Dissertation). University of Regina.

Del Rio, P., & Alvarez, A. (2007). Inside and Outside the Zone of Proximal Development. An Ecofunctional Reading of Vygotsky. In The Cambridge Companion to Vygotsky (pp. 276-303). Cambridge: Cambridge University Press.

Dewey, J. (1997). *Experience and Education*. New York: Touchstone. (Original work published 1938)

Dysthe, O., Hertzberg, F., & Løkensgard Hoel, T. (2011). *Skriva för att lära. Skrivande i högre utbildning* [Writing to learn: Writing in Higher Education] (2nd ed.; S. Andersson, Trans.). Lund: Studentlitteratur.

Evans, C. (2013). Making sense of assessment feedback in higher education. *Review of Educational Research*, *83*(1), 70–120. doi:10.3102/0034654312474350

Gee, J. P. (2007). *What Video Games Have to Teach us About Learning and Literacy*. New York, NY: Palgrave Macmillan.

Gros, B. (2016). The design of smart educational environments. *Smart Learning Environments*, *3*(1), 15. doi:10.118640561-016-0039-x

Hattie, J., & Timperley, H. (2007). The power of feedback. *Review of Educational Research*, *77*(1), 81–112. doi:10.3102/003465430298487

Hwang, G. J. (2014). Definition, framework and research issues of smart learning environments – a context-aware ubiquitous learning perspective. *Smart Learning Environments*, *1*(1), 4. doi:10.118640561-014-0004-5

Hwang, G. J., Lai, C. L., & Wang, S. Y. (2015). Seamless flipped learning: A mobile technology-enhanced flipped classroom with effective learning strategies. *Journal of Computers in Education*, *2*(4), 449–473. doi:10.100740692-015-0043-0

Jordi, R. (2011). Reframing the concept of reflection: Consciousness, experiential learning, and reflective learning practices. *Adult Education Quarterly*, *61*(2), 181–197. doi:10.1177/0741713610380439

Kearney, M., Schuck, S., Burden, K., & Aubusson, P. (2012). Viewing mobile learning from a pedagogical perspective. *Research in Learning Technology*, *20*(1), n1. doi:10.3402/rlt.v20i0.14406

Kennedy, M., & Dunn, T. J. (2018). *Improving the use of technology enhanced learning environments in higher education in the UK: A qualitative visualisation of students' views*. Contemporary Educational Technology.

Koehler, M. J., Mishra, P., & Cain, W. (2013). What is technological pedagogical content knowledge (TPACK)? *Journal of Education*, *193*(3), 13–19. doi:10.1177/002205741319300303

Koschmann, T. (1996). Paradigm shifts and instructional technology: An introduction. *CSCL: Theory and Practice of an Emerging Paradigm*, *12*(4), 18-19.

McIntosh, P. (2010). *Action research and reflective practice*. London: Routledge. doi:10.4324/9780203860113

Ott, M., & Freina, L. (2015). A Literature Review on Immersive Virtual Reality in Education: State Of The Art and Perspectives. *The 11th International Scientific Conference eLearning and Software for Education.*

Reinholz, D. (2016). The assessment cycle: A model for learning through peer assessment. *Assessment & Evaluation in Higher Education*, *41*(2), 301–315. doi:10.1080/02602938.2015.1008982

Sadler, D. R. (1989). Formative assessment and the design of instructional systems. *Instructional Science*, *18*(2), 119–144. doi:10.1007/BF00117714

Schön, D. (1987). Educating the Reflective Practitioner. Jossey-Bass Publishers.

Spector, J. M. (2014). Conceptualizing the emerging field of smart learning environments. *Smart Learning Environments*, *1*(1), 2.

Tomkins, A. (2009). "It was a great day when…": An exploratory case study of reflective learning through storytelling. *Journal of Hospitality, Leisure, Sport and Tourism Education*, *8*(2), 123–131. doi:10.3794/johlste.82.198

Topping, K. J. (2005). Trends in peer learning. *Educational Psychology, 25*(6), 631–645. doi:10.1080/01443410500345172

Topping, K. J., Smith, E. F., Swanson, I., & Elliot, A. (2000). Formative peer assessment of academic writing between postgraduate students. *Assessment & Evaluation in Higher Education, 25*(2), 149–169. doi:10.1080/713611428

Vygotsky, L. S. (1978). *Mind in Society: Development of Higher Psychological Processes* (M. Cole, Trans.). Academic Press.

Wegerif, R. (2007). *Dialogic education and technology: Expanding the space of learning* (Vol. 7). Springer Science & Business Media. doi:10.1007/978-0-387-71142-3

Wenger, E. (1998). *Communities of Practice - Learning, Meaning, and Identity*. New York: Cambridge University Press. doi:10.1017/CBO9780511803932

Wiliam, D. (2011). What is assessment for learning? *Studies in Educational Evaluation, 37*(1), 3–14. doi:10.1016/j.stueduc.2011.03.001 PMID:22114905

Wiliam, D. (2013). Assessment: The bridge between teaching and learning. *Voices from the Middle, 21*(2), 15.

Wong, L. H., Chai, C. S., Aw, G. P., & King, R. B. (2015). Enculturating seamless language learning through artifact creation and social interaction process. *Interactive Learning Environments, 23*(2), 130–157. doi:10.1080/10494820.2015.1016534

Wong, L. H., & Looi, C. K. (2011). What seams do we remove in mobile-assisted seamless learning? A critical review of the literature. *Computers & Education, 57*(4), 2364–2381. doi:10.1016/j.compedu.2011.06.007

Zhu, Z. T., Yu, M. H. & Riezebos, P. (2016). A research framework of smart education. *Smart Learning Environments, 3*(1), 4.

# Introduction

The seven chapters in this book are focusing on virtual and mobile learning activities in higher education for student-centered learning and in what way teachers can design and use different learning activities, both blended and mobile, for self-directed and motivated 'smart' education. Another focus is on how the students perceive the activities and how the outcomes can be analysed using with adaptive, resource-enriched, and technology-embedded tools and intelligent technologies that are appropriate for students learning and active participation. The word 'smart' is an acronym for self-directed, motivated, adaptive, resource-enriched, and technology-embedded, and refers to wisdom as bounding together the ability of using and motivating self-directed learning, knowledge building, problem solving, critically reflections, collaborating and evaluating different circumstances with resource-enriched and technology-embedded tools (Hwang, 2014; Zhu, Yu & Riezebos, 2016).

Digitization has undergone a number of paradigm shifts over some decades where structures, processes and behaviours have changed from the ground, both in research, in education and in the society (Koschmann, 1996; Wegerif, 2007). Smart mobile and smart television are usually used in our society and our daily speech, in this book, also smart mobile learning activities, smart education, smart pedagogy and smart learning in higher education are mentioned. The use of technology-enhanced learning, TEL has increased – from a centralized technology-push strategy where the learning content is only used by a predefined group of students (Chatti, Agustiawan, Jarke & Specht, 2010) – to be delivered via a virtual learning environment as a gateway to a variety of resource-enriched and technology-embedded tools, such as lecture material, lecture recordings and / or images, online face-to-face webinars, F2F, online quizzes, chat, blogs, discussion forums, and other online resources, i.e. interactive white-board (Amhag, 2016a; 2016b; 2017; 2020).

Since 2002, I have served as a university teacher, course leader and examiner/ assessor both in Teacher Education at distance and on campus and in further education of teachers, as well as in graduate courses and undergraduate levels in the field of Education. My research has focus on computer-supported collaborative learning, formative peer assessment processes and interactive mobile learning activities among students in higher education and at distance. I have also been a part of the editorial board during 2013-2018 of the journal Educational research in Sweden, http://pedagogiskforskning.se. For my university teaching at distance, I received Malmö University Teaching Award 2010 with the students' motivation: "She has a great capacity to teach at distance and is fully conversant with digital communication. She is knowledgeable, serious, demanding and which is very stimulating for us students. Her open approach in daily contact with us makes you always feel welcome with questions and opinions."

All chapters in this book are based on own research studies based on previous research about virtual and mobile learning activities with different smart devices such as laptops, tablets, virtual glasses, and smartphones (Amhag, 2011; 2012; 2013a; 2013b; 2016a; 2016b; 2017; 2020; Amhag, Hellström & Stigmar, 2019; Amhag & Jakobsson, 2009). In the chapters, I will highlight the results of my research in relation to previous and recent research in the fields of interactive virtual and mobile learning activities, computer-supported collaborative learning, formative peer assessment processes among students in higher education. The selected articles for the review are from searches in different databases in education and social sciences and Libsearch that allow searching at almost all library databases, such as Web of Knowledge, ERIC, Scopus and Google Scholar, as well as from studies cited by these authors of the articles and from previous used peer review articles published in the current field with relevant keywords for each focus of the article.

## REFERENCES

Amhag, L. (2011). *Students' Argument Patterns in Asynchronous Dialogues for Learning. I SITEs Research Book 2011. In Research Highlights in Technology and Teacher Education 2011*. Society for Information Technology & Teacher Education.

Amhag, L. (2012). High school students' argument patterns in online peer feedback. Handbook of Research on Didactic Strategies and Technologies for Education: Incorporating Advancements, 2, 711-723.

Amhag, L. (2013a). High school students' argument patterns in online peer feedback. *K-12 Education. Concepts, Methodologies, Tools, and Applications, 1*, 209–221.

Amhag, L. (2013b). *Creativity in and between Collaborative Peer Assessment Processes in Higher Distance Education. I Creative Education, 4(7A2).* doi:10.4236/ce.2013.47A2011

Amhag, L. (2016a). Mobile technologies for student centered learning in a distance higher education program. In *Wearable Technology and Mobile Innovations for Next-Generation Education,* (pp. 184-199). IGI Global. https://www.igi-global.com/book/wearable-technology-mobile-innovations-next/142108

Amhag, L. (2016b). Mobile technologies for student centered learning in a distance higher education program. *Blended Learning: Concepts, Methodologies, Tools, and Applications, 4*, 802–817. doi:10.4018/978-1-5225-0069-8.ch010

Amhag, L. (2017). Mobile-Assisted Seamless Learning Activities in Higher Distance Education. *International Journal of Higher Education, 6*(3), 2017. doi:10.5430/ijhe.v6n3p70

Amhag, L. (2020). Student Reflections and Self-Assessments in Vocational Training Supported by a Mobile Learning Hub. *International Journal of Mobile and Blended Learning, 12*(1), 1–16. doi:10.4018/IJMBL.2020010101

Amhag, L., Hellström, L., & Stigmar, M. (2019). Teacher Educators' Use of Digital Tools and Needs for Digital Competence in Higher Education. *Journal of Digital Learning in Teacher Education, 35*(4), 203–220. doi:10.1080/21532974.2019.1646169

Amhag, L., & Jakobsson, A. (2009). Collaborative Learning as a Collective Competence when Students Use the Potential of Meaning in Asynchronous Dialogues. *Computers & Education, 52*(3), 656–667. doi:10.1016/j.compedu.2008.11.012

Bain, J.D., Ballantyne, R., Mills, C. & Lester, N.C. (2002). *Reflecting on practice: Student teachers' perspectives*. Flaxton: Post Pressed.

Bakhtin, M. M. (1981). *The Dialogic Imagination: Four Essays by M. M. Bakhtin* (C. Emerson & M. Holquist, Trans.). University of Texas Press.

Bakhtin, M. M. (1986/2004). Speech Genres & Other Late Essays (V. W. McGee, Trans., Vol. 9). Austin, TX: University of Texas Press.

Bandura, A. (1977). Self-efficacy: Toward a unifying theory of behavioral change. *Psychological Review*, *84*(2), 191–215. doi:10.1037/0033-295X.84.2.191 PMID:847061

Bandura, A. (1982). Self-efficacy mechanism in human agency. *The American Psychologist*, *37*(2), 122–147. doi:10.1037/0003-066X.37.2.122

Bandura, A. (1984). Recycling Misconceptions of Perceived Self-efficacy. *Cognitive Therapy and Research*, *8*(3), 231–255. doi:10.1007/BF01172995

Bandura, A. (2002). Growing primacy of human agency in adaption and change in the electronic era. *European Psychologist*, *7*(1), 2–16. doi:10.1027//1016-9040.7.1.2

Baran, E. (2014). A review of research on mobile learning in teacher education. *Journal of Educational Technology & Society*, *17*(4), 17.

Boud, D., Cohen, R., & Sampson, J. (2001a). Peer learning in higher education: Learning from and with each other. In Introduction: Making the move to peer learning. Routledge.

Boud, D., Cohen, R., & Sampson, J. (2001b). Peer learning in higher education: Learning from and with each other. In Designing peer learning. Routledge.

Boud, D., Cohen, R., & Sampson, J. (2001c). Peer learning in higher education: Learning from and with each other. In Strategies for peer learning: some examples. Routledge.

Chatti, M. A., Agustiawan, M. R., Jarke, M., & Specht, M. (2010). Toward a personal learning environment framework. *International Journal of Virtual and Personal Learning Environments*, *1*(4), 66–85. doi:10.4018/jvple.2010100105

Chen, N. S., Cheng, I. L., & Chew, S. W. (2016). Evolution is not enough: Revolutionizing current learning environments to smart learning environments. *International Journal of Artificial Intelligence in Education*, *26*(2), 561–581. doi:10.100740593-016-0108-x

Compeau, D. R., & Higgins, C. A. (1995). Computer self-efficacy: Development of measure and initial test. *Management Information Systems Quarterly*, *19*(2), 189–211. doi:10.2307/249688

Couros, A. V. (2006). *Examining the open movement: Possibilities and implications for education* (Dissertation). University of Regina.

Del Rio, P., & Alvarez, A. (2007). Inside and Outside the Zone of Proximal Development. An Ecofunctional Reading of Vygotsky. In The Cambridge Companion to Vygotsky (pp. 276-303). Cambridge: Cambridge University Press.

Dewey, J. (1997). *Experience and Education*. Touchstone. (Original work published 1938)

Dysthe, O., Hertzberg, F., & Løkensgard Hoel, T. (2011). *Skriva för att lära. Skrivande i högre utbildning* [Writing to learn: Writing in Higher Education] (2nd ed., S. Andersson, Trans.). Studentlitteratur.

Evans, C. (2013). Making sense of assessment feedback in higher education. *Review of Educational Research*, *83*(1), 70–120. doi:10.3102/0034654312474350

Gee, J. P. (2007). *What Video Games Have to Teach us About Learning and Literacy*. Palgrave Macmillan.

Gros, B. (2016). The design of smart educational environments. *Smart Learning Environments*, *3*(1), 15. doi:10.118640561-016-0039-x

Hattie, J., & Timperley, H. (2007). The power of feedback. *Review of Educational Research*, *77*(1), 81–112. doi:10.3102/003465430298487

Hwang, G. J. (2014). Definition, framework and research issues of smart learning environments – a context-aware ubiquitous learning perspective. *Smart Learning Environments*, *1*(1), 4. doi:10.118640561-014-0004-5

Hwang, G. J., Lai, C. L., & Wang, S. Y. (2015). Seamless flipped learning: A mobile technology-enhanced flipped classroom with effective learning strategies. *Journal of Computers in Education*, *2*(4), 449–473. doi:10.100740692-015-0043-0

Jordi, R. (2011). Reframing the concept of reflection: Consciousness, experiential learning, and reflective learning practices. *Adult Education Quarterly*, *61*(2), 181–197. doi:10.1177/0741713610380439

Kearney, M., Schuck, S., Burden, K., & Aubusson, P. (2012). Viewing mobile learning from a pedagogical perspective. *Research in Learning Technology*, *20*(1), n1. doi:10.3402/rlt.v20i0.14406

Kennedy, M., & Dunn, T. J. (2018). *Improving the use of technology enhanced learning environments in higher education in the UK: A qualitative visualisation of students' views*. Contemporary Educational Technology.

Koehler, M. J., Mishra, P., & Cain, W. (2013). What is technological pedagogical content knowledge (TPACK)? *Journal of Education, 193*(3), 13–19. doi:10.1177/002205741319300303

Koschmann, T. (1996). Paradigm shifts and instructional technology: An introduction. *CSCL: Theory and Practice of an Emerging Paradigm, 12*(4), 18-19.

McIntosh, P. (2010). *Action research and reflective practice*. Routledge. doi:10.4324/9780203860113

Ott, M., & Freina, L. (2015). A Literature Review on Immersive Virtual Reality in Education: State Of The Art and Perspectives. *The 11th International Scientific Conference eLearning and Software for Education.*

Reinholz, D. (2016). The assessment cycle: A model for learning through peer assessment. *Assessment & Evaluation in Higher Education, 41*(2), 301–315. doi:10.1080/02602938.2015.1008982

Sadler, D. R. (1989). Formative assessment and the design of instructional systems. *Instructional Science, 18*(2), 119–144. doi:10.1007/BF00117714

Schön, D. (1987). Educating the Reflective Practitioner. Jossey-Bass Publishers.

Spector, J. M. (2014). Conceptualizing the emerging field of smart learning environments. *Smart Learning Environments, 1*(1), 2

Tomkins, A. (2009). "It was a great day when…": An exploratory case study of reflective learning through storytelling. *Journal of Hospitality, Leisure, Sport and Tourism Education, 8*(2), 123–131. doi:10.3794/johlste.82.198

Topping, K. J. (2005). Trends in peer learning. *Educational Psychology, 25*(6), 631–645. doi:10.1080/01443410500345172

Topping, K. J., Smith, E. F., Swanson, I., & Elliot, A. (2000). Formative peer assessment of academic writing between postgraduate students. *Assessment & Evaluation in Higher Education, 25*(2), 149–169. doi:10.1080/713611428

Vygotsky, L. S. (1978). *Mind in Society: Development of Higher Psychological Processes*. Academic Press.

Wegerif, R. (2007). *Dialogic education and technology: Expanding the space of learning* (Vol. 7). Springer Science & Business Media. doi:10.1007/978-0-387-71142-3

Wenger, E. (1998). *Communities of Practice - Learning, Meaning, and Identity*. Cambridge University Press. doi:10.1017/CBO9780511803932

Wiliam, D. (2011). What is assessment for learning? *Studies in Educational Evaluation*, *37*(1), 3–14. doi:10.1016/j.stueduc.2011.03.001 PMID:22114905

Wiliam, D. (2013). Assessment: The bridge between teaching and learning. *Voices from the Middle*, *21*(2), 15.

Wong, L. H., Chai, C. S., Aw, G. P., & King, R. B. (2015). Enculturating seamless language learning through artifact creation and social interaction process. *Interactive Learning Environments*, *23*(2), 130–157. doi:10.1080/10494820.2015.1016534

Wong, L. H., & Looi, C. K. (2011). What seams do we remove in mobile-assisted seamless learning? A critical review of the literature. *Computers & Education*, *57*(4), 2364–2381. doi:10.1016/j.compedu.2011.06.007

Zhu, Z. T., Yu, M. H. & Riezebos, P. (2016). A research framework of smart education. *Smart Learning Environments, 3*(1), 4.

# Chapter 1
# Smart Mobile Learning Activities


## ABSTRACT

*The rapid technical development with new media forms and increased mobility is integrated into our everyday lives, as well as in more digitalized higher education and at distance. A new research area has been developed on mobile learning (m-learning) about the integration of self-directed and motivated opportunities. This chapter describes smart mobile learning activities with an emphasis on the importance of the connection by using resource-enriched and technology-embedded mobile devices for student-centered learning that allow students' to learn self-directed and motivated to obtain learning materials at anywhere and anytime, what learning benefits are being observed among students and teachers, and how different issues are being addressed. Methodically, it illustrates different frameworks for mobile learning and theoretically is the analysis of excerpts based on dialogical theories. The findings display that the space for m-learning offers many opportunities, as well as challenges, to design smart "mobile pedagogy" with a focus on student-centered learning.*


DOI: 10.4018/978-1-7998-4183-8.ch001

## BACKGROUND

Smart mobile learning offers numerous opportunities for student-centered learning by resource-enriched and technology-embedded enhanced devices such as laptops, mobile phones, and smart mobile phones with Bluetooth, mobile applications and faster internet transmission for self-directed and motivated with adaptive, resource-enriched, and technology-embedded opportunities. The word 'smart' is an acronym for self-directed, motivated, adaptive, resource-enriched, and technology-embedded, and refers to wisdom as bounding together the ability of using and motivating self-directed learning, knowledge building, problem solving, critically reflections, collaborating and evaluating different circumstances with resource-enriched and technology-embedded tools (Hwang, 2014; Zhu, Yu & Riezebos, 2016).

Digitization have gone through several paradigm shift where structures, processes and behaviours are fundamentally changed, as well in education as in the society, thereby changing even the teaching. The research of mobile learning has significantly increased over the last decade (Alrasheedi & Capretz, 2018; Baran, 2014; Kearney, Schuck, Burden & Aubusson, 2012; Lee & Salman, 2012; Marin, Jääskelä, Häkkinen, Juntunen, Rasku-Puttonen & Vesisenaho, 2016; Ozdamli & Cavus, 2011). The authors argue that the learning paradigm of higher education has changed with the potential to transform the way to more active student-centered learning with self-directed and collaborative processes with other students. It allows students to adapt and manage the content, scope, and spaces of their learning and have control over the time and place where they can access learning materials and participate, discuss and collaborate, as well as share knowledge and experiences with other peers.

This chapter expands the knowledge about smart mobile learning activities with an emphasis on the importance of the connection by using resource-enriched and technology-embedded mobile devices that allow students to learn self-directed and collaboratively to obtain learning materials at anywhere and anytime. The following questions are addressed:

- In what way can teachers a) design and b) use different smart mobile learning activities and tools that are appropriate for student-centered learning and active participation?
- How do the students experience the smart mobile activities and the smart tools for their learning?

- In what way can the smart mobile activities and tools be analyzed comparing to the students' performance?

Digital technologies, by contrast to traditional technologies, are unstable because of the rapidly changings, they are changeable and pervasive because of their using in many different ways in everyday life, and opaque when the inner work are hidden from other users (Koehler, Mishra & Cain, 2013). Several boundaries exist, such as lack of resource-enriched and technology-embedded groundings, sustainable integration into formal educational contexts, and, particularly, lack of smart mobile learning pedagogical abilities among teachers (Baran, 2014; Hwang, 2014; Kaliisa, & Picard, 2017; Zhu, Yu & Riezebos, 2016). Likewise, poor attitudes among students and teachers, as well as need of technically and pedagogically support and training in digital competence (Amhag, Hellström & Stigmar, 2019). A high level of digital competence requires an exemplary digital practice, characterized by good technical infrastructure, teachers with high technical-pedagogical knowledge, continuous professional development and a well-functioning technology-embedded mediated communication and administration (Olofsson, Fransson & Lindberg, 2019).

The nature of higher education has two constants or boundaries: space and time. The place of learning has been a requirement to learn in fixed, scheduled time spaces in school buildings and classrooms, often complemented with an optional learning management system, LMS enabling the teachers to organize and structure course materials for the students to be more flexible when they learn. The challenges teachers are facing with integrating various media forms depend on their digital competence to organizing and implementing different synchronous and asynchronous learning activities (e.g. Amhag, 2016; Buxton, Burns & De Muth, 2012; De Wever, Van Keer, Schellens & Valcke, 2009; Kearney et al., 2012).

The difference between synchronous and asynchronous learning spaces is that synchronous learning activities are momentary, because they are direct and oral. What is unique is that students can participate in a wireless and mobile manner in real time, and discuss, collaborate and negotiate, as well as have oral examination online. In comparison, asynchronous learning activities are delayed, and usually written. These activities are often taking place in the LMS where course documents and instructions, written discussions forum and critical review of different texts, as well as recorded lectures and flipped classroom videos are accessible online. Unique here is that the written documents, texts, and recordings are published before or afterwards the activity. This content reveals the extent of spaces for students' participation and motivation, collaborative peer assessment processes, and the teachers' arrangement of the course (Amhag, 2013b; Amhag & Jakobsson, 2009). All these processes can support student-centered learning and collaborative learning in a more digitalized higher education and at distance, instead of merely focusing on how new media techniques can make education more effective with blended learning activities or detrimental solitary trainings (e.g. Amhag, 2011; 2012; 2013a; Lee & Salman, 2012; Rockinson-Szapkiw, Courduff, Carter & Bennett, 2013; Sana, Weston & Cepeda, 2013).

However, smart m-learning can be seen as a key to the future era of e-learning with the potential to exceed spatial and temporal constraints by linking specific activities to specific locations at specific times (Al-Adwan, Al-Madadha & Zvirzdinaite, 2018; Kearney et al., 2012). Other research studies show that there is a need for continuing innovative solutions for the teachers and teacher teams as an important part of teachers' professional competence of using resource-enriched and technology-embedded mobile devices in higher education (Amhag, Hellström & Stigmar, 2019). Teachers' digital competence vary in teaching and it is based on teachers' own value frameworks, but teachers' abilities are also dependent on local contextual conditions and decisions (Olofsson, Fransson & Lindberg, 2019). Likewise, in underlying pedagogical theories and skills for student-centered and collaborative learning, critical thinking, as well as increasing the active participation, flexibility and freedom feelings for the students (Amhag, 2013a; 2013b; 2016a; 2016b; Tømte, Enochsson, Buskqvist & Kårstein, 2015). Critical thinking is both a process and a result that is best understood from an individual perspective (Garrison et al., 2001). That is, the acquisition of deep and meaningful understanding as well as content-specific critical investigation abilities, skills and dispositions. Assessing the quality of critical thinking within a certain educational context is the responsibility of the teachers. Therefore, essential is to expand the knowledge about smart mobile learning activities with an emphasis on using resource-enriched and technology-embedded mobile devices that allow students to learn self-directed and collaboratively anywhere and anytime.

## PREVIOUS RESEARCH OF M-LEARNING

The media development has expanded spaces online with active involvement and opportunities for smart mobile teaching and learning, observation and documentation, participation and communication, as well as innovation of global learning spaces. Selected articles for review of previous research were obtained from searches in databases in education and social sciences such as ERIC, Libsearch etc. and from studies cited by these authors and from previously used peer review articles published in the relevant field with keywords: mobile learning and higher education. According to Kearney et al. (2012), the space of m-learning offers numerous opportunities, as well as challenges in higher education, including virtual spaces, created on "mobile pedagogy". The highlighted opportunities for mobile learning are that they are contextualized, situated, and participatory, as well as the occurrence of active processes, mediated by wearable tools.

Pegrum, Oakley and Faulkner (2013) use various `space´ with the terms: electronic learning (*e-learning*), mobile learning (*m-learning*), and ubiquitous learning (*u-learning*). E-learning is learning through digital technology; m-learning is through portable means such as handheld laptops, tablets, or smartphones; and u-learning addresses possibilities for mobile techniques providing support regardless of place and time. The researchers emphasize that mobile devices can support a variety of teaching methods, but it is important to plan how to use them. For example, the ability to use mobile devices in different contexts such as in classrooms, online webinars, and work-based professional trainings, field trips, or wherever a learning situation can take place, to create opportunities for mobile learning. For example, a case study by Marin et al. (2016) demonstrated that tablet devices were conceived as mediators and cognitive tools that enhanced the creation of u-learning and m-learning spaces from the teachers' point of view.

A 10-year longitudinal study in an online bachelor's and master's pharmacy programs by Englund, Olofsson and Price (2017) show a clear difference between novice and experienced teachers in higher education. Novice teachers initially held more teacher-focused conceptions, but they changed their ideas faster than experienced colleagues who tended to exhibit little to no changing in their conceptions. Therefore, central for successful implementation of educational technologies in higher education are conceptions of and approaches to the pedagogical surplus value in teaching and learning online based on pedagogical theories and methods.

Another study by Alrasheedi and Capretz (2018) of a meta-analysis of 19 research studies in the area of m-learning, show that the critical success factors were the technical competence of educators, the development of assessment techniques, and institutional support. The success of m-learning was only based on perceived benefits from students' perspectives. This result neglects other important users such as the teachers, instructors and members of the university management and administration.

Additional systematic research review by Kaliisa and Picard (2017) published between 2010 and 2016 on m-learning in higher education in Africa to explore the applications, impact and challenges of mobile technology supported learning, show increased collaboration between student and teachers, student participation and engagement, as well as fostering of the learning communities. A change in the teachers' approaches to mobile teaching also occurred. The significant challenges are incompatibility of mobile devices and poor technological infrastructure, lack of access to modern mobile devices and pedagogical skills among teachers, as well as poor attitudes among students and teachers.

Supplementary research by a quantitative survey among 160 medical students by Briz-Ponce, Pereira, Carvalho, Juanes-Méndez and García-Peñalvo (2017) about different factors that influence students' behavior to use mobile technologies for learning, show a correlation with a strong attitude towards using mobile technology for learning (57%) and willingness to recommend it (40.5%). However, the main factor affecting their social influence had a variance of 31.9% in their willingness to adopt mobile technology for learning.

A study at two Swedish universities (Amhag, Hellström & Stigmar, 2019) through a digital survey included 16 questions among one hundred five teacher educators with closed- and open-ended questions to evaluate their competence of how they effectively practice ICT in teaching situations. Theoretically the TPACK model and computer self-efficacy were used. The results show that the majority of the teacher educators (N = 105) rated their digital competence as medium (54.8%), just under a fifth as low (16.3%) and just over a quarter as high (27.9%). However, the teacher educators do not primarily use digital tools for educational purposes, therefore, they need extensive and continuous educational support to understand the potential of digital tools in education and discover the pedagogical surplus value in their own teaching and for students learning.

Above the research studies, I want to demonstrate that the use of digital tools must be qualified and developed professionally by the technical staff at the university with an institutional support for teachers about underlying pedagogical skills and theories, as well as didactic strategies (Lakkala & Ilomäki, 2015). Attitudes towards m-learning technology is also an important factor to identify strengths and weaknesses and facilitate the development of the technology infrastructure and determining whether or not students and teachers are ready to use m-learning (Al-Emran, Elsherif & Shaalan,

2016). The aim is also to increase the students understanding of the skills, dispositions, assignments, tutoring and examinations with a clear focus on knowledge for teaching-learning contexts where communication technologies are increasingly pivotal (Forbes & Khoo, 2015).

## DESIGN OF SMART MOBILE LEARNING ACTIVITIES

Important question is how teachers can design smart "mobile pedagogy" in higher education and at distance with different mobile learning activities that are appropriate for student-centered learning and active participation. The design of the course is of great importance to its quality. Therefore, the design of mobile learning has led to even more multifaceted teaching profession in higher education and at distance.

The core characteristics of mobile learning, according to Ozdemir and Cavus (2011) include:

a) Portable size of mobile tools for learning everywhere.
b) Ubiquitous and more spontaneous than other learning forms.
c) Blended learning which combines face-to-face, F2F classroom lectures and mobile online methods.
d) Interactive agent for the process of coming to know.
e) Collaboration, which enable students to learn in the right place at the right time, that is, the authentic joy of learning.
f) Instant information that enables students to quickly zone into information with e.g. definitions, formula, and equations, etc.
g) M-learning is more private because of independently access of information and to connect and download from other learners.

All these features must be carefully planned, prepared, observed, checked, evaluated and constantly modified by the teachers. Hattie (2009) emphasizes the importance of visible learning among teachers and students who are the most important actors in the context and the interactions between them. According to Hattie, teaching is about getting knowledge about how the students' learning develops and are changing the teaching after the students' progression. An open communication and reciprocity between teachers and students about the knowledge content, the teaching methods and the learning activities that happens or not, seems to be the foundation of Hattie's perspective, and is the key to good study performance.

The same key factors should also be used in mobile teaching and at distance. Teachers need even to have knowledge about mobile learning activities with mobile technology based on "mobile pedagogy". Then mobile learning has the potential to support students to learn professionally. The basic design of mobile learning, according to Ozdemir and Cavus (2011), consist of five ground rules:

1. The students should be in focus and the courses should be built on the students' interests, experiences and needs.
2. The teacher role has changed from just being an expert and lecturer of others' expertise to moderate or facilitate different contrasting research positions.
3. The content should be decided in consultation with all stakeholders such as students, teachers, colleagues at the institution, and peers, supported with multimedia tools e.g. graphics, recorded videos and other presentation programs.
4. The learning environment should be designed applicably to obtain various learning experiences with open course content available for cell phones, laptops and tablets, with recurring online interactions between students-students and students-teachers.
5. Assessment of the course content can be done through written reports, recorded oral presentations, and discussions online as well as online exams during a specified period. In addition, students should reflect and evaluate their own efforts and others through different peer feedback processes.

Biesta (2004, p. 70-71) argue that the teacher role has been redefined as moderating or supporting / facilitating learning. He is also emphasising that "the language of education has largely been replaced by a language of *learning"*. This language need to change to both a language *of* education and *for* education with a focus on relationships, trust and responsibility that truly are educational. Language is practice, and is something we do and matters to education, because the languages about education regulate what can be said and done, and what cannot be said and done.

The talk *about* and *with* learning in education has changed, emphases Biesta (2004). Adult education has become lifelong learning and learning society, instead of talking about permanent or recurrent adult education. The teacher role for integrating mobile learning, found Barans (2014) analysis of 37 research articles in teacher education six results:

1. An increasing trend in integrating mobile learning in teacher education contexts.
2. Theoretical and conceptual perspectives are barely reported.
3. Variations exist in insights, attitudes and usage patterns.
4. Engagement with mobile learning and devices is mainly reported as being helpful.
5. Challenges were scarcely reported.
6. Several pedagogical affordances, as literature discussions, knowledge exchange, peer feedback processes and different problem scenarios, are supporting mobile learning integration into teacher education settings.

*Figure 1. Methods for integrating about and with mobile learning in teacher training (Baran, 2014, p. 28)*

| **Teacher training *about* mobile learning** | **Teacher training *with* mobile learning** |
|---|---|
| • Hands-on explorations of mobile learning<br>• Developing mobile lesson plans<br>• Micro-teaching mobile lessons<br>• Enacting mobile lessons in the classrooms<br>• Reflecting on mobile lessons<br>• Planning mobilized curriculum<br>• Attending to communities of practice | • Collaborating with peers, colleagues, teacher educators and supervisors<br>• Accessing teacher education content anytime anywhere<br>• Reflecting on teaching<br>• Sharing classrooms practice<br>• Using peer feedback<br>• Customizing teacher training content |

Figure 1 summarizes methods for integrating *about* and *with* mobile learning in teacher training (Baran, 2014, p. 28).

An earlier study by Tolmie and Boyle (2000), which I have used in my research since 2005 and in my university teaching (Amhag, 2013b; 2016;

2017), is still valid on broad previous research about factors influencing the success of computer mediated communication, CMC, environments in university teaching. Following eight key aspects are highlighted:

1. The size of the group is important. Communication works better in groups of six students. The dynamics are promoted as the critical level increases in the individual contributions, as well as the continuous engagement of all participants. In smaller groups, a power relationship often occurs. In larger groups, subgroups are often formed.
2. Knowledge of other course participants is a key for successful collaboration. Early, the group participants need to meet face-to-face, F2F and to some extent get to know each other. Physically hits at the beginning of a mobile activity contribute to more successful knowledge exchanges.
3. Student experiences about communication work better if they are experienced correspondents. Knowledge exchanges and personal opinions with a link to the assignment with clear deadlines are needed for better working conditions in which they are involved.
4. Clarity about the task and the students' understandings how to work with the task they are engaged in, especially if this understanding is shared with other fellow students.
5. Ownership of task is provided when the students can give peer feedback in CMC, as well as negotiate face-to-face, F2F about the task and opportunity for continuing renegotiation later on.
6. Need for a guide of the LMS and the different tools. It is better if there is a clear function for each tool which cannot be served more easily in another way.
7. Type of LMS and
8. Prior experience of CMC, may be factors, but important levels are unclear in the research.

The designs of mobile learning show that it is important with varied education and learning with scaffolding-, peer learning- and collaborative knowledge processes (Scardamalia, 2004). Scaffolding is a kind of "thinking type" to promote clear and analytic written and oral dialogues, designed to provide procedural facilitation to address different problem solving or suggestions from other students and teachers. Generally, critical questions should be based on course learning goals and developed from the criteria of knowledge. Then can the dialogues take several "thinking forms", such as literature discussions, knowledge exchange, peer feedback and different scenarios with critical incidents or problems, case studies, role-play, and debate.

Scaffolds are adaptable and can easily be added or modified to support a particular knowledge process or activities provided by the teacher, or more competent peer, to support the student. Therefore, the zone of proximal development, ZPD (Vygotsky, 1978) has become synonymous in the literature with the term scaffolding. Scaffolding has provided a perspective and a language in which teaching can easily be redefined as facilitating and supporting learning (Biesta, 2004).

For instance, show the study of Ciampa (2014) that providing scaffold experiences can support students' learning and development. Important motivational factors were teamwork and opportunities to work with other students. They could share thoughts and ideas, collaborate with peers and become active participants in a digital community of practice. Hattie and Timperley (2007) are raising three effective feedback questions:

1. Where am I going? (What are the goals?).
2. How am I going? (What progress is being made toward the goal?).
3. Where to next? (What activities need to be undertaken to make better progress?).

These three questions correspond to the design of *feed up, feed back* and *feed forward*. The questions and design are including; better strategies to complete the task or obtain more information; error detection skills; tackling more tasks that are challenging or appreciating "higher order thinking skills".

Richardson and Ice (2010) compared three different instructional strategies as "thinking forms": a case study, a debate, and an open discussion, and how these discussion questions engaged students for meaningful learning, as well as the connection between student's levels of critical thinking and the instructional strategy. The result shows that the students preferred open discussions (47%), followed by debate (36%) and case discussions (17%). However, the analysis of critical thinking achievement levels displays that the students had generally lower critical posts on the open discussions (61%), compared with case discussions (81%) and debate (78%). The result show that students are not always fully aware of their metacognitive strengths and abilities, such as solving problems understanding concepts, paying attention, remembering and reflecting. Likewise, how they can use their learning strategies to experience, think, analyze and test... which gives new experiences etc. However, the open discussions can first and foremost be seen as an ongoing knowledge process. It can also be an indication of a pattern when students are getting used to the open format to debate and discuss or choose the least complex, or with the easiest instructional strategy.

Another study by Heflin, Shewmaker and Nguyen (2017) with three different designs of LMS with or without mobile technology on the students' engagement, critical thinking and attitudes towards collaboration, show, on the one hand, that the students' responses in mobile devices showed significantly less critical thinking than those who used a keyboard or wrote the responses by hand. On the other hand, mobile technology was associated with positive student attitudes of collaborative learning, but with increased disengagement during the class. Perhaps, the teachers must be clearer about what reflects the critical thinking process and the means to create cognitive presence, for example, give response on particular problems, presenting ideas or suggesting a solution.

Evidence of higher-order thinking is analysed in the study by Meyer (2003) based on graduate students' experiences in using course-related discussions, both face-to-face, F2F in class and online. But only the analysis of higher-order thinking was based on a content analysis of the threaded online discussions. Each posting was coded as one of the four cognitive-processing categories described by Garrison et al. (2001), based on the practical inquiry model by Dewey (2004) including:

1. *Triggering* event include an issue, dilemma, or problem that emerges from experience, is identified or recognized.
2. *Exploration* include the shift between the private, reflective world of the individual and the social exploration of ideas.
3. *Integration*, is characterized by constructing meaning from the ideas generated in the exploratory phase.
4. *Resolution*, is characterized by the dilemma or problem by means of direct or mediated action.

The analysis shows 18% triggering questions, 51% exploration, 22% integration, and 7% resolution questions. Only 3% were social responses. The result shows that teachers need to be clearer about what shall be discussed, for example, encouraging students to solve particular problems, presenting their ideas or suggesting a solution to the issues discussed, to prove that students receive the intellectual higher-order thinking that higher education values highly.

In order to increase the level of critical thinking and higher-order thinking skills in higher education and discover the value of a broader meaning content, is continuing scaffolding needed by teachers about what reflects the critical thinking process and the means to create cognitive presence (Dewey, 2004), as well as collaborative learning processes among students (Amhag, 2011; 2012; 2013a). Increasingly, as teachers begin to understand the mobile technologies, learning possibilities and "mobile pedagogy" strategies for integrating mobile learning into higher education, the role of teacher to integrating mobile devices becomes crucial in addressing students' active learning and participation, critical thinking and higher-order thinking skills as well as collaborative peer assessment processes.

## METHOD OF MOBILE LEARNING

The qualitative method of the mobile learning activities for self-directed, motivated, adaptive, resource-enriched, and technology-embedded smart education has an emphasis on the integration of opportunities and the importance of the connection by using resource-enriched and technology-embedded mobile devices for student-centered learning. The growth of new resource-enriched and technology-embedded wearable tools is challenging for higher education and the institutions. The idea of smart m-learning is that the learning contexts also can be created self-directed by students and occurring in different places and at different times, and not restricted to formal scheduled learning settings in a classroom at the university. Moreover, there is a need of investigating smart mobile pedagogical opportunities and challenges in higher education with principles of authentic, motivational, collaborative and self-directed learning, based on well-researched socio-cultural perspectives. Methodically, illustrates two frameworks for mobile learning activities. A systematic analysis, from both a pedagogical and a technical perspective is crucial for ensuring the appropriate use, benefits and implementation of smart mobile learning activities (Ally & Prieto-Blázquez, 2014).

### Framework for Mobile Learning

The framework by Kearney, Schuck, Burden and Aubusson (2012) is a model to analyse, highlight and explore the experiences of mobile learning. The framework is extended from Koole's model (2009) based on socio-cultural understandings from a pedagogical perspective, especially referring to enhance collaboration, access to information and deeper contextualisation of learning. Pedagogy is central and technology is only distinctive about the learning afforded by the technology. The framework identifies three distinctive features of m-learning: *authenticity*, *collaboration* and *personalisation*, illustrated in figure 2.

*Figure 2. Framework of Kearny et al. (2012, p. 8) comprising three distinctive characteristics of m-learning experiences, with sub-scales*

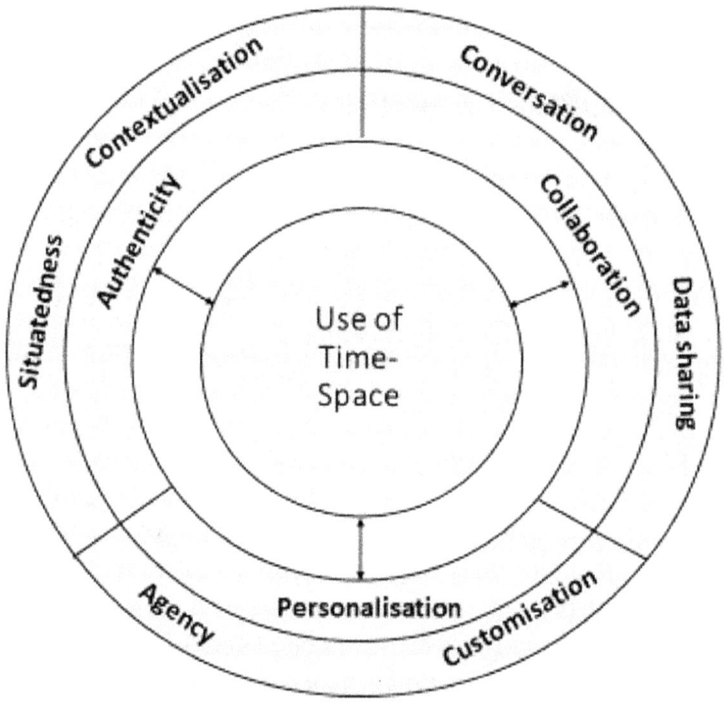


1. The *authenticity* feature highlights opportunities for contextualised, participatory and situated learning, providing the real world relevance and personal meaning to the students.
2. The *collaboration* feature captures the conversational and connected aspects by making rich data sharing and dialogic interactions with

more capable peers or adults with pedagogical emphasis on scaffolding, mediated by mobile devices.

3. The *personalisation* feature has implications for ownership, agency / action and customized / modified self-directed learning drawing on motivational theory, embedded in the unique time space contexts of mobile learning.

The conclusion of the framework is that the students' experiences of the characteristics: authenticity, collaboration and personalization are strongly influenced by the teachers organization of the spatial place and time-based aspects of m-learning with blended learning activities face to face, F2F classroom lectures and computer-supported collaborative learning strategies (Kearny et al., 2012). However, the teacher needs to take into account the student centered space where learning takes place and the teachers' competence to design m-learning. The teacher team and the course assignments are further important factors. Likewise, to explore in more detail the use of time-space, and how it can be organised to optimise student centred learning, mediated by mobile tools.

## Framework of Collaborative Learning

A framework of dialogic levels, related to the *collaboration* feature in the framework of Kearny et al. (2012), is from a study (Amhag & Jakobsson, 2009) among 40 student teachers and their contributions (N=919) in web-based courses over a nine-month period in Teacher Education with blended learning activities. The purpose of the study was to examine what significance the students' dialogues have to be able to develop a collective competence of collaboration. The students were divided into groups of five to six where they worked both individually and collaboratively with problem-based course assignments, group responses on their contributions and their collaborative discussions in the LMS discussion fora.

The analysis of the dialogical exchanges between the students to develop a collective competence of collaboration was based on Bakhtin's (1981; 1986/2004) specific approach to understand dialogues. Bakhtin (1981) distinguish between *authoritative discourse* and *inner persuasive discourse*, by using the concepts of *active* or *passive understanding.*

*Authoritative discourse* includes monological utterances, for example, religious, political or moral texts, as well as from a superior power as an adult, a parent or a teacher. *Inner persuasive discourse* obtains its power through being covered partly of one's own words and partly of others' words.

The *passive* understanding reproduces merely speakers or writer's words or thoughts, whilst *active* understanding creates a basis for response, argumentation, agreement, sympathy, objection etc. The analysis was also using Rommetveit's (2003) the concept of *meaning potentials* as a space of meaning-mediating possibilities that emerge during dialogic interactions between students.

1. The first dialogic level: Passive and authoritative, characterises an accepting or confirming discourse (Bakhtin, 1981). As Bakhtin states, "its authority was already acknowledged in the past. It is a prior discourse" (p.342). The students are mainly passively reproducing and re-expressing each other's ideas and thoughts: "Do you prefer as a teacher some of the students ..." or general thoughts: "I think you have taken care of the problem well ..." or social confirmation: "Yes, you might be right about ...". The dialogues are monological without any questioning or developing previous contributions to the discussion. At this level, the students are avoiding contradictory understandings and are failing to explain the possible meaning potentials as a basis for learning (Rommetveit, 2003).
2. The second dialogic level: Persuasive and preliminary negotiation, characterises an accepting and confirming discourse; but gradually the students are questioning what previously has been said or adding new opinions. "I think you are raising an important issue that is not highlighted in the report, namely ...", "I think your text is more consistent with your reality than the article we should read about ...", "I got stuck for that you said about... ". The inner and outer struggle between differing points of view and values develops in the discussion. In this particular form of discourse, the students' utterances partly consist of their own words and voices and partly of other's (Bakhtin, 1981). However, the possible meaning potentials are infrequently made explicit, and are not used as a tool for enhanced learning (Rommetveit, 2003).
3. The third dialogic level: Persuasive and co-authorial negotiation, characterises more actively questions what was previously stated or further developing the discussion through providing new opinions or examples (Bakhtin, 1981). "Your example clearly show that Vygotsky's theories of learning and development are in line with your reality when you describe clearly about...", "I have similar experiences with one of my pupil, but unfortunately it has not gone as well like your...". The students

became shareholders and co-authors with an active understanding through negotiations. In this situation, the dialogic interactions often succeed in making the meaning potentials explicit and visible (Rommetveit, 2003), which in turn create increased prerequisites for the students to use them as a basis for learning and development to a higher degree than before. This mediated learning process can be characterized as "mediation on knowledge", which includes reflections on their own and others' understandings and experiences, an event that has a crucial role in the learning process.

## ANALYSIS OF MOBILE LEARNING

The qualitative analysis had focus on what learning benefits are being observed based on the two framework who allow students' to learn self-directed and motivated when they obtain learning materials at anywhere and anytime, and their using's are being faced among students and how different issues are being addressed, as well as afterwards the activities for teachers' assessment.

Theoretically, is the analysis of mobile learning based on socio-cultural approach, were students' dialogues, interactions and interplay, creates important factors for both students own learning, as well as the group's learning and knowledge processes, mediated by use of tools (Wertsch, 1998). Learning always arises as a product of a social community of practice where students are involved in different types of learning activities and processes to create meaning (Wenger, 1998). Important is the *community of practice*, which is maintained by the participants' mutual engagement, common interests and joint enterprise, as well as a shared repertoire with a set of rules, means and working methods. The students' who writes or speaks is co-dependent on those who read or listen as co-authors in a collaborative construction of meaning. From a technical perspective, learning is created and adapted by the use of tools, as well as the mutually learning tools are modified by the way they are used for learning (ibid. 1998).

### Analysis of Collaborative Processes for Learning

The analysis of the collaborative processes for learning show that the students were successively developing a competence to use others' utterances as a tool for learning, but also as an extended, collective competence to collaborate within the group. In that way, all group members became shareholders and co-authors in a joint construction of meaning (Amhag & Jakobsson, 2009). Overall, all student groups developed some kind of collective competence to collaborate, and they used this ability as a tool for learning. The exchange of views can be regarded as a two-sided act between the student's experiential texts and other literary-related words and voices (Rommetveit, 2003, p. 214). The students start a negotiation between different views of opinions and argue more for their statements in different ways than they did earlier and are reconnecting more to the original texts. However, the development was inconsistent in different groups, but also varying within the sample group throughout the nine months of participation. The analysis also show that the dialogues were mostly at level one or two and only uncommonly at level three. In some groups, the development of the collective competence to collaborate was problematic, and in these groups, there existed a tendency to remain at a lower dialogical level (Amhag & Jakobsson, 2009, pp. 18-19). Three different levels of thematic patterns are summed up in Table 1.

*Table 1. Summary of the three levels of thematic patterns in the dialogues (Amhag & Jakobsson, 2009, p. 17)*

| Dialogic Level | The levels of thematic pattern in the dialogue |
|---|---|
| Passive and authoritative | · accepting and confirming<br>· passively reproducing<br>· monological and authoritative<br>· failure to explicate the possible meaning potential in the dialogue as a basis for learning and development |
| Persuasive and preliminary negotiation | · accepting, confirming and questioning<br>· elements of passively reproducing posts<br>· negotiations<br>· responses create possible meaning potentials<br>· failure to use meaning potential as a basis for learning and development |
| Persuasive and co-authorial negotiation | · accepting, confirming or actively questioning and a desire to develop the discussion<br>· few or no elements of reproducing posts<br>· others' statements reworded to own words<br>· participants are shareholders and co-authors in the account<br>· negotiations<br>· responses create possible meaning potentials |

The implications of these findings indicate that course assignments should be more visible and explicit in mobile activities for the students with scaffolding processes by teachers to promote clear and analytic written and oral dialogues. In this process, the three dialogic levels can be used as a metacognitive tool for students in order to improve the efficiency of the group, as well as analysing their own dialogic interactions retrospectively. At that time, the students could easier develop the ability to independently identify the meaning potentials for enhanced learning and development (Rommetveit, 2003). The meaning potential of the text is not only developed by the relationship between the writer and the reader, it is realized when it is used in other ways with others, and provide an expanded space for all the possible ways to develop a collective competence to collaborate (Amhag & Jakobsson, 2009, p. 20).

## Analysis of Argumentation Processes for Learning

The analysis of the argumentation processes for learning is related to the *authenticity* feature in the framework of Kearny et al. (2012). The empirical data is from a study (Amhag, 2011, 2012, 2013a) among 30 students, teachers and their contributions (N=253) in a web-based course over ten weeks. Data was collected from five student groups' asynchronous argumentation, relating to authentic cases of teacher leadership with a focus on the extent they used own and others' texts meaning content in the LMS discussion forum.

The analysis of the meaning content was based on Toulmin's argument pattern, TAP (1958, pp. 98, 101, 103) how writers and readers can deal with texts, and how they can use the resources of texts to determine what they mean – or rather, some possible meanings – and how it can be analysed from an argument model containing six elements. Three elements of Toulmin's argument pattern are mandatory: C (claim), D (data) and W (warrant). Three elements are more optional elements: Q (qualifier), R (rebuttal) and B (backing). All the mandatory elements in the basic model (C, D & W) are required to describe an authentic argument pattern and for the analysis of it, as well as more and less of the optional elements (Q, R, B).

The logical relationship between the elements is practically important (cf. the logic of rhetoric: logos, pathos, and ethos). However, the argument model is a simplification of the complexity and the authentic found in an argumentation. Various suggestions and solutions that are found in the meaning content are part of the learning process (Toulmin, 1958). The task for the teacher is to show students how to present their ideas in an understandable and coherent manner, above all, based on these data, warrant and claims of the mandatory elements. An illustration of TAP is given in Figure 3.

*Figure 3. Toulmin's argument pattern, TAP (1958, p. 104)*

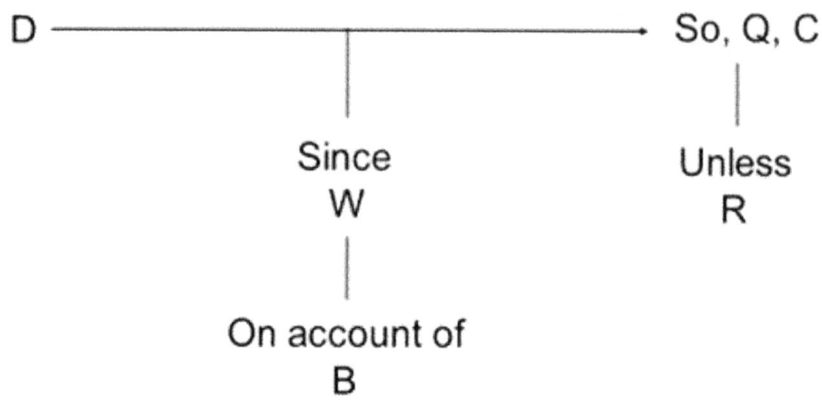


## Mandatory elements:

1. The basic model's first mandatory element, claim (C), has a superior position with a relation to something, e.g. determining or justification of norms or values that people hold or desire for acceptance of the claim.
2. The second mandatory element, data (D), includes the information on which the claim is based on, e.g. previous research, personal experience, common sense or statements used as evidence to support the claim.
3. The third mandatory element, warrant (W), includes explicit or implicit arguments that explain the relationship between data and claim, usually with the words: because or since.

Optional elements:

1. The first optional element, qualifier (Q), relates to the claim and indicates the degree of strength in the claim by distinctive comments, e.g. with the words: therefore, probably, maybe or so.
2. The second optional element, rebuttal (R), connects to the qualifier (Q) with statements or facts that either contradict the claim, data or rebuttal or qualify an argument, e.g. with the words: but or unless.

3. The third optional element, backing (B), can be directly connected to warrant (W) with often implicit motives underlying claims, e.g. with the words: because of or on account of.

An illustration of the revised version of Toulmin's argument pattern, TAP (1958) is given in Figure 4.

*Figure 4. Revised version of Toulmin's argument pattern, TAP (1958)*

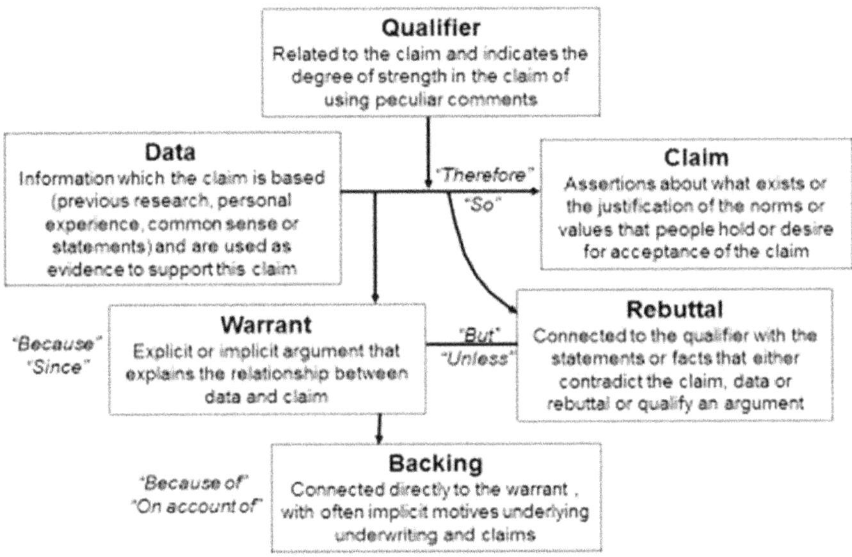


Before the analyse of the contributions (N=253) among 30 students asynchronous argumentation relating to authentic cases of teacher leadership, I was revising an own version of Toulmin's (1958) argument pattern with the three mandatory elements and the three optional elements, to deeper understand the relationships between them, inspired on the developments of the specific features in TAP by Kneupper (1978) and Simon et al. (2006). The focus in the analysis of the meaning content in the students' contributions (N=253) was on the specific features to which extent students had made use of Toulmin's (1958) mandatory elements; C (claim), D (data) and W (warrant), as well as the optional elements; Q (qualifier), R (rebuttal) and B (backing), and how the different elements in the same argument are related to each other.

The result shows overall, that over half of the students (63%) use the highest number of argument elements (CDWB, CDWR, CDWQ and CDWB) in their argumentations. Nevertheless, there are large differences between the five student groups A, B, C, D and E. Group C had the highest number (25%) of argument elements (CDWB, CDWR, CDWQ and CDWB), compared with only 15% in group D. There are also variations between the lowest elements (CD, CW, CR, DR and WB), 38% in group B and only 4% in group E. Likewise, a difference with the three elements (CDW, CDR, CWR and DWR), 32% in group B and only 11% in group E. A revised version of TAP is given in Figure 4.

Furthermore, the result of the number of written, asynchronous arguments (N=253) shows that the students' argumentation containing only two or three elements had the character of an authoritative discourse with monological words such as accepting and confirming statements or reproducing text or are failing to explain the possible meaning content (Bakhtin, 1981). The meaning content displays also a lack of relationship between the mandatory elements; C (claim), D (data) and W (warrant) and the optional elements; Q (qualifier), R (rebuttal) and B (backing) (Toulmin, 1958). The numbers of written, asynchronous arguments are summed in Table 2.

*Table 2. The number of written, asynchronous arguments (N=253) with the elements C, D, W, Q, R, B in five student groups (N=30)*

| | Group A n=7 | Group B n=5 | Group C n=6 | Group D n=6 | Group E n=6 | N 30 |
|---|---|---|---|---|---|---|
| Selective analysis | 63 (25%) | 61 (24%) | 58 (23%) | 34 (13%) | 37 (15%) | 253 100% |
| CD, CW, CR, DR, WB | 15 (28%) | 20 (38%) | 12 (22%) | 4 (8%) | 2 (4%) | 53 (21%) |
| CDW, CDR, CWR, DWR | 10 (27%) | 12 (32%) | 6 (16%) | 5 (14%) | 4 (11%) | 37 (15%) |
| CDWB, CDWR, CDWQ, CDWB | 38 (23%) | 29 (18%) | 40 (25%) | 25 (15%) | 31 (19%) | 163 (64%) |

However, the highest space of arguments between the students' claim with critical aspects or justification of norms or values, or other data with previous research, personal experience, common sense or statements, and warranties between data and claim, demonstrate more credible and convincing evidence based on their own and others' words. Students began to see contradictions and boundaries between different arguments and opinions. The relation between thought and words, becomes a movement from thought to word and from word to thought.

The implications of these findings show that the argument patterns that developed in the students (N=30) contributions (N=253) provide examples of how the meaning content in the arguments can be distinguished, identified and characterized between the mandatory and optional elements (Amhag, 2011, 2012, 2013a). In the exchange of views between the students, a dialogical argument pattern is formed through the chain of different opinions formed by voices with neutral, other and own words and the approach using the elements of TAP: C, D and W, and more or less with Q, R and B. Moreover, the use of Toulmin's (1958) argument model displays a greater background and evidence of how "arguing to learn" and "responding to learn" can be promoted, evaluated and developed in higher education.

## CONCLUSION

In the analysis of the results of collaborative processes for learning and argumentative processes for learning by using smart mobile activities, three important results appear, not only in individual utterances, but also in the group wise.

Firstly, the social and dialogic interactions can be understood as both an individual and collective competence that students develop when they write their own texts and read others', and take part of their own and others' experiences but also other authors' meaning content (Bakhtin, 1981; Toulmin, 1958). Moreover, an individual and collective competence develops by arguing, giving feedback, discuss and collaborate with different course assignments (Amhag, 2011; 2012; 2013a).

Secondly, the value of what the students write about or how creative they are when formulating the texts is determined to which extent they use their own words that broaden and further develop the opinions of other students and authors meaning content (Amhag, 2013b). Then it becomes realizable to them to reflect on and critically examine their own and others' texts in a new and different way, which was not previously possible. A form of higher-order thinking.

Thirdly, smart mobile learning activities are more dependent on clear and adaptive course design and various support and self-directed collaborative working methods (Baran, 2014; Hwang, 2014; Zhu, Yu & Riezebos, 2016). The teacher's tutoring and feedback to support is also important to motivate and challenge students in their learning in collaboration with other students (Amhag, 2016a; 2016b; Amhag & Jakobsson, 2009).

## REFERENCES

Al-Adwan, A. S., Al-Madadha, A., & Zvirzdinaite, Z. (2018). Modeling Students' Readiness to Adopt Mobile Learning in Higher Education: An Empirical Study. *The International Review of Research in Open and Distributed Learning*, *19*(1). doi:10.19173/irrodl.v19i1.3256

Al-Emran, M., Elsherif, H. M., & Shaalan, K. (2016). Investigating attitudes towards the use of mobile learning in higher education. *Computers in Human Behavior*, *56*, 93–102. doi:10.1016/j.chb.2015.11.033

Ally, M., & Prieto-Blázquez, J. (2014). What is the future of mobile learning in education? *International Journal of Educational Technology in Higher Education*, *11*(1), 142–151.

Alrasheedi, M., & Capretz, L. F. (2018). *Determination of critical success factors affecting mobile learning: A meta-analysis approach.* arXiv preprint arXiv:1801.04288

Amhag, L. (2011). *Students' Argument Patterns in Asynchronous Dialogues for Learning. I SITEs Research Book 2011. In Research Highlights in Technology and Teacher Education 2011*. Society for Information Technology & Teacher Education.

Amhag, L. (2012). High school students' argument patterns in online peer feedback. Handbook of Research on Didactic Strategies and Technologies for Education: Incorporating Advancements, 2, 711-723.

Amhag, L. (2013a). High school students' argument patterns in online peer feedback. *K-12 Education. Concepts, Methodologies, Tools, and Applications*, *1*, 209–221.

Amhag, L. (2013b). *Creativity in and between Collaborative Peer Assessment Processes in Higher Distance Education. I Creative Education, 4(7A2)*, 94–104. doi:10.4236/ce.2013.47A2011

Amhag, L. (2016a). Mobile technologies for student-centered learning in a distance higher education program. In *Wearable Technology and Mobile Innovations for Next-Generation Education,* (pp. 184-199). IGI Global. https://www.igi-global.com/book/wearable-technology-mobile-innovations-next/142108

Amhag, L. (2016b). Mobile technologies for student-centered learning in a distance higher education program. *Blended Learning: Concepts, Methodologies, Tools, and Applications*, *4*, 802–817. doi:10.4018/978-1-5225-0069-8.ch010

Amhag, L., Hellström, L., & Stigmar, M. (2019). Teacher Educators' Use of Digital Tools and Needs for Digital Competence in Higher Education. *Journal of Digital Learning in Teacher Education*, *35*(4), 203–220. doi:10.1080/21532974.2019.1646169

Amhag, L., & Jakobsson, A. (2009). Collaborative Learning as a Collective Competence when Students Use the Potential of Meaning in Asynchronous Dialogues. *Computers & Education*, *52*(3), 656–667. doi:10.1016/j.compedu.2008.11.012

Bakhtin, M. M. (1981). *The Dialogic Imagination: Four Essays by M. M. Bakhtin* (C. Emerson & M. Holquist, Trans.). Austin: University of Texas Press.

Bakhtin, M. M. (1986/2004). Speech Genres & Other Late Essays (V. W. McGee, Trans.; Vol. 9). Austin: University of Texas Press.

Baran, E. (2014). A review of research on mobile learning in teacher education. *Journal of Educational Technology & Society*, *17*(4), 17.

Biesta, G. (2004). Against learning. Reclaiming a language for education in an age of learning. *Nordisk Pedagogik*, *24*, 70–82.

Briz-Ponce, L., Pereira, A., Carvalho, L., Juanes-Méndez, J. A., & García-Peñalvo, F. J. (2017). Learning with mobile technologies–Students' behavior. *Computers in Human Behavior*, *72*, 612–620. doi:10.1016/j.chb.2016.05.027

Buxton, E. C., Burns, E. C., & De Muth, J. E. (2012). Instructional Design and Assessment. Professional Development Webinars for Pharmacists. *American Journal of Pharmaceutical Education*, *76*(8), 1–7. doi:10.5688/ajpe768155 PMID:23129854

Ciampa, K. (2014). Learning in a mobile age: An investigation of student motivation. *Journal of Computer Assisted Learning*, *30*(1), 82–96. doi:10.1111/jcal.12036

De Wever, B., Van Keer, H., Schellens, T., & Valcke, M. (2009). Structuring asynchronous discussion groups: The impact of role assignment and self-assessment on students' levels of knowledge construction through social negotiation. *Journal of Computer Assisted Learning*, *25*(2), 177–188. doi:10.1111/j.1365-2729.2008.00292.x

Dewey, J. (2004). *How we think*. New Delhi: Cosmo Publications.

Englund, C., Olofsson, A. D., & Price, L. (2017). Teaching with technology in higher education: Understanding conceptual change and development in practice. *Higher Education Research & Development*, *36*(1), 73–87. doi:10.1080/07294360.2016.1171300

Forbes, D., & Khoo, E. (2015). Voice over distance: A case of podcasting for learning in online teacher education. *Distance Education*, *36*(3), 335–350. doi:10.1080/01587919.2015.1084074

Garrison, D. R., Anderson, T., & Archer, W. (2001). Critical thinking, cognitive presence, and computer conferencing in distance education. *American Journal of Distance Education*, *15*(1), 7–23. doi:10.1080/08923640109527071

Hattie, J. A. C. (2009). *Visible Learning: a synthesis of over 800 meta-analyses relating to achievement*. London: Routledge.

Heflin, H., Shewmaker, J., & Nguyen, J. (2017). Impact of mobile technology on student attitudes, engagement, and learning. *Computers & Education*, *107*, 91–99. doi:10.1016/j.compedu.2017.01.006

Hwang, G. J. (2014). Definition, framework and research issues of smart learning environments – a context-aware ubiquitous learning perspective. *Smart Learning Environments*, *1*(1), 4. doi:10.118640561-014-0004-5

Kaliisa, R., & Picard, M. (2017). A Systematic Review on Mobile Learning in Higher Education: The African Perspective. *Turkish Online Journal of Educational Technology*, *16*(1), 1–18.

Kearney, M., Schuck, S., Burden, K., & Aubusson, P. (2012). Viewing mobile learning from a pedagogical perspective. *Research in Learning Technology*, *20*(1), n1. doi:10.3402/rlt.v20i0.14406

Kneupper, C. W. (1978). Teaching Argument: An Introduction to the Toulmin Model. *College Composition and Communication, 29*(3), 237–241. doi:10.2307/356935

Koehler, M. J., Mishra, P., & Cain, W. (2013). What is technological pedagogical content knowledge (TPACK)? *Journal of Education, 193*(3), 13–19. doi:10.1177/002205741319300303

Koole, M. L. (2009). A model for framing mobile learning. *Mobile Learning: Transforming the Delivery of Education and Training, 1*(2), 25-47.

Lakkala, M., & Ilomäki, L. (2015). A case study of developing ICT-supported pedagogy through a collegial practice transfer process. *Computers & Education, 90*, 1–12. doi:10.1016/j.compedu.2015.09.001

Lee, K., & Salman, R. (2012). The Design and Development of Mobile Collaborative Learning Application Using Android. *Journal of Information Technology and Application in Education. JITAE, 1*(1), 1–8.

Marin, V. I., Jääskelä, P., Häkkinen, P., Juntunen, M., Rasku-Puttonen, H., & Vesisenaho, M. (2016). Seamless Learning Environments in Higher Education with Mobile Devices and Examples. *International Journal of Mobile and Blended Learning, 8*(1), 51–68. doi:10.4018/IJMBL.2016010104

Meyer, K. A. (2003). Face-to-face versus threaded discussions: The role of time and higher-order thinking. *Journal of Asynchronous Learning Networks, 7*(3), 55–65.

Ozdamli, F., & Cavus, N. (2011). Basic Elements and Characteristics of Mobile Learning. *Procedia: Social and Behavioral Sciences, 28*, 937–942. doi:10.1016/j.sbspro.2011.11.173

Pegrum, M., Oakley, G., & Faulkner, R. (2013). Schools going mobile: A study of the adoption of mobile handheld technologies in Western Australian independent schools. *Australasian Journal of Educational Technology, 29*(1). doi:10.14742/ajet.64

Richardson, J. C., & Ice, P. (2010). Investigating students´ level of critical thinking across instructional strategies in online discussions. *Internet and Higher Education, 13*(1-2), 52–59. doi:10.1016/j.iheduc.2009.10.009

Rockinson-Szapkiw, A. J., Courduff, J., Carter, K., & Bennett, D. (2013). Electronic versus traditional print textbooks: A comparison study on the influence of university students' learning. *Computers & Education, 63*, 259–266. doi:10.1016/j.compedu.2012.11.022

Rommetveit, R. (2003). On the Role of "a Psychology of the Second Person" in *Studies of Meaning, Language, and Mind. Mind, Culture, and Activity. International Journal (Toronto, Ont.), 10*(3), 203–218.

Sana, F., Weston, T., & Cepeda, N. J. (2013). Laptop multitasking hinders classroom learning for both users and nearby peers. *Computers & Education, 62*, 24–31. doi:10.1016/j.compedu.2012.10.003

Scardamalia, M. (2004). CSILE/Knowledge forum®. *Education and Technology: An Encyclopedia, 183*, 192.

Simon, S., Erduran, S., & Osborne, J. (2006). Learning to Teach Argumentation: Research and development in the science classroom. *International Journal of Science Education, 28*(2-3), 235–260. doi:10.1080/09500690500336957

Tolmie, A., & Boyle, J. (2000). Factors influencing the success of computer mediated communication (CMC) environments in university teaching: A review and case study. *Computers & Education, 34*(2), 119–140. doi:10.1016/S0360-1315(00)00008-7

Tømte, C., Enochsson, A. B., Buskqvist, U., & Kårstein, A. (2015). Educating online student teachers to master professional digital competence: The TPACK-framework goes online. *Computers & Education, 84*, 26–35. doi:10.1016/j.compedu.2015.01.005

Vygotsky, L. S. (1978). *Mind in Society: Development of Higher Psychological Processes.* Academic Press.

Wenger, E. (1998). *Communities of Practice - Learning, meaning and Identity.* New York: Cambridge University Press. doi:10.1017/CBO9780511803932

Wertsch, J. V. (1998). *Mind as Action.* Oxford: Oxford University Press.

Zhu, Z. T., Yu, M. H. & Riezebos, P. (2016). A research framework of smart education. *Smart Learning Environments, 3*(1), 4.

# Chapter 2
# Smart Mobile Learning Environment


## ABSTRACT

*Digital technology is promoting a vision for self-directed, motivated, adaptive, resource-enriched, and technology-embedded smart higher education, as in this chapter about a smart mobile learning environment. A smart learning environment shall encourage mobile and blended prerequisites and activities across various dimensions, including the notion that students can learn anywhere and anytime and easily switch learning contexts to another or a variety of scenarios. Methodically, the qualitative data illustrates a smart mobile learning hub, MLH, for student-centered learning, both in and out of the university and during practical training in the profession by using smart devices such as mobile laptop, tablet, or smart mobile. Theoretically, the analysis joins the research tradition of computer-supported collaborative learning, CSCL, complemented with computer self-efficacy, CSE. The result show that it is important in the design of smart learning environment to motivate a variety of students so they can be self-directed and adaptive in joining the resource-enriched and technology-embedded education.*


DOI: 10.4018/978-1-7998-4183-8.ch002

## BACKGROUND

University teachers take often for granted that the students are active on an individual and voluntary basis and already are able to increase and discover the value of collaboration, dialogue exchanges, as well as reflections of own learning and self-assessments afterwards for knowledge development (Amhag & Jakobsson, 2009; Amhag, 2013b). Dialogic exchanges between students do not developed only on their own. It requires more and other support from teachers to progress their competence of presenting topics, exchanging ideas and give/receive feedback from other students and teachers, as well as create critical reflections and self-assessments afterwards.

This chapter increases the knowledge about the design of a smart mobile learning hub, MLH for student-centered learning both in- and out-off the university and during practical training in the profession by using smart devices such as mobile laptop, tablet or smart mobile phone. The MLH is a kind of mobile portfolio that goes beyond simple application of technology by integrating smart technology with smart pedagogy (Spector, 2014; Zhu, Yu & Riezebos, 2016). The word 'smart' is an acronym for self-directed, motivated, adaptive, resource-enriched, and technology-embedded, and refers to wisdom as bounding together the ability of using and motivating self-directed learning, knowledge building, problem solving, critically reflections, collaborating and evaluating different circumstances in a resource-enriched learning environment with technology-embedded tools (Hwang, 2014; Zhu, Yu & Riezebos, 2016).

The goal of MLH is to provide the advantages of collaborative and reflective activities into student-centered learning in higher education by a smart self-directed and motivated learning environment which is resource-enriched with technology-embedded tools. The following questions are addressed:

- In what way can teachers a) design and b) use different smart mobile learning environment with mobile learning activities and wearable tools that are appropriate for student-centered learning and active participation?
- How do the students experience the smart mobile activities and the wearable tools for their learning?
- In what way can the smart mobile activities and tools be analyzed comparing to the students' performance?

The user interface of a smart learning environment should be based on that all students are using different social media and digital resources. In particular, the design with different place, based on individual and collective learning circumstances (Amhag & Jakobsson, 2009; Amhag, 2013b; Gros, 2016). The design of a smart learning environment, revised from Couros (2006, p. 172) and Hwang (2014, p. 7), is given in Figure 1 for more and less networking students.

*Figure 1. Framework of smart learning environment revised from Couros (2006, p. 172) and Hwang (2014, p. 7)*

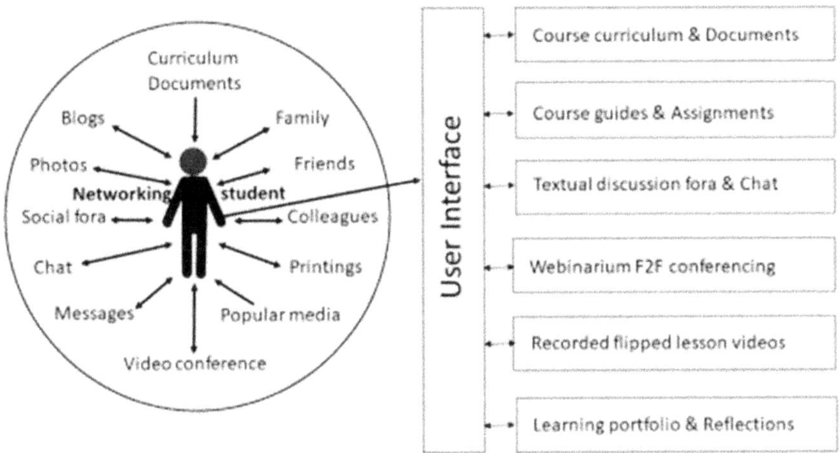


The framework of a smart learning environment illustrates that it is important to create a context-aware and blended learning context, mixed with in-class lectures reviewing course documents at the university, and followed up with out-of-class online mobile-assisted learning activities, e.g. webinars F2F conferencing; teacher recorded flipped lesson videos; peer feedback processes; textual discussion fora; chat for collaborative knowledge exchanges; as well as within individual learning portfolio for reflections and self-evaluations; in addition to teachers tutoring or guidance. However, it is a challenging issue for teachers in higher education to adapt the user interface with different modules to meet student-centered learning needs in a smart learning environment with smart pedagogy.

## PREVIOUS RESEARCH OF SMART LEARNING ENVIRONMENT

The rapid development of mobile communication technology has resulted in several challenges faced by current educational systems and teachers in higher education, such as an increased focus on student-centered learning and mobile technology learning, but also the setting for formal and informal learning (Wong & Looi, 2011). Informal learning is used to supplement or reinforce formal learning from various higher education programs. Informal learning methods should be easily accessible and available to students via wireless technology. According to Chen, Cheng and Chew (2016), the time allocation of formal learning in higher education is changed up to 50 percent with mobile technology. Informal learning can then be used for the other 50 percent with blended learning activities, accessible from a smart learning environment.

Selected articles for review of previous research were obtained from searches in databases in education and social sciences such as ERIC, Libsearch etc. and from studies cited by these authors and from previously used peer review articles published in the relevant field with keywords: learning environment and higher education.

In recent years higher education has performed various Technology-Enhanced Learning, TEL-projects, e.g. in Malaysia, Singapore, Australia, South Korea, New York, Finland and United Arab Emirates. According to Chatti, Agustiawan, Jarke and Specht (2010), TEL initiatives still have a centralized technology-push approach in which learning content is pushed to a predefined group of students in closed Learning Management System, LMS. They are arguing for a new vision for learning and a shift toward a more open and student-pull model for learning that can support students to take control over their learning experiences by creating and managing their own Personal Learning Environment, PLE with a reuse and combination of different sources to create new functions for learning.

Chan, Roschelle, Hsi, Kinshuk, Sharples, Brown, et al. (2006) has been studying how TEL can move one-to-one technically enhanced learning, towards seamless learning space. One-to-one TEL means that the students are using at least one mobile device with support of *e-learning* through digital electronic tools, and *m-learning* through mobile devices and wireless transmission. Instead of associate the two terms e-learning and m-learning with simplified understanding to facilitate learning by delivering instructional content, they are putting high value on active, productive, creative and collaborative methods. They share a vision of global research, inviting other research groups to collaborate in ongoing, mobile activities.

Therefore, there are different challenges with current learning environments to transform the interface to be a smart learning environment with new technological tool functions with required pedagogical shift to reshape student-centered learning behaviours and teachers' teaching methods (Chen et al., 2016). As a result, educators in higher education are facing increasing problems in preparing and structuring formal courses to accommodate various networking students with self-directed and motivational learning activities at different levels of knowledge.

Spector (2014) highlights that a smart learning environment should be "effective, efficient and engaging" for a wide variety of students with different levels of prior knowledge, different backgrounds, and different interests, as well as offer both individual and collaborative challenges and formative feedback based on educational strategies. It is not enough for students in higher education to only get self-regulated course assignments and interact on their own anywhere and at anytime. It requires the access to the core plan, course guides and course literature with continuing support for strategies of feedback processes, supportive tools and the right learning suggestions, at the right time and in the right form (Hwang, 2014). It is also highly desirable for the design of a smart learning environment to motivate different students, recognising their competencies, learning styles and interests (Hwang, Lai & Wang, 2015; Spector, 2014).

The intention is to operationalize each characteristics and potential criteria to create appropriate performance measures and participations, compared to traditional, non-smart learning environments with techno-centric point of view (Gros, 2016; Spector, 2014). To support progressive development and refinement of smart learning environments, evaluations with both formative and summative aspects should be made, e.g. regular and systematic collection and analysis of students and teachers expectations and how their perceptions change over time. According to Spector (20124, p. 9) the smart learning environment should be developed by educational research to reach *effectiveness, efficiency, engagement, flexibility, adaptability,* and *reflectiveness*:

*...effectiveness (an ability to achieve recognized goals and objectives), efficiency (the ability to be effective without exorbitant costs and extreme effort), engagement (the willingness to collaborate with and learn from others), flexibility (the willingness to try new things), adaptability (the ability to adjust to different situations and make appropriate adjustments), and reflectiveness (the ability to recognize successes and failures and learn from mistakes).*

Another perspective is the concept of learning ecology which is an important part of smart learning environments that goes beyond a simplified techno-centric point of view (Barron, 2006; Gros, 2016). Central is to understand that technology is embedded within the students' usual life experiences and networking by maintaining social relationships.

Excerpts of adolescent students are illustrating different pathways for learning interest (Barron, 2006). In the result, five types of self-initiated learning processes are identified:

1. Searching for text-based information resources.
2. Creating new interactive activities contexts such as projects.
3. Searching for structured learning opportunities such as courses.
4. Exploration of media.
5. Development of mentorship or knowledge relationships.

The framework of learning ecology by Barron (2006) highlights the necessity to better understand how learning out-of-school relates to learning in-school or other formal organizations, and vice versa. Three assumptions of learning ecology are concretized in three dimensions:

1. The different resources must sustain and encourage the learning interest.
2. The student shall not only choose, but also develop and create learning opportunities for themselves when they are interested, if they have time, freedom and resources to learn.
3. Interest driven learning activities are boundary-crossing and self-supporting.

The view of learning ecology understands the student as the main player in their networking by maintaining social relationships and creating meanings in physical and virtual contexts (Barron, 2006).

In summary, a smart learning environment should generally contribute to and support learning in different ways, but the learning environment should also be quality-audited and integrate necessary improvements and evaluate the curriculum or course objectives needed for students to be well-equipped and prepared for new types of professions and future requirements. (Hwang, 2014; Hwang, Lai & Wang, 2015; Spector, 2014). However, modern information and communication technology is facing a major challenge for the design and development of smart learning environments for higher education. Therefore, universities can have benefit from "thinking out the box" by teaching students with mixed learning activities, blending with in-class and out-of-class, and integrating work experiences that involve the profession or business.

## DESIGN OF SMART MOBILE LEARNING HUB

A smart learning environment will be illustrated by a design of a mobile learning hub, MLH, providing mobile and blended learning and activities across various dimensions at distance and spaces for learning blended with in-class and out-of-class, including the notion that students can learn anywhere and anytime, and easily switch learning contexts to another or a variety of scenarios (Amhag, 2019). It is important that the MLH promotes theoretical and practical topics, collaboration, reflections and self-assessments encouraging students to find their own ways of learning and to act and think critically, and professionally, as an integral part of the higher education program. The design of a MLH can easily be replicated and accessible from a smart learning environment with different digital devices.

The goal of a smart learning environment as a MLH, illustrated in Figure 2, is to provide different support organized in modules which are accessible from the student' laptops, tablets, and cell phones. This MLH was organized with a main folder per semester with subfolders for different course materials and activities, where the students could download and access e.g. feedback processes, recorded flipped lesson videos and webinars F2F, as well as individual learning portfolio from their practical training in their new profession with different tasks.

There were also folders in which they could post their written reflections and self-assessments during the different courses. The MLH had also a link to the e-meeting system hosted for mobile online face-to-face, F2F webinars, where the student could discuss their theoretical readings and practical experiencing's, as well as participating in tutoring and scaffolding delivered by experienced teachers. Within the MLH, there were also a folder containing a link to the different recordings of the webinar sessions available afterwards

*Figure 2. The mobile learning hub, MLH, accessible from different digital devices (Amhag, 2019)*

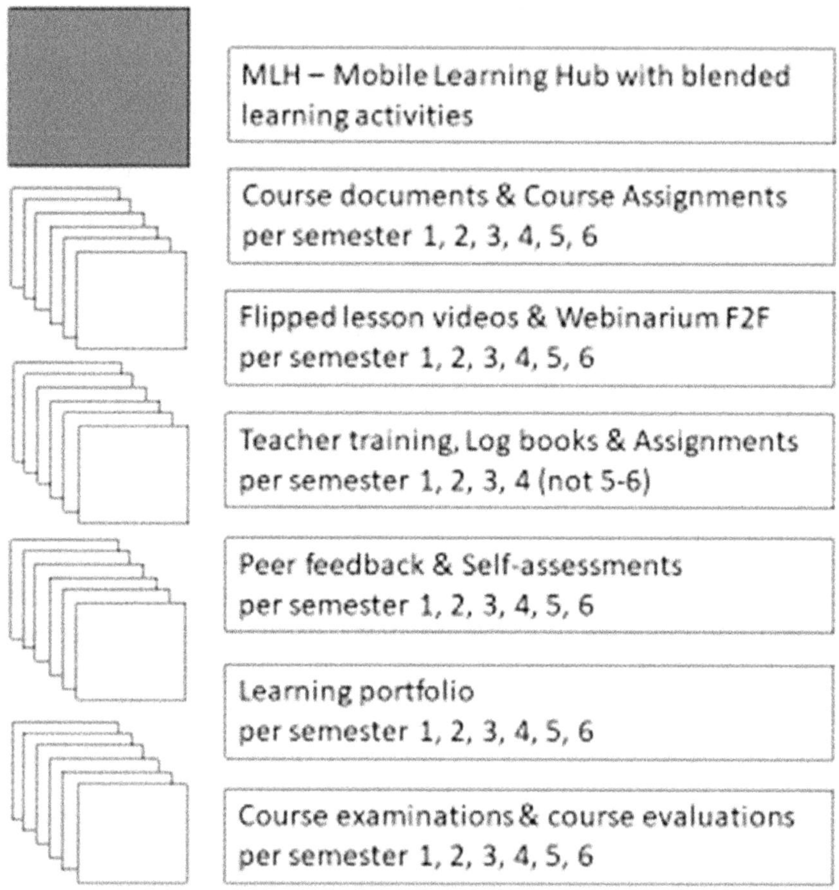


for further critical review. Likewise, the students could use these recordings as input for their reflections and self-evaluations of their learning.

## METHOD OF SMART MOBILE LEARNING ENVIRONMENT

Methodically, the qualitative data illustrate and analyses students using of the smart mobile learning hub, MLH for student-centered learning both in- and out-off the university and during practical training in the profession by using smart devices such as mobile laptop, tablet or cellphone. Following three preliminary and partial set of characteristics: *necessary, highly desirable* and *likely,* are used to divide the design of smart learning environment (Spector, 2014, p. 7).

1. *Necessary* is when; a) effectiveness reaches students generally acceptable or desirable learning outcomes; b) efficiency shows cost-effective initial investment, support and maintenance over a five-year period; c) scalability is over a small number of limited and restricted try-outs; d) autonomous response make the students become more organized and aware of their own learning goals, processes and results.
2. *Highly desirable* is; a) engagement to motivating and maintaining continued interest and participation of a variety of students; b) flexible and adaptable changes, such as joining the course, introducing different resources or adding additional goals; c) adaptive to specific learning needs by recognizing competencies, learning methods and interests; d) personal in providing assignments and / or formative feedback when needed or progressing rapidly.
3. *Likely* is when: a) conversations and engagement in students' dialogue exchanges can promote group negotiations on relevant topics and problem based situations; b) reflection and self-evaluation is based on the student's progress and performance with different mobile learning activities that can be modified to improve overall efficiency but also the students' self-efficacy; c) innovation through using new and emerging technologies creatively can support smart learning and teaching; d) self-organization to reorganize resources and control functions to improve performance over time, based on data automatically collected and used to refine how the environment interacts with students during different circumstances.

Hwang (2014) adds three overall potential criteria for a smart learning environment:

a) *Context-aware* with a focus into students' learning situations or the context in the real environment where the students are, which means that the system can provide teacher support based on course goals and the students' circumstances online and off-line;
b) *Direct and adaptive support* to students by immediate analyses of the students' needs from different perspectives, as well as the online and real-

world contexts in which they are situated. Moreover, students can actively provide various individual and collective support, including tutoring, guidance, course guides, peer feedback processes, formative assessment and different learning tools as online webinars F2F conferencing and teacher recorded flipped classroom videos;

c) *Adaptive user interface* for organizing the course subject content and exchange information to meet the students' different learning styles and conditions to be able to interact with the learning environment via mobile devices such as laptops, smartphones or tablets and mobile applications.

## ANALYSIS OF MOBILE LEARNING ENVIRONMENT

The analysis of the qualitative empirical data is taken from the design of the mobile learning environment in Vocational Teacher Education (Amhag, 2016a; 2016b). All course content had strong links between vocational training and education. The study examined how 22 adult students experienced the tension between their professional occupation and the studies in higher education to be vocational teachers and in what way their experience-based knowledge could be utilized during their school-based practical vocational training.

Qualitative research interviews were conducted with six representative students (5 women, 1 man). All of them had been working for several years in their occupation. Three of them were already working as informal vocational teachers (without teacher education), and only one of them had previously studied in higher education. Before the study, the students signed an agreement to participate in the study and returned the agreement via e-mail.

Theoretically, the analysis joins the research tradition of Computer Supported Collaborative Learning, CSCL with emphasis on that it is not possible to understand learning solely from individual actions. CSCL is complemented with Computer Self-Efficacy, CSE concerned with individuals' media and information literacy. An overview of the theories is given in Table 1.

CSCL is based on socio-cultural theory, that learning always arises as a product of a social community of practice in which our understanding of language, communication, culture, and various aspects of the social context for learning and development is central. Wenger (1998) consider sociocultural theory of learning in terms of *communities of practice,* CoP constituted by students´negotiated engagement and joint enterprise, as well shared repertoire. There is also a question of collective appropriation of tools through language, and how students use language as a tool for learning. Wenger describes assumptions of learning and the nature of knowledge with four hypotheses:

1. We are social beings which is a central aspect of learning.
2. Knowledge is a matter of the competence to evaluate.
3. Knowing is a matter of participating in the pursuit of such valuation.
4. Meaning is our ability to experience the world and engage with it meaningfully.

Theoretically, the concept of *communities of practice,* CoP (Wenger, 1998) is concretized into four key concepts: *meaning, practice, community* and *identity.* An overview is given in Table 1.

1) *Meaning* is learning as experiences – refers to the students' way of talking about their abilities, individually and collectively, and to experience the life and the world as meaningful.
2) *Practice* is learning as doing – refers to the students' way of talking about their shared experiences, practices and social resources, networking's, and perspectives that can sustain mutual engagement in action.
3) *Community* is learning as belonging – refers to a way of talking about social configurations in which our creativities are defined as worthy of application, and our suggestions and participation are recognizable as competencies.
4) *Identity* is learning as becoming – refers to a way of talking how learning changes the unique person they are and creates personal narratives of becoming. The development is arising in the tension between spaces of academic studies, teaching practices and as a professional, e.g. as hairdresser, seller, waiter, chef, builder or mechanic.

The theoretical approach of self-efficacy is the students' belief about his or her ability to perform a given task (Bandura, 2002). This approach is related to Computer Self-Efficacy, CSE, which is a key variable that may determine students' intentions to use information technology, IT successfully. Research show that self-efficacy instruments have positive and strong influence of efficacy beliefs on achievement and persistence with regard to specific, criterial tasks and to meet the technological demands of an online course (Puzziferro, 2008, p. 73). The concept gives the opportunities to challenge different efficacies and make assessments of students' ability to apply knowledge, and manage and evaluate the mobile learning activities, individually and collectively (Bandura, 2002).

Bandura stresses "self-precepts of efficacy influence thought patterns, actions, and emotional arousal" (1982, p. 122) which are shaping the students' outcomes, and expectations of their individual performance ability. Bandura (1984) distinguishes between the component skills in practice, for example the difference between driving a car in freeway traffic and navigating twisting mountain roads. It is comparable with the individual and collective performance by using recorded flipped-lesson videos and participating in mobile online webinars F2F, as well the use of mobile applications such as laptop, tablet or cell phone to develop CSE, which can be seen as a level of media and information literacy.

Theoretically, CSE is based on the theory of Bandura (1977, p. 194) that efficacy expectations vary on several dimensions that give important performance consequences and are concretized by Compeau and Higgins (1995) three interrelated dimensions: *magnitude, strength* and *generalizability*. An overview is given in Table 1.

1) *The magnitude* of CSE refers to the students' cognitive knowledge processes, based on the ability to communicate, manage information, understand ideas and concepts, as well as analyse and evaluate knowledge content both blended and online.
2) *The strength* of CSE refers to the students' ability to exchange experiences and perform various tasks blended in-class and out-of-class and how to learn with technology that can facilitate some of the problems that students encounter.
3) *Generalizability* of CSE refers the degree to which studies are limited to a specific area of a learning activity, or academic literacy, and use of different software as recorded flipped lesson videos and mobile online webinars F2F and different mobile applications.

According to CSCL and CoP perspectives, students' dialogues, interactions, and interplay constitute a determining factor for their learning and knowledge development in higher education programs. An overview is given in Table 1.

## Analysis of Excerpts

The following excerpts are from a group of six vocational student teachers in higher education and their experienced tension between spaces of their

*Table 1. Overview of Communities of Practice, CoP (Wenger1998), and Computer Self-Efficacy, CSE (Compeau & Higgins, 1995)*

| Communities of practice, CoP (Wenger, 1998) | Computer self-efficacy, CSE (Compeau & Higgins, 1995) |
|---|---|
| *Meaning* is learning as experiencing – refers to the students way of talking about their abilities, individually and collectively, and to experience the life and the world as meaningful. | *Magnitude of CSE* – refers to the students' cognitive knowledge processes, based on the ability to communicate, understand ideas and concepts, as well as analyse and evaluate knowledge content both blended and online. |
| *Practice* is learning as doing –refers to the students' way of talking about their shared experiences, practices and social resources, networking's, and perspectives that can sustain mutual engagement in action. | *Strength of CSE* – refers to the students' ability to exchange experiences and perform various tasks blended in-class and out-of-class and how to learn with technology that can facilitate some of the problems that students encounter. |
| *Community* is learning as belonging – refers to a way of talking about social configurations in which our creativities are defined as worthy of application, and our suggestions and participation are recognizable as competencies. | *Generalizability* of CSE – refers the degree to which studies are limited to a specific area of a learning activity, or academic literacy, and use of different software as recorded flipped lesson videos and mobile online webinars F2F and different mobile applications. |
| *Identity* is learning as becoming – refers to a way of talking how learning changes the unique person they are and creates personal narratives of becoming (e.g. self-efficacy). The development is arising in the tension between spaces of academic studies, teaching practices and as a professional.<br>Note: The students learning in *community of practice* by using mobile technology have impact on their *computer self-efficacy, CSE.* Therefore, expands the dimension of *identity* over both CoP and CSE. | |

academic studies, teaching practises and as vocational teachers in any upper secondary school in Sweden, as well as in what way their experience-based knowledge could be utilized during their school-based practical vocational training.

**Student 1**, a student teacher for Restaurant and Food Program, has no experience as a vocational teacher, and has worked 20 years in different restaurant business as a waiter. At first, she felt that she had no substance to add or relate to in the first course:

*The meeting with the academic world, from having worked for several years in my profession and not having studied earlier in higher education, was a bit of a shock first and I felt that I had no substance to add or relate to in the courses. Nevertheless, it is more a learning process that has occurred inside myself, where I not only see the specific professional skills within the restaurant business. If I hadn´t my professional experiences, I would not have been able to gain insight or have discussions at various meetings about how my profession works. There is actually a lot of feedback to myself I have had, things that It took me some time before I changed my mind a little bit.*

Student 1 experienced the meeting with the academic studies as traumatic. She had nothing to add or relate to from her twenty professional years into the academic studies in the first course about social relations, conflict management and educational leadership. *Meaning* is learning as experiencing, and to try-out the abilities through reading, writing and discussing with others. (Wenger, 1998). After a while, student 1 could discover her own learning process with a lot of own feedback to be able to discuss how her profession works within the student group and with teachers. This *practice* is learning by doing, but it took some time for her to reflect and talk about her experiences, practices and perspectives in her restaurant profession for a school practice (Wenger, 1998). Her *identity* and learning as becoming, was discovered when she realized that learning changed her and created narratives of becoming as a vocational teacher within her. The development of self-efficacy arose in the tension between the spaces of academic studies, teaching practices and as becoming a professional teacher.

After three courses, each with four weeks of practical teacher training at a school, student 1 felt more confident about becoming a professional teacher (Wenger, 1998). She thanks the mixed course design with mixed learning activities and feedback processes.

*Before the practical teacher training at a school, I was wondering about: How does the pupils work, where are they in their learning, do they have some kind of difficulties or do they need to be challenged? These thoughts I did not have at the beginning of the education. I will thank the mixed course design with blended learning activities. I took with me some activities to the pupils, they are often working in groups and they can easily record a certain sequence on each other when they are practising in the dining room. The next lesson they can review a small movie clip and respond to it. I have called it "find five errors", and ask them to find five errors together, often it is small things. But the response on practical issues is quite different and the pupils are learning to give feedback as well. It is also something I learned in the teacher education. Sometimes it is written response, sometimes oral, sometimes in group and sometimes in full class. We have also used some recordedflipped-lesson videos that some teachers have used in the education.*

Student 1 is first reflecting about the pupils learning style and prerequisites when she is answering the question about which course modules she has most benefit from the professional knowledge. The progression of student 1's *magnitude* of CSE has developed and reflects her cognitive knowledge processes based on her ability to communicate with other students and teachers, managing blended learning activities, as well as understand how to use recordings of pupils learning in practice and concepts of different feedback processes (Compeau & Higgins, 1995). Moreover, her *strength* of CSE has also advanced when she is letting the pupils learn with technology as with recorded flipped-lesson videos that can facilitate some of the problems they encounter, and exchange experiences, as well as perform various tasks blended in-class and out-of-class by reviewing small movie clip trying to find five errors, as well as respond to what can be improved (Compeau & Higgins, 1995).

**Student 2**, a student teacher for the Handicraft program in hairdressing, has some experiences as a vocational teacher, mixed with has own hairdressing salon for 15 years. She tries to link her hairdresser profession during the practical teacher training with recorded flipped-lesson videos.

*I try to tie my professional skills into my teaching practice because I also teach in history that is intertwined in hairdressing about tradition and development. I think that recorded flipped-lesson videos is practical to use, that a smaller group gather in the same place, it is clearly visible in front of the computer who has a "finger with" or not. It quickly becomes a receipt for whether they understood or not. Last week I was gone and they had to do a task and record and publish what they did in the learning environment. It's a very smooth way! It is also a way for those students who have difficulty in writing for one reason or another. They can show what they have done, even if they have not written four pages. They have learned something and can describe with pictures and speeches.*

Student 2 is highlighting her own *meaning* to learn through experiencing (Wenger, 1998) when she is using recorded flipped-lesson videos in the teaching practices with the pupils about tradition and development in hairdressing. She observes that the pupils' discussions in front of the computer quickly becomes a receipt of their understandings or not, and who has a "finger with" in hairdressing. She also understands what the pupils have done, even if they had not written four pages. Instead, they can explain their works oral or with pictures. The statement "It's a very smooth way" is an echo of student 2´s media and information literacy as an achieved level of *generalizability* of CSE (Compeau & Higgins, 1995) when the pupils are using recordings and online publishing as learning tools. Moreover, learning processes are developing in practice by doing and collaborating in groups. This way sustains mutual engagement in action and their creativities are recognizable as belonging in the *community of practice* (Wenger, 1998).

**Student 3**, a student teacher for the Handicraft program in stylist and makeup, work as an informal vocational teacher. She highlights the use of flipped teaching and learning.

*I like the flipped-lesson videos very much, because you come prepared and can use the lessons more effectively, than just sitting and listening. What you are listening to can many times be read in the literature. During the follow-up webinars F2F, you can ask questions and take part of other student's thoughts, so it is very good! Especially, when it is distance studies it is good to use it. I use flipped-lesson videos in my school because we do not have so many textbooks. It is easy to record different parts about stylist and makeup, it is a good alternative.*

*How did you experience to be examined orally in webinar F2F online? [in course 3 about reading and writing difficulties]*

*I think it's great, what I could have done better myself was to prepare a media presentation, which I had not done. Just talking about what I wrote about and only having a paper as support is not the same. It is better to have some kind of presentation that everyone can follow. As a teacher, we are used to talk a lot during the lessons with the pupils, but one always use some support, the white board or something else. Otherwise, it is great with webinars F2F, because it is easier to leave the work for a while, than to take a full day off for an exam at the university.*

Student 3 demonstrates the *strength* of CSE when evaluating recorded flipped-lesson videos. She points to the value of being prepared for the webinars F2F online and using the lessons more effectively by asking questions and sharing other students' thoughts (Compeau & Higgins, 1995). She has also reached the level of *generalizability* of CSE (ibid.) by using own flipped-lesson videos as teacher for the pupils about stylist and makeup as an alternative because they do not have many textbooks. She thinks it is easy to record different parts.

On the question, how she experienced the exam orally in the form of webinar F2F online, she realizes that her oral presentation had been more meaningful if she had used a media presentation as support that all in the group could follow. This *meaning* in *practice* through experiencing and evaluating the exam online and orally, she brings with her both in the academic studies and as a vocational teacher. Moreover, her *identity* has changed, ascended and developed in the tension between spaces of academic studies, teaching practices and as a professional (Wenger, 1998).

## CONCLUSION

The result of smart learning environment has shown a set of features based on the three preliminary and partial characteristics: *necessary, highly desirable* and *likely* (Spector, 2014, p. 7), illustrated in three representative excerpts.

Firstly, it is highly desirable for the design of a smart learning environment to motivate and maintain continued interest and participation of a variety of students so they can be flexible and adaptable in joining the course (Spector, 2014). Moreover, it is highly desirable for the design to be adaptive on specific learning needs by recognising students' competencies, learning styles and interests for academic studies, both theoretically and practically for the future profession (Hwang, Lai & Wang, 2015; Spector, 2014). Furthermore, it is *necessary* to reach students generally acceptable or desirable learning outcomes (Spector, 2014), as well as support the students' beliefs of their computer self-efficacy; and performance ability (Bandura, 1982; Compeau & Higgins, 1995). As Bandura (1982) emphasizes, self-efficacy and performance ability are influenced thought patterns, actions, and emotional arousal. They are shaping the students' expectations and expands the space of learning and developing in a creative manner. In particular, guide students to do the right thing, in the right way, at the right time, and in the right place, based on individual and collective learning circumstances to accommodate various networking students with motivational and mixed learning activities at different levels of prior knowledge, different backgrounds, and different interests (Amhag, 2013b; Amhag & Jakobsson, 2009; Chen et al., 2016; Gros, 2016; Spector, 2014).

Secondly, it is *highly desirable* for a smart learning environment to provide smart educational strategies, e.g. personal assignments and formative feedback from peers and teachers, as well as collaborative conversations and engagement in dialogue exchanges. Moreover, shall it be easy accessing the core plan, course guides and course literature with continuing support of feedback processes, reflections and self-evaluations of the student's progress and performance with different mobile learning activities. These mobile learning activities should be evaluated and modified to improve the overall efficiency with supportive tools and the right learning suggestions, at the right time and in the right form (Hwang, 2014; Hwang, Lai & Wang, 2015; Spector, 2014).

Thirdly, it is *highly desirable* for a smart learning environment to develop and evaluate the smart educational strategies on educational research to reach *effectiveness, efficiency, engagement, flexibility, additivity,* and *reflectiveness* (Spector, 2014). Therefore, it is important to do regular and systematic collection and analysis of students and teachers expectations and how their perceptions change over time. *Necessary* for a smart learning environment is to be cost-effective based on initial investment, support and maintenance over a five-year period (Spector, 2014). Frequently, the universities will have benefit from "thinking out the box" by challenging and teaching students with mobile and blended learning activities, mixed with in class and out-of-class, by using *community of practice* integrating work experiences involving both academic studies and practises, as well as the profession or business (Amhag, 2013b; 2016a; 2016b; 2019; Amhag & Jakobsson, 2009; Wenger, 1998).

## REFERENCES

Amhag, L. (2013b). *Creativity in and between Collaborative Peer Assessment Processes in Higher Distance Education. Creative Education, 4(7A2),* 94–104. doi:10.4236/ce.2013.47A2011

Amhag, L. (2016a). Mobile technologies for student centered learning in a distance higher education program. In *Wearable Technology and Mobile Innovations for Next-Generation Education,* (pp. 184-199). IGI Global. https://www.igi-global.com/book/wearable-technology-mobile-innovations-next/142108

Amhag, L. (2016b). Mobile technologies for student centered learning in a distance higher education program. *Blended Learning: Concepts, Methodologies, Tools, and Applications*, *4*, 802–817. doi:10.4018/978-1-5225-0069-8.ch010

Amhag, L. (2020). Student Reflections and Self-Assessments in Vocational Training Supported by a Mobile Learning Hub. *International Journal of Mobile and Blended Learning*, *12*(1), 1–16. doi:10.4018/IJMBL.2020010101

Amhag, L., & Jakobsson, A. (2009). Collaborative Learning as a Collective Competence when Students Use the Potential of Meaning in Asynchronous Dialogues. *Computers & Education*, *52*(3), 656–667. doi:10.1016/j.compedu.2008.11.012

Bandura, A. (1977). Self-efficacy: Toward a unifying theory of behavioral change. *Psychological Review*, *84*(2), 191–215. doi:10.1037/0033-295X.84.2.191 PMID:847061

Bandura, A. (1982). Self-efficacy mechanism in human agency. *The American Psychologist*, *37*(2), 122–147. doi:10.1037/0003-066X.37.2.122

Bandura, A. (1984). Recycling Misconceptions of Perceived Self-efficacy. *Cognitive Therapy and Research*, *8*(3), 231–255. doi:10.1007/BF01172995

Bandura, A. (2002). Growing primacy of human agency in adaption and change in the electronic era. *European Psychologist*, *7*(1), 2–16. doi:10.1027//1016-9040.7.1.2

Barron, B. (2006). Interest and self-sustained learning as catalysts of development: A learning ecology perspective. *Human Development*, *49*(4), 193–224. doi:10.1159/000094368

Chan, T.-W., Roschelle, J., Hsi, S., Kinshuk, Sharples, M., Brown, ... Hoppe, U. (2006). One-to-one technology-enhanced learning: An opportunity for global research collaboration. *Research and Practice in Technology-Enhanced Learning*, *1*(1), 3–29. doi:10.1142/S1793206806000032

Chatti, M. A., Agustiawan, M. R., Jarke, M., & Specht, M. (2010). Toward a personal learning environment framework. *International Journal of Virtual and Personal Learning Environments*, *1*(4), 66–85. doi:10.4018/jvple.2010100105

Chen, N. S., Cheng, I. L., & Chew, S. W. (2016). Evolution is not enough: Revolutionizing current learning environments to smart learning environments. *International Journal of Artificial Intelligence in Education*, *26*(2), 561–581. doi:10.100740593-016-0108-x

Compeau, D. R., & Higgins, C. A. (1995). Computer self-efficacy: Development of measure and initial test. *Management Information Systems Quarterly*, *19*(2), 189–211. doi:10.2307/249688

Couros, A. V. (2006). *Examining the open movement: Possibilities and implications for education* (Dissertation). University of Regina.

Gros, B. (2016). The design of smart educational environments. *Smart Learning Environments, 3*(1), 15. doi:10.118640561-016-0039-x

Hwang, G. J. (2014). Definition, framework and research issues of smart learning environments - a context-aware ubiquitous learning perspective. *Smart Learning Environments, 1*(1), 4. doi:10.118640561-014-0004-5

Hwang, G. J., Lai, C. L., & Wang, S. Y. (2015). Seamless flipped learning: A mobile technology-enhanced flipped classroom with effective learning strategies. *Journal of Computers in Education, 2*(4), 449–473. doi:10.100740692-015-0043-0

Puzziferro, M. (2008). Online technologies self-efficacy and self-regulated learning as predictors of final grade and satisfaction in college-level online courses. *American Journal of Distance Education, 22*(2), 72–89. doi:10.1080/08923640802039024

Spector, J. M. (2014). Conceptualizing the emerging field of smart learning environments. *Smart Learning Environments, 1*(1), 2

Wenger, E. (1998). *Communities of Practice - Learning, Meaning, and Identity*. New York: Cambridge University Press. doi:10.1017/CBO9780511803932

Zhu, Z. T., Yu, M. H. & Riezebos, P. (2016). A research framework of smart education. *Smart Learning Environments, 3*(1), 4.

# Chapter 3
# Smart Learning With Seamless Activities


## ABSTRACT

*The new vision for self-directed, motivated, adaptive, resource-enriched, and technology-embedded smart higher education has promoted smart learning with mobile-assisted seamless activities to learn across time and locations, individual and collective, from one scenario to another including formal and informal learning through smart mobile devices. Methodologically, the collective and ubiquitous leaning for student-centered learning is examined qualitatively with empirical data of how smart education are enhancing students' individual and collaborative learning, rather than focusing on using only technological devices. Theoretically, the analysis is based on the concept of mobile-assisted seamless learning activities, MSL, grounded in six dimensions of actual learning. The findings display that smart learning with mobile-assisted seamless mediated learning activities improves with the design of before-, in-, and after-class stages with a focus on contextual, adapted, and self-directed seamless learning activities to promote the students' capabilities to learn, collaborate, and critically solve problems in different situations and contexts.*


DOI: 10.4018/978-1-7998-4183-8.ch003

## BACKGROUND

Smart education is a new global educational paradigm and a concept that describes learning in a digital age based on smart pedagogy for smart learning (Zhu, Yu & Riezebos, 2016). The point of departure is based in foundations on smart devices and intelligent technologies for accessing course documents, course literature, inquiry, communication and collaboration, as well as construction and evaluation. This is made possible by improved wearable technologies, faster internet transmission, and smart mobile devices through wireless networks (e.g. Amhag, 2016; 2017; Lee & Salman, 2012; Marin, Jääskelä, Häkkinen, Juntunen, Rasku-Puttonen & Vesisenaho, 2016).

This article progresses the knowledge about the design of smart learning with seamless activities including both in classroom and out of classroom with teacher recoded flipped lesson videos, in online webinars with verbal face-to-face, F2F communications and parallel textual chat exchanges with other students and teachers for their seamless learning and teaching. The article demonstrates in representative excerpts seamless learning activities and how they can increase student-centered learning and bridge between smart pedagogy and intelligent technologies in different professional teaching practices. The following questions are addressed:

- In what way can teachers a) design and b) use different smart learning with seamless activities and wearable tools that are appropriate for student-centered learning and active participation?
- How do the students experience the smart learning with seamless activities and the wearable tools for their learning?
- In what way can the smart learning with seamless activities and tools be analyzed comparing to the students' performance?

The word 'smart' is an acronym for self-directed, motivated, adaptive, resource-enriched, and technology-embedded, and refers to wisdom as bounding together the ability of using and motivating self-directed learning, knowledge building, problem solving, critically reflections, collaborating and evaluating different circumstances with resource-enriched and technology-embedded tools (Hwang, 2014; Zhu, Yu & Riezebos, 2016).

'Smart learning' focuses on student-centered learning based on context-aware ubiquitous learning more than on devices. The features of smart learning include formal and informal learning, social and collaborative learning, personalized and situated learning, as well as application and content focus

(Lee, Zo & Lee, 2014). Nevertheless, the mobile devices should be effective and intelligent for tailored learning based on advanced IT infrastructure, e.g. context-aware ubiquitous learning system with GPS and learning system for guiding (Hwang, 2014; Kim, Cho & Lee, 2012; Kukulska-Hulme & Viberg, 2018; Scott & Benlamri, 2010; Zhu, Yu & Riezebos, 2016).

'Smart education' is based on smart pedagogy to make the students engaging and motivating in their learning and increase their independence in more open, collaborative and augmented environment with individually and collectively richer and smarter context (Zhu, Yu & Riezebos, 2016). In this way, smart higher education has expanded spaces and opportunities for mobile teaching and learning, observation and documentation, as well as participation and creativeness. The space of smart learning is transformed into flexible and smart technology-enhanced settings where students should be the key creator in the learning space design that can support various learning modes, e.g. formal, informal, ad hoc, and virtual learning (Scott & Benlamri, 2010). Three main educational goals should be included:

1. Provide a learning environment to enhance collaborative learning and face-to-face interactions between students and teachers.
2. Creating new patterns of social and intellectual interactions.
3. Provide activity-based resources that promote knowledge dissemination and sharing.

A seamless learner is expected to explore, identify and seize boundless opportunities across contexts, seamlessly and integrally, which are extending students' learning space through accessing different resources in the smart learning environment (Wong & Looi, 2011; Wong, 2012).

The "seamless" concept is defined as continuous experiences of learning and purposely bridging the multidimensional learning outcomes over a combination of places, times, technologies, or social settings (Hwang, Lai & Wang, 2015). The concept has change from considering separate and distinct parts – e.g. in-class and out-of-class, at school and during free time, academic at school and non-academic at practice, formal and informal learning, or on- and off-campus experiences – to being one part bound together (Kuh, 1996; Wong & Looi, 2011). Students are encouraged to take advantage of learning resources that exist both inside and outside of the classroom and use their life experiences to make meaning of introduced materials.

In recent years, flipped learning and teaching has received increased attention from interdisciplinary higher education and educators around the world (Lin & Hwang, 2018). The concept of the flipped classroom has been implemented in many different disciplines in higher education, such as in social and medical sciences (Akçayır & Akçayır, 2018). Mainly the focus is on the students, not the teacher, to progress the in-class practicing time and interactions to improve students' self-efficacy for higher education, performance and motivation with support of flipped classroom. The easiest definition of teacher-recorded flipped lessons or flipped classroom is: "Inverting the classroom means that events that have traditionally taken place inside the classroom now take place outside the classroom and vice versa" (Lage, Platt & Treglia, 2000, p.32). The core idea of flipped classroom is to invert the common instructional approach, as homework before inside the classroom, instead of after, by using teacher-recorded lesson videos with various topic content, concepts and instructions. The flipped lesson videos can be accessed from any mobile devices, available at anytime and anywhere, prior to the class learning activities.

"Class" becomes the room at the university or in the mobile online webinars integrating face-to-face, F2F conferencing with a predefined aim of using real-time experiences and literature discussions with guidance from a teacher. The potential of mobile online webinars F2F is that everyone can see and hear each other's verbally through discussions, while at the same time communicating via textual chat and notes. Furthermore, the synchronous online webinars F2F can be recorded for later asynchronous viewing online within the Learning Management System, LMS in order to provide students with the opportunity to take a step back, reflect, self-assess and compare various contributions. The concept removes the teacher-recorded lessons and instructions from the classroom at the university or in online webinars F2F in order to allow better use of the in-class time during the online webinars F2F with discussions, tutoring and scaffolding in student-centered learning (Bishop & Verleger, 2013; Lage et al., 2000; Long, Logan & Waugh, 2014).

Learning is usually defined as the knowledge process of obtaining professional competence and understandings (Gros, 2016), resulting in a new ability to do something, and an understanding of something that was previously not understood. Competence is sometimes described in terms of possessing specific skills, understanding in terms of possessing in depth knowledge as a kind of higher-order thinking (Amhag, 2013b). However, it is important to research about how smart education based on smart pedagogy for smart learning with flipped teaching and learning in a more wireless form of higher education are enhancing students' individual and collaborative learning. Empirical evidence is needed on the significance of how different conditions of mobile-assisted seamless mediated learning activities can contribute to the broadening of smart education based on smart pedagogy for smart learning.

## PREVIOUS RESEARCH OF SEAMLESS LEARNING

Advances in mobile technology in higher education has changed students' learning actions and redesigned the teaching methods. The rapid development of wireless education has also developed new research topics, such as; Technology-Enhanced Learning (TEL) as a media or tools providing flexibility in the mode of learning (Zhu, et al., 2016); seamless learning (Wong & Looi, 2011); mobile learning (Alrasheedi & Capretz, 2018; Amhag, 2016; Kearney, Schuck, Burden & Aubusson, 2012); and ubiquitous learning (Chan, Roschelle, Hsi, Kinshuk, Sharples, Brown, et al., 2006; Hwang, 2014); for both formal and informal learning (Hwang & Wu, 2014; Scott & Benlamri, 2010). Selected articles for review of previous research were obtained from searches in databases in education and social sciences such as ERIC, Libsearch etc. and from studies cited by these authors and from previously used peer review articles published in the relevant field with keywords: seamless learning and higher education.

The concept of Mobile-assisted Seamless Learning activities, MSL, expands spaces of e-learning, m-learning and u-learning, about time and place, from one scenario to another, between individual and collaborative learning, as well as formal and informal learning, supported by smart technological devices at anytime and anywhere (Amhag, 2016; 2017; Hwang, Lai & Wang, 2008; Kim, et al., 2012). Seamless learning space include scenarios of a collective and an individual process, across time and locations, ubiquitous access to learning resources, encompassing physical and digital worlds, engaging multiple types of devices, and integrating different approaches to teaching and learning. Nevertheless, the success of mobile-assisted seamless learning heavily depends on teachers' learning designs (Wong & Looi, 2011).

Ubiquitous learning (*u-learning*) is blended with mobile, augmented and seamless learning, synonymously used for the ubiquitous phenomenon of learning at anytime and anywhere without limitations (Kim, Cho & Lee, 2012; Virtanen, Haavisto, Liikanen & Kääriäinen, 2018). Three phenomenon of learning should be included:

1. A situation of ubiquitous learning activities which can be conducted in a different space and time for each student or student groups.

2. Ubiquitous distributed experiences in different time and space.
3. Teaching materials accessible from any mobile devices, available at anytime and anywhere.

The rapid development of mobile communication technology has resulted in several challenges faced by current educational systems and teachers in higher education, such as an increased focus on student-centered learning and mobile technology learning, but also the practice for formal and informal learning (Wong & Looi, 2011). Informal learning is used to supplement or reinforce formal learning from various higher education programs. Informal learning methods are easily accessible and available to students via the Internet, resulting in a change in the time allocation of formal learning in the education up to 50 percent (Chen, Cheng & Chew, 2016).

To bridge formal and informal aspects of learning is when students negotiate in-school and out-of-school learning spaces (Wong, Chai, Aw & King, 2015). The findings indicate that student participation significantly improved, but teachers must plan and stimulate online interactions and negotiations, as well as create artefacts, such as teacher-recorded flipped videos, instructions and examples of problem-based situations. In addition, there is a growing gap about the importance of prior formal and informal knowledge for students learning both in-school, out-of-school and mobile online, as well as an insufficient matching between individual career choices and work development (Chen, et al., 2016).

Research trends of flipped classroom studies from a review of journal publications during 2008 to 2017 based on the technology-enhanced learning model by Lin and Hwang (2018), show that most studies of flipped teaching in medical courses mainly emphasized basic knowledge understandings and skills training, while little attention was paid to developing students' higher order thinking skills. Another large-scale systematic review of 71 Web of Science articles on the flipped classroom about the advantages and challenges for both students and teachers by Akçayır and Akçayır (2018) demonstrates improvements of student learning performance. Some potential challenges need to be addressed to implement the flipped classroom, such as the quality of the instructional videos by keeping the content interesting and brief, as well as providing feedback during the out-of-class activities and preparations before in-class activities.

Additional study display that the flipped classroom may promote students' creativity, especially with regard to ability, flexibility and novelty (Al-Zahrani, 2015). Difficulties were particularly related to teachers' preparation of the flipped strategy, and the students' advantage of the flipped lessons, as well as having adequate e-learning tools and follow-up with meaningful activities in the in-class time. The study by Lee and Choi (2019) also indicates significant and strong learning outcomes and experienced learning readiness through flipped classroom with video material than if they received reading materials. Among several student factors, self-direction was affected. Three methods of pre-class content learning between interactive online tutorials, video lectures, and textbook readings show the study by Jensen, Holt, Sowards, Heath Ogden and West (2018) that video lectures offer a small advantage to overall student learning over interactive online tutorials and textbook readings. The value of the various activities have significance for the student's cognitive processes, regardless of whether the setting is traditional in-class or out-of-class with flipped teaching display the study by DeLozier and Rhodes (2017).

However, relatively little new technology learning approaches and instructional models have been implemented in higher education with any significant learning outcomes. Foremost, teachers need to plan and apply seamless activities to systematically promote the artefacts' quality and online interactions between students (Wong, Chai, Aw & King, 2015). In particular, points Hwang and Wu (2014) out that some teachers still doubt the effectiveness of using smart technologies in school settings. Their statistical data show that mobile technology was rarely used in several subject domains, such as astronomy, physics, chemistry and arts. Moreover, has new technology learning often been used without adequate training and support among teachers (Amhag, Hellström & Stigmar, 2019; Spector, 2014).

Contrary, show the review of seven publications between 2008 to 2012 about technology-enhanced learning and their applications and impacts that mobile learning is promising in improving students' learning achievements, motivations and interests (Hwang &Wu, 2014). Another review of mobile collaborative language learning studies (Kukulska-Hulme & Viberg, 2018), including 33 articles published in 21 peer-reviewed journals during 2012–16, present a convincing benefits of collaboration to improve negotiation of meaning and opportunities for feedback, increased motivation, engagement and enjoyment, as well as mutual encouragement, reduction in nervousness and embarrassment. A few negative results are risk of distraction, safety concerns, feelings of uncertainty and technical problems.

A critical aspect is that the research studies often are conducted on a small scale in a privileged context, for example among experienced or enthusiastic teachers and interested researchers, and peer review accepted articles in technical journals. An example is the case study by Marin et al. (2016) which show that the tablet devices were using as mediators and cognitive tools by the pupils that enhanced the creation of ubiquitous and seamless learning spaces from the teachers' point of view; the pupils' perspective is not included in the study. Another case study by Lan and Lin (2016) show notable improvements in two groups of Chinese language in teachers' test-based communication performance. The online group in the study made significantly fewer errors and had more mutual collaboration through the various individual and collective support in their LMS, compared to the classroom group.

Additional case study by Laru and Järvelä (2015) is designing the integrated use of multiple social software tools and face-to-face activities to support self-regulated learning. The result show that pedagogically grounded instructional design is needed in order to effectively use new technologies. Even a study on workplace learning display that the companies have failed to capture the features of the new learning environment and verify its impact on the assumption (Lee, Zo & Lee 2014). The companies have focused on traditional e-learning environment, and failed to adapt the educational needs of employees and technology-oriented organizational focus.

Regardless of how valuable the teaching methods may be, the higher education sector is known to be extremely slow to make changes and implement technological and educational advances (Amhag, Hellström & Stigmar, 2019). Moreover, the necessary pedagogical changes to make actual use of these technological advances are even slower.

## DESIGN OF SMART LEARNING WITH SEAMLESS ACTIVITIES

Several researches begin to pay attention to the importance and necessity of authentic and seamless activities in which students work with problem based situations from the area of profession (Hwang et al. 2008; Zuh et al., 2016). In order to situate students' smart learning with smart education, it is important to design learning that combine both actual and virtual learning environments. Zhu and He (2012, p. 6) describes that:

*The essence of smart education is to create intelligent environments by using smart technologies, so that smart pedagogies can be facilitated as to provide personalized learning services and empower learners, and thus talents of wisdom who have better value orientation, higher thinking quality, and stronger conduct ability could be fostered.*

Based on this definition of smart education, the following research framework is proposed by Zhu, Yu and Riezebos (2016) revised in Figure 1. The framework defines three essential elements in smart education: smart learning environments, smart pedagogies, and smart learners. Smart education give emphasis to the ideology for quality-enhanced education. Therefore, renamed as smarter education, which address to smart pedagogies as methodological approach and smart learning environments as technological approach (Zhu, Yu & Riezebos, 2016). The goal is to advance the education to educate smart learners as results. Smart learning environments should be significant influenced by smart pedagogies, e.g. socio-cultural- and cognitive theories, to support the development of smart learners (Amhag, 2017).

*Figure 1. Research framework of smart education revised from Zhu, Yu and Riezebos (2016, p. 17)*

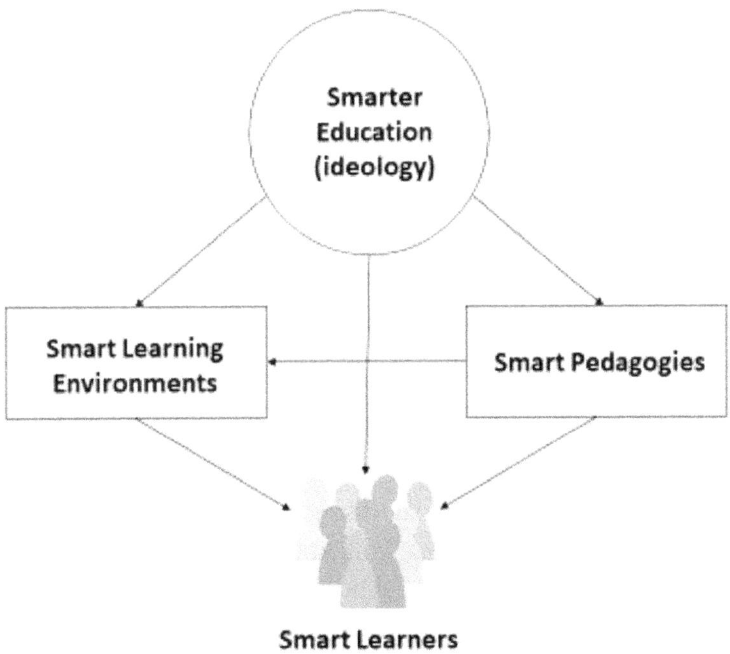

Essential is also to engage the students in varied learning processes to adapt their self-efficacy, attitudes and learning methods to the situation of learning seamlessly in view of mobile technology-supported learning activities as part of the formal curriculum. A technology-based learning model of flipped classrooms include before-class-, in-class-, and after-class stages (Hwang, Lai & Wang, 2015, p. 460), illustrated in Figure 2.

*Figure 2. Technology-based Learning model for flipped classroom (Hwang et al., 2015, p. 460)*

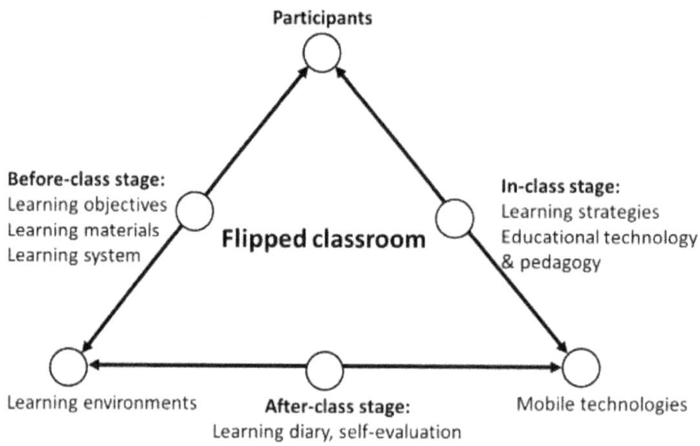


1. The before-class stage includes learning objectives, learning materials, learning system, and online discussion fora to engage students in self-learning at home. Form of teaching material means that the adopted teaching material can be downloaded before the in-class, including instructional videos, animations or e-books, learning tasks and course literature.
2. The in-class stage includes learning strategies and educational technology and pedagogy to engage students in higher order thinking. Learning strategies are classified into issue discussion, practicing or doing exercises, mind tool-based learning (e.g. concept maps), problem-based learning, inquiry-based learning, personal projects or group projects (e.g. reports, cases) and peer-to-peer and peer-to-teacher interactions in all learning spaces.

3. The after-class stage includes learning diary, submission of personal projects or group projects with reflections and self-evaluations, after-course evaluations, without activity.

## METHOD OF SMART LEARNING WITH SEAMLESS ACTIVITIES

Methodologically, the collective and ubiquitous leaning for student-centered learning is examined qualitatively with empirical data of how smart education are enhancing students' individual and collaborative learning, rather than focusing on using only technological devices. The result show that the fusion of technology and didactic pedagogy involves active participation between students and teachers with support of seamless activities e.g. teacher recorded flipped lesson videos, online webinars face-to-face, F2F, peer feedback processes with formative assessment and other online course materials (Amhag, 2016a; 2016b; 2017). As well as a portfolio for self-reflection and lifelong learning, and individual and collective teaching methods that are transmitted seamlessly to students as they move from one learning context to another (Amhag, 2020; Chen, et al., 2016).

The purpose of smart learning didactic is to support the students for new knowledge, even when they are engaged in leisure activities. Following ten key features can be defined as smart learning (Hwang, 2014; Zhu, Yu & Riezebos, 2016, p.11):

1. Location-aware: the location in real time is important data that the systems need in order to adapt the content and situation to the learner;
2. Context-aware: are exploring different activity scenarios and information;
3. Socially-aware: are sensing social relationships;
4. Interoperable: setting standards for different resources, services and platforms;
5. Seamless connection: are providing continuous service when any device connects;
6. Adaptable: are pushing learning resources according to access, preference and demand;
7. Ubiquitous: are predicting learner demands until clearly expressed, providing visual and transparent access to learning resources and services;

8. Whole record: are recording learning path data to mine and analyse in depth, then providing reasonable assessment, suggestions and pushing on-demand service;
9. Natural interaction: are transferring the senses of multimodal interaction, including position and facial expression recognition;
10. High engagement: are immersion in multidirectional interactive learning experiences in technology-enriched environments.

Smart pedagogy emphasises the active engagement of students in their own learning, learner responsibility, metacognitive skills, and a dialogical and collaborative model of smart teaching and learning. This pedagogy is based on content, inquiry, communication and collaboration, as well as construction and evaluation. Smart learning focuses on student-centered learning based on context-aware ubiquitous learning, blended with mobile, augmented and seamless learning, more than on devices (Amhag, 2016a; 2016b; 2017; Chan et al., 2006; Hwang, 2014; Hwang, Lai & Wang, 2008; Kim, et al., 2012; Kukulska-Hulme & Viberg, 2018; Scott & Benlamri, 2010; Zhu, Yu & Riezebos, 2016).

The "seamless" concept is defined as continuous experiences of learning and purposely bridging the multidimensional learning outcomes over a combination of places, times, technologies, and different settings (Hwang, Lai & Wang, 2015; Kuh, 1996). Students are encouraged to take advantage of learning resources that exist both inside and outside of the classroom and use their life experiences to make meaning of introduced materials. The success of mobile-assisted seamless learning activities, MSL heavily depends on teachers' learning designs (Wong & Looi, 2011). There are five principles for teachers to design seamless flipped learning:

1. *Engaging students in self-learning* at anywhere and anytime with instructional course materials, such as recorded flipped lessons and study guides before the class time to gain knowledge at an understanding level.
2. *Designing off-class learning activities* to engage students in content knowledge of real problems and the collection from the field, literature and everyday life experiences on the applying, analysing, and evaluating levels.
3. *Designing in-class learning activities* to engage students in higher order thinking based on what they have learned from the flipped lessons and what they have observed or collected from the field, literature or their

daily-life experiences on the applying, analysing, evaluating, and even creating levels.

4. *Encouraging peer-to-peer and peer-to-teacher interactions* in all learning spaces, at home, at the university, professional practice, and other real-world spaces.
5. *Mobile communication technologies* are used to seamlessly connect the self-learning at home, critically review and applying in practice for high-order thinking tasks in the class, and peer-to-peer and peer-to-teacher interactions across these learning spaces.

In summary, the result show that smart mobile-assisted seamless learning activities is created on two different types of technology: smart devices and intelligent technologies (Gros, 2016; Kim, Cho & Lee, 2012; Lee, Zo & Lee, 2014). Smart devices refer to artefacts that display certain characteristics of commonly used computers, including artificial intelligence (not necessarily); for example, the internet of things, portable technology in the form of accessories such as glasses, wristwatches, backpack or even clothes. The use of intelligent technologies, such as cloud computing, learning analytics or big data analysis, focuses on how learning data can be captured, analysed and directed towards improving learning and teaching, and supporting the development of individual and adaptable learning. A systematic analysis, from both smart pedagogy with five principles for teachers to develop and analyse smart seamless flipped learning, is crucial for ensuring the appropriate use, benefits and implementation of smart education with MSL (Ally & Prieto-Blázquez, 2014).

## ANALYSIS OF SMART LEARNING WITH SEAMLESS ACTIVITIES

The design of smart learning with seamless activities is from two groups of vocational student teachers at a university in Sweden (Amhag, 2017). The qualitative data collection consists of observations of 22-recorded online webinars F2F among 40 vocational student teachers divided into groups of 18 and 22 participants, and 12 interviews (six from each group, including both women and men). The analysis is based on the concept of MSL with six dimensions of actual learning (Wong & Looi, 2011; Wong, Chai, Aw & King, 2015):

1) Formal and informal of learning is when students negotiate in-school and out-of-school learning spaces.
2) Personal and social learning is the knowledge process of obtaining professional competence and understandings.
3) Learning across time at any time without limitations.
4) Learning across locations at anywhere without limitations.
5) Ubiquitous knowledge access, blended with different space and time for each student or student groups.
6) Physical and digital spaces where students can access learning materials, participate, discuss and collaborate, as well as share knowledge and experiences with other students.

The students were studying the same three first courses of six in Vocational Teacher Education Program with both in-class and out of online webinars F2F, or with and without teacher-recorded flipped lessons (Amhag, 2017). All three courses started the before-class stage with accessible course curriculum, schedule and literature. The in-class stage included presentations of course goal and assignments, grouping with collaborative exercises to get to know each other and different lessons at the university lasting two days. The students also received an introduction and guidelines for the LMS and the e-meeting system, and the required equipment (webcam, microphone/headset, and text-based chat). During the three courses, students worked both individually and in groups with four or five students, using problem-based course assignments with deadlines. The courses were ended with one day of examinations also at the university.

Online webinars F2F were scheduled in cooperation with the students at the start of the course, with a defined date and time for each group. During the online webinars F2F, the students received follow-up on the course starting part, and they discussed theoretical concepts from the course literature and experiences between teaching practices and professions, as well as tutoring and scaffolding in different course assignments. A majority of the webinars were recorded and made available in the students' LMS to provide the opportunity to take a step back, reflect, self-assess, and compare various contributions. The students could also have parallel chat communications during the webinars online to support each other and ask text-based questions when someone else was talking.

Group 1, summarised in Table 1, had 12 online webinars F2F. Some of the webinars were made available for students to attend as per their own needs

*Table 1. Summary of the design in Group 1 using mobile online webinars F2F during the three first courses in the Vocational Teacher Education Program (Amhag, 2017)*

| Group 1 | | 15 students |
|---|---|---|
| Spring semester 2012 | Length | Course 1 - Learning outcome about social relations, conflict management and educational leadership. |
| 08/02/2012 | 00:31:06 | Webinar: Follow-up of course start and tutoring in technology and course assignments of social relations, one group. |
| 08/02/2012 | 00:52:01 | Webinar: Follow-up of course start and tutoring in technology and course assignments of social relations, one group. |
| 07/05/2012 | 00:30:59 | Webinar: Tutoring in educational leadership, three groups, drop-in |
| Date | Length | Course 2 - Learning outcome about syllabus, vocational didactics and assessment |
| 07/11/2012 | 02:14:27 | Webinar: Literature of language-oriented teaching, three groups, 44 min / group |
| 14/11/2012 | 00:35:41 | Webinar: Literature of professional didactics, one group |
| 15/11/2012 | 00:40:30 | Webinar: Literature of professional didactics, one group |
| 21/11/2012 | 02:12:23 | Webinar: Theory of Assessment & Grading, three groups, 25 min / group |
| 29/11/2012 | 00:54:23 | Webinar: Theory of Formative assessment, three groups, drop-in |
| 04/12/2012 | 00:39:09 | Webinar: Theory of Summative assessment, three groups, drop-in |
| Date | Length | Course 3 - Learning outcome about development, learning and special education |
| 23/01/2013 | 00:23:47 | Webinar: Literature of Read & writing disabilities, one group |
| 23/01/2013 | 00:20:44 | Webinar: Literature of Read & writing disabilities, one group |
| 25/01/2013 | 00:34:35 | Webinar: Literature of Read & writing disabilities, one group |

and preferences through flexible drop-in available at anywhere. All webinars thus varied in length from 20 to 54 minutes.

Group 2, summarised in Table 2, had 13 online webinars F2F, and four group wise examinations of a course assignment. Five of the online webinars F2F were complemented by teacher-recorded flipped lessons lasting 20–30 minutes. These were made available 1 week before the follow-up online webinar F2F and contained introductions of theories and concepts, along with reading instructions. Some of the online webinars F2F were made available for students to attend as per their own needs and preferences through flexible drop-in available at anywhere. All online webinars F2F thus varied in length from 25 to 70 minutes.

*Table 2. Summary of the design in Group 2 using mobile online webinars F2F complemented with teacher-recorded flipped lessons during three courses in the Vocational Teacher Education Program (Amhag, 2017)*

| Group 2 | | 18 students |
|---|---|---|
| Spring semester 2013 | | Course 1 - Learning outcome about social relations, conflict management and educational leadership. |
| Three webinars<br>Not recorded | | Follow-up of course start and tutoring in technology and course assignments of social relations |
| Date | Length | Course 2 - Learning outcome about syllabus, vocational didactics and assessment |
| 02/15/2013 | 00:27:46 | Flipped lesson: Theory of Pedagogy & Didactic, follow-up of course start |
| 02/25/2013 | 01:16:27 | Webinar: Teaching & Education, five groups, drop-in |
| 03/15/2013 | 00:19:13 | Flipped lesson: Theory of Formative assessment |
| 03/21/2013 | 00:19:51 | Flipped lesson: Theory of Assessment & Grading |
| 03/21/2013 | 01:14:01 | Webinar: Assessment & Grading, three groups, 25 min / group |
| 03/25/2013 | 01:00:59 | Webinar: Assessment & Grading, two groups, 30 min / group |
| 05/07/2013 | 00:55:06 | Webinar: Tutoring of the two last course assignments, five groups, drop-in |
| Date | Length | Course 3 - Learning outcome about development, learning and special education |
| 09/09/2013 | 00:28:05 | Flipped lesson: Theory of Read & writing disabilities, follow-up course start |
| 10/14/2013 | 00:47:49 | Webinar: Literature of Read & writing disabilities, five groups, drop-in |
| 10/29/2013 | 01:04:57 | Webinar: Examination of Read & writing disabilities, two groups, 32 min / group |
| 10/31/2013 | 00:46:22 | Webinar: Examination of Read & writing disabilities, one group |
| 10/31/2013 | 00:42:36 | Webinar: Examination of Read & writing disabilities, one group |
| 10/31/2013 | 00:56:22 | Webinar: Examination of Read & writing disabilities, one group |
| 12/10/2013 | 00:34:24 | Flipped lesson: Theory of Teaching & Education of vocational students |
| 12/19/2013 | 00:39:50 | Webinar: Tutoring of the last course assignments, five groups, drop-in |

## Analysis of Excerpts Group 1

The first three excerpts addresses student teachers in Group 1 and their experiences and views of mobile online webinars F2F during the first three courses in Vocational Teacher Education Program (Amhag, 2017). Two conditions are compared, a) online webinars F2F and real-time chat communications, b) the elements of part a, but complemented by teacher-recorded flipped lessons before the online webinars F2F.

Theoretically, the study refers to the research concept of mobile-assisted seamless learning, MSL with mediated learning at anytime and anywhere, and easily switch learning contexts to another, or a variety of scenarios. A key component of this idea is that each student is using a personal device as a mediator. The results raise some challenges and implications for individual and collaborative learning access in the form of online webinars F2F, textual chat communications and teacher-recorded flipped lesson videos.

Student 1a, in the Hotel and Tourism program, specialisation conference, described her experiences with online webinars F2F:

*It took too much time to get the webinars up and running during the first course, and they all had different questions, and a lot of task switching. This sometimes created confusion. Support before them was also lacking. In terms of literature we would, for example, read two books and highlight something interesting, and then formulate a question. I had no idea how to create those questions.*

*Therefore, I wish there were some kind of preparation before the webinars, perhaps a mini lecture, to hear what others says. I could learn from that. It would also be useful to be able to get the page numbers of important parts in the literature; there were few examples of interesting content and which issues should be discussed further.*

Student 1a raises the issue that the MSL in-class stage should offer individual challenges and formative feedback that support conversation and dialogue exchanges during the online webinars F2F (Hwang, Lai & Wang, 2015). Such as getting support in academic reading and writing, as well as critical questioning the literature. Mobile devices, such as personal laptops, tablets, or cell phones, could function as a 'learning hub' for experiencing seamless teaching and learning with different modules in their LMS for discussions and theoretically- and practically exchanges and other collaborative functions, such as online webinars F2F and chat communications (Looi, Wong, So, Seow, Toh, Chen et al., 2009; Spector, 2014). The devices should bridge physical and digital spaces to support students who are less academically inclined, especially in their academic reading and writing.

The importance of linking students' in-class and out-of-class experiences is to create academic achievement with seamless activities through formal and informal learning, across time and location, as well as with more ubiquitous knowledge access in different space and time for each student or student groups in the form of flipped lessons before the online webinars F2F (Wong & Looi, 2011; Wong, 2013).

Student 1b, in the Business and Administration program, referred to the digital ability among teachers and students:

*Most webinars were very technology-centred. I constantly heard: 'do you see me?', 'can you hear me?', 'now it's gone' [laughing]. The systems depend on the habits of both teachers and students, and requires us to be able to listen and be prepared to discuss. Everyone must take responsibility. Otherwise, it will be messy and slow.*

Student 1b raises some initial problems that also were confirmed in the observations occurring at the start of the use of mobile online webinars F2F. The e-meeting system should be context-aware for teacher support online and recordings off-line with direct and adaptive support including tutoring, guidance, course guides, peer feedback processes, formative assessment and different learning tools, as well as have adaptive user interface for organizing the course subject content and interacting tools (Hwang, 2014).

In this study, the e-meeting system was unreliable because of a problematic mobile connection. Some students were logging in and out, which led to the repetitious, 'do you see me?' and 'can you hear me?' Accessing the voice audio and web camera requires a stable mobile connection. Moreover, the teachers were initially unfamiliar with the online technique and how to support the students. Mediating by technology for seamless learners should offer the potential to be able to explore, identify, and seize infinite latent opportunities in collaboration with other students and in a structured way (Chan et al., 2006; Wong & Looi, 2011). This should be present rather some of what appeared in the observations during the webinars F2F, such as being inhibited by logging in and out, constantly shifting content, unnecessary repetition of formalities (e.g. number of pages, font size), or unclear supervision enabling more independent reading of the study guide and literature.

Student 1c, in the Health Care program, emphasised being able to learn at anywhere and anytime and easily switch learning contexts by using a tablet.

*I think it has been great not to have to go to the physical university; many students live far away. This is a new way for me to meet everyone [by tablet] without being at the university. However, there were some teething problems in the malfunctioning. Sitting with two devices [laptop and tablet] and not being able to access the e-meeting system made me stressed. On top of that, I had telephone contact with a classmate who also couldn't connect. It was frustrating to be prepared and not be able to get in. Otherwise, it was great!*

In this excerpt, student 1c emphasizes, in addition to the initial technical problems, the importance of using smart education, which address to smart pedagogies as methodological approach and smart learning environments as technological approach (Zhu, Yu & Riezebos, 2016). The notion of seamless learning research, 'learning anytime, anywhere,' is not 'learning everytime, everywhere' (Wong & Looi, 2011; Wong et al., 2015). The goal is to empower and support students to learn wherever and whenever they are stimulated to learn, in different contexts. These spaces consist of scenarios in which students are active, productive, creative, and collaborative across different devices and settings (Chan, Roschelle, Hsi, Kinshuk, Sharples, Brown et al., 2006). Seamless learning changed their approach to learning and development in and between moments of teaching practices and as professionals, e.g. as hairdresser, seller, chef, or vocational teacher.

## Analysis of Excerpts Group 2

The following three excerpts address student teachers in Group 2 and their experiences and views of mobile online webinars F2F prepared with teacher-recorded flipped lesson videos during the first three courses in Vocational Teacher Education Program (Amhag, 2017).

Student 2a, a student teacher in the Hairdressing program and also working at a personally owned salon, was close to dropping out of the educational program if the support online had not existed:

*Without webinars, I don't think I would have continued my studies. In particular, all the documents [papers and reports] posted to the LMS and preparations [flipped lessons] before the follow-up webinars provided a sense of reality. I wish there were more flipped lessons or other types of tutoring and scaffolding. I also think it was convenient to be able to participate somewhat quickly and easily at work and I was able to take a short time to look through webinars afterwards. I think it was good and I would have liked additional offerings!*

The student's statements reflected the importance of social arrangements for meaningful learning and not only provide self-learning, self-motivated and individual support, but also collaborative learning with other students and teachers. A potential pitfall can also be seen in these seamless activities when the students were provided the opportunity to interact within their LMS, but were not given support for deepening their understanding through textual knowledge, this could have been a cause for dropout. The online documents and teacher-recorded flipped lessons, as pre-lessons prior to the follow-up online webinars F2F, developed a greater sense of authenticity.

In the before-class stage, students could download study guides, research articles, and reports from the National Agency for Education in Sweden. In the in-class stage, the student highlights 'cross-time and cross-location' and socio-constructivist learning of 'formal learning in informal settings' (Hwang, Lai & Wang, 2015; Wong & Looi, 2011; Wong et al., 2015). An online webinar involves the full, unique individual in a dynamic interplay of participation and reification of smart learning. This is possible when students directly meet other students and teachers mobile online F2F, and discuss how they should deal with course assignments with theoretical concepts from the course literature, and experiences between teaching practices and as a working professional.

Student 2b, a student teacher in the Hotel and Tourism program who was working half time as a flight attendant, commented:

*The webinars and flipped lessons were very beneficial! For me this is somewhat special because I work as a flight attendant, but there is also benefit for students who may want to be able to close time gaps. Even the chat communications worked very well in the groups. It was fun to have peer feedback, and we also had some time to respond to the course assignments. I enjoyed it and the peer feedback was a great support!*

Student 2b highlighted the teacher-recorded flipped lessons, posted 1 week before the follow-up online webinars F2F, which were also recorded and accessible afterwards in the LMS after-class stage (Hwang, Lai & Wang, 2015). These recordings gave good leeway for the student to later take part in clarification and discussions related to the course content. Even the peer learning activities were appreciated for providing peer feedback on classmates' course assignments and their corresponding work in the group's discussion forum in the LMS within 1 week (e.g. Amhag, 2013b; Amhag & Jakobsson, 2009). The students had opportunities to contribute actively to the course documents and literature, flipped lessons recordings, mobile online webinars F2F, and text-based chat communications. They could also give and receive peer feedback in the LMS discussion forums.

In this way, students could also practice and value their understanding of academic reading and writing, and creatively formulating their critical reviews of others. The design extended the space of the learning flow in the LMS with the combination of textual documents, preparation, and recordings of online webinars F2F for learning alliances. The ubiquitous knowledge access was blended with different space and time for each student or student groups and bridged gaps between formal and informal learning, extending time for the former into the latter, and embracing the opportunities of out-of-school learning driven by the students' personal interests (Chan et al., 2006; Wong & Looi, 2011; Wong et al., 2015).

Student 2c, a student teacher in the Handicraft program and specialising in makeup and skin therapy, thinks generally:

*I thought it worked well. Everyone could see and hear each other and ask questions. It was also easier to participate because we did not need to be physically at the university. I definitely wish more teachers could work in this way. Now is also the time for using mobile, online lessons and presentations at distance. We, as teachers, also want that with our own students and give them the possibility to show their presentations from home. In this way, they don't miss anything if they are not at school for whatever reason.*

Student 2c emphasised the mobile online examination F2F and the importance of using the LMS in-class stage for seamless flipped learning engaging students in self-learning at anywhere and anytime. The design of in-class learning activities included reviews of course documents, lectures and assignments of real problems. The design of out-of-class learning activities had focus on engaging students in higher-order-thinking, encouraging peer-to-peer and peer-to-teacher interactions in all learning spaces, as well as seamlessly connect across all learning spaces (Hwang, Lai & Wang, 2015). This student wished that more teachers would proceed to switch learning contexts between personal and social, as well as have in-school and out-of-school learning spaces by using mobile online webinars F2F and teacher-recorded flipped lesson videos with digital devices as a mediator (Chan, et al., 2006; Looi et al., 2009; Wong & Looi, 2011).

It is important that smart learning involve the interplay between local contexts; in this study, these were the preparations and presentations from home or work before and during the examinations. This is a sort of global context online when students can see and hear each other's arguments F2F during the online webinars and recordings, from different contexts. These mobile-assisted mediated activities for collaborative learning extend one-off learning to ongoing learning and trigger a shift from consuming to producing (Wong & Looi, 2011; Wong et al., 2015).

## Analysis of Course Evaluations

After one year of studies, the study was complemented with a course evaluation about the students' views on how the MSL activities contributed to their learning (Amhag, 2017). The two course evaluations was given after 1 year of studies (in January 2013 for Group 1, in June 2013 for Group 2). In Group 1: 9 answers from 18 students (50%), in Group 2: 15 answers from 22 students (68%).

*Table 3. Two course evaluation results after 1 year of studies on students' views of how mobile-assisted seamless learning activities contributed to their learning (Amhag, 2017)*

| Seamless Mediated Learning Activities | Group 1 (50%) 1-3 Disagree- Partly agree | Group 1 (50%) 4-6 Agree – Strongly agree | Group 2 (68%) 1-3 Disagree- Partly agree | Group 2 (68%) 4-6 Agree – Strongly agree |
|---|---|---|---|---|
| Lessons at course start | 22% | 78% | 33% | 67% |
| Webinars online F2F | 25% | 75% | 27% | 73% |
| Flipped lessons | not included | not included | 13% | 87% |
| Repeated flipped lessons | not included | not included | 20% | 80% |
| Active in webinars | 33% | 67% | 20% | 80% |
| Active in the group´s learning | 67% | 33% | 10% | 90% |

The most prominent result, illustrated in Table 3, in the comparison in both groups shows that the majority of the students strongly agree that F2F online webinars (75% and 73%) contributed to their learning. This was despite Group 1 having technical problems with the e-meeting system owing to a problematic mobile connection and teachers' unfamiliarity with the online technique online and how to support the students. However, the majority of the students in Group 2 noted the teacher-recorded flipped classroom videos (87%) and the majority of these students (80%) had retrospectively reviewed and reflected on the meaning of the contents. The major differences between the two groups' results appear especially with regard to the groups' collaborative learning with peer feedback and with making creative use of their critical review of others presentations and discussions; 90% of the students in Group 2 strongly agreed about their activities in the group´s learning, though only 33% in Group 1 did. Perhaps this was due to the initial technical problems and the teachers' unfamiliarity with the system. The two groups' activities during the webinars (67% and 80%) by discussing different perspectives and their experiences of university lecturers at course start (78% and 67%) also show differences, albeit to a lesser degree (Amhag, 2017).

In the after-class stage, it is important to investigate the effects of the learning management system and the course qualities during the course based on the students' learning performance and perceptions of various seamless activities in order for teachers to be able to make course improvement and develop more efficient and smart education. An evaluation can easily be carried out on the students' perception of their learning and collaboration in the groups, how the feedback processes and problem solutions work and own self-evaluations, as well as other technical and pedagogical aspects.

The presented study (Amhag, 2017) has shown the importance of the design of before-, in- and after-class stages, especially sharing of knowledge in online webinars F2F and textual chat communications, as well as critical review of recorded webinars and teacher-recorded flipped lesson videos for enhancing students' individual and collaborative learning. The concept of mobile-assisted seamless learning activities, MSL, across different contexts, seamlessly has a potential for strengthening the space between flipped learning and flipped teaching by extending students' learning activities between home and school to their daily-life contexts (Hwang, Lai & Wang, 2015; Wong & Looi, 2011). Smart education emerges when teachers take into account the knowledge creation metaphor of smart learning that highlights competencies in producing knowledge in collaboration.

## CONCLUSION

Based on previous research and the presented study of smart learning with mobile-assisted seamless learning activities in before-class, in-class and after-class stages (Hwang, Lai & Wang, 2015), four levels of abilities in smart education students will meet and master in future higher technology-enhanced education. The abilities should have focus on student-centered learning based on context-aware ubiquitous and blended learning with mobile, augmented and seamless flipped learning activities, more than on mobile devices (Zhu, Yu & Riezebos, 2016):

1) Basic knowledge and context-aware core skills such as in academic reading and writing, critical review and self-assess learning (Amhag, 2017; 2019; Laru & Järvelä, 2015).
2) Comprehensive abilities such as critical higher-order thinking, problem-solving, as well as analysing and making judgments and decisions on different complex situations (Amhag, 2013b, 2016a; 2016b; Hwang, Lai & Wang, 2015).
3) Adapted expertise to master ICT information and smart learning spaces such as in digital literacy, creativity and innovation skills in which the literacy, creativity and innovation will occur (Amhag, 2017; Chen et al., 2016; Hwang, 2014; Hwang, Chu, Yin & Ogata, 2015; Looi et al., 2009; Scott & Benlamri, 2010; Spector, 2014; Wong & Looi, 2011).
4) Collaborative intelligence to communicate clearly and effectively peer-to-peer and peer-to-teacher in all learning spaces, and reflect and self-assess about how to share, negotiate and transmit the results or outputs (Amhag, 2020; Amhag, & Jakobsson, 2009; Hwang & Wu, 2014; Kukulska-Hulme & Viberg, 2018; Looi et al., 2009; Spector, 2014; Wong & Looi, 2011; Wong, Chai, Aw & King, 2015).

The four abilities 1) basic knowledge and context-aware core skills, 2) comprehensive abilities, 3) adapted expertise and 4) collaborative intelligence should have focus on student-centered learning based on context-aware ubiquitous and blended learning with mobile, augmented and seamless flipped learning activities. The findings show that to improve students' excellence of lifelong learning should university teachers have focus on contextual, adapted and self-directed seamless learning activities to promote the students' capabilities to learn, collaborate and critically solve problems in different situations and contexts (Hwang, Lai & Wang, 2015). With the development of technologies, and within a modern society, and smart higher education will confront many challenges, such as smart pedagogical theory, smart educational technology leadership, teachers' flipped teaching and learning leadership, mobile educational structures, and smart educational ideology (Zhu, Yu & Riezebos, 2016). Therefore, it is necessary to value the importance of seamless flipped learning and teaching and the design of before-class-, in-class- and after-class stages with a focus on student-centered collaborative learning.

## REFERENCES

Akçayır, G., & Akçayır, M. (2018). The flipped classroom: A review of its advantages and challenges. *Computers & Education*, *126*, 334–345. doi:10.1016/j.compedu.2018.07.021

Ally, M., & Prieto-Blázquez, J. (2014). What is the future of mobile learning in education? *International Journal of Educational Technology in Higher Education*, *11*(1), 142–151.

Amhag, L. (2013b). *Creativity in and between Collaborative Peer Assessment Processes in Higher Distance Education. Creative Education, 4(7A2)*, 94–104. doi:10.4236/ce.2013.47A2011

Amhag, L. (2016a). Mobile technologies for student-centered learning in a distance higher education program. In *Wearable Technology and Mobile Innovations for Next-Generation Education,* (pp. 184-199). IGI Global. https://www.igi-global.com/book/wearable-technology-mobile-innovations-next/142108

Amhag, L. (2016b). Mobile technologies for student-centered learning in a distance higher education program. *Blended Learning: Concepts, Methodologies, Tools, and Applications*, *4*, 802–817. doi:10.4018/978-1-5225-0069-8.ch010

Amhag, L. (2017). Mobile-Assisted Seamless Learning Activities in Higher Distance Education. *International Journal of Higher Education*, *6*(3), 2017. http://ijhe.sciedupress.com. doi:10.5430/ijhe.v6n3p70

Amhag, L. (2020). Student Reflections and Self-Assessments in Vocational Training Supported by a Mobile Learning Hub. *International Journal of Mobile and Blended Learning*, *12*(1), 1–16. doi:10.4018/IJMBL.2020010101

Amhag, L., Hellström, L., & Stigmar, M. (2019). Teacher Educators' Use of Digital Tools and Needs for Digital Competence in Higher Education. *Journal of Digital Learning in Teacher Education*, *35*(4), 203–220. doi:10.1080/21532974.2019.1646169

Amhag, L., & Jakobsson, A. (2009). Collaborative Learning as a Collective Competence when Students Use the Potential of Meaning in Asynchronous Dialogues. *Computers & Education*, *52*(3), 656–667. doi:10.1016/j.compedu.2008.11.012

Bishop, J. L., & Verleger, M. A. (2013). *The Flipped Classrom: A Survey of the Research*. Paper presented at the 120th ASEE Conference & Exposition.

Chen, N. S., Cheng, I. L., & Chew, S. W. (2016). Evolution is not enough: Revolutionizing current learning environments to smart learning environments. *International Journal of Artificial Intelligence in Education*, *26*(2), 561–581. doi:10.100740593-016-0108-x

DeLozier, S. J., & Rhodes, M. G. (2017). Flipped classrooms: A review of key ideas and recommendations for practice. *Educational Psychology Review*, *29*(1), 141–151. doi:10.100710648-015-9356-9

Gros, B. (2016). The design of smart educational environments. *Smart Learning Environments*, *3*(1), 15. doi:10.118640561-016-0039-x

Hwang, G. J. (2014). Definition, framework and research issues of smart learning environments – a context-aware ubiquitous learning perspective. *Smart Learning Environments*, *1*(1), 4. doi:10.118640561-014-0004-5

Hwang, G. J., Chu, H. C., Yin, C., & Ogata, H. (2015). Transforming the educational settings: Innovative designs and applications of learning technologies and learning environments. *Interactive Learning Environments*, *23*(2), 127–129. doi:10.1080/10494820.2014.998863

Hwang, G. J., Lai, C. L., & Wang, S. Y. (2015). Seamless flipped learning: A mobile technology-enhanced flipped classroom with effective learning strategies. *Journal of Computers in Education*, *2*(4), 449–473. doi:10.100740692-015-0043-0

Hwang, G. J., & Wu, P. H. (2014). Applications, impacts and trends of mobile technology-enhanced learning: A review of 2008–2012 publications in selected SSCI journals. *International Journal of Mobile Learning and Organisation*, *8*(2), 83–95. doi:10.1504/IJMLO.2014.062346

Jensen, J. L., Holt, E. A., Sowards, J. B., Heath Ogden, T., & West, R. E. (2018). Investigating strategies for pre-class content learning in a flipped classroom. *Journal of Science Education and Technology*, *27*(6), 523–535. doi:10.100710956-018-9740-6

Kearney, M., Schuck, S., Burden, K., & Aubusson, P. (2012). Viewing mobile learning from a pedagogical perspective. *Research in Learning Technology*, *20*(1), n1. doi:10.3402/rlt.v20i0.14406

Kim, T., Cho, J. Y., & Lee, B. G. (2012). Evolution to smart learning in public education: a case study of Korean public education. In *IFIP WG 3.4 International Conference on Open and Social Technologies for Networked Learning* (pp. 170-178). Springer.

Kuh, G. D. (1996). Guiding principles for creating seamless learning environments for undergraduates. *College Student Development*, *37*(2), 135–148.

Kukulska-Hulme, A., & Viberg, O. (2018). Mobile collaborative language learning: State of the art. *British Journal of Educational Technology*, *49*(2), 207–218. doi:10.1111/bjet.12580

Lage, M. J., Platt, G. J., & Treglia, M. (2000). Inverting the classroom: A gateway to creating an inclusive learning environment. *The Journal of Economic Education*, *31*(1), 30–43. doi:10.1080/00220480009596759

Laru, J., & Järvelä, S. (2015). Integrated use of multiple social software tools and face-to-face activities to support self-regulated learning: a case study in a higher education context. In *Seamless learning in the age of mobile connectivity* (pp. 471–484). Singapore: Springer. doi:10.1007/978-981-287-113-8_24

Lee, J., & Choi, H. (2019). Rethinking the flipped learning pre-class: Its influence on the success of flipped learning and related factors. *British Journal of Educational Technology*, *50*(2), 934–945. doi:10.1111/bjet.12618

Lee, K. & Salman, R. (2012). The Design and Development of Mobile Collaborative Learning Application Using Android. *Journal of Information Technology and Application in Education, 1*(1), 1-8.

Lin, H. C., & Hwang, G. J. (2018). Research trends of flipped classroom studies for medical courses: A review of journal publications from 2008 to 2017 based on the technology-enhanced learning model. *Interactive Learning Environments*, 1–17. doi:10.1080/10494820.2018.1545672

Long, T., Logan, J., & Waugh, M. (2014). Students' Perceptions of Pre-class Instructional Video in the Flipped Classroom Model: A Survey Study. In *Proceedings of Society for Information Technology & Teacher Education International Conference 2014*. AACE.

Looi, C.-K., Wong, L.-H., So, H.-J., Seow, P., Toh, Y., Chen, W., ... Soloway, E. (2009). Anatomy of a mobilized lesson: Learning my way. *Computers & Education*, *53*(4), 1120–1132. doi:10.1016/j.compedu.2009.05.021

Marin, V. I., Jääskelä, P., Häkkinen, P., Juntunen, M., Rasku-Puttonen, H., & Vesisenaho, M. (2016). Seamless Learning Environments in Higher Education with Mobile Devices and Examples. *International Journal of Mobile and Blended Learning*, *8*(1), 51–68. doi:10.4018/IJMBL.2016010104

Scott, K., & Benlamri, R. (2010). Context-aware services for smart learning spaces. *IEEE Transactions on Learning Technologies*, *3*(3), 214–227. doi:10.1109/TLT.2010.12

Spector, J. M. (2014). Conceptualizing the emerging field of smart learning environments. *Smart Learning Environments, 1*(1), 2.

Virtanen, M. A., Haavisto, E., Liikanen, E., & Kääriäinen, M. (2018). Ubiquitous learning environments in higher education: A scoping literature review. *Education and Information Technologies*, *23*(2), 985–998. doi:10.100710639-017-9646-6

Wong, L. H. (2012). A learner-centric view of mobile seamless learning. *British Journal of Educational Technology*, *43*(1), E19–E23. doi:10.1111/j.1467-8535.2011.01245.x

Wong, L. H., Chai, C. S., Aw, G. P., & King, R. B. (2015). Enculturating seamless language learning through artifact creation and social interaction process. *Interactive Learning Environments*, *23*(2), 130–157. doi:10.1080/10494820.2015.1016534

Wong, L. H., & Looi, C. K. (2011). What seams do we remove in mobile-assisted seamless learning? A critical review of the literature. *Computers & Education*, *57*(4), 2364–2381. doi:10.1016/j.compedu.2011.06.007

Zhu, Z. T., Yu, M. H. & Riezebos, P. (2016). A research framework of smart education. *Smart Learning Environments, 3*(1), 4.

# Chapter 4
# Peer Learning Activities in Smart Education


## ABSTRACT

*Peer learning strategies in higher education have been developed and extended in different trends and forms, as well as in various contexts of learning, on campus and in mobile frameworks. Commonly, peer learning activities are introduced by university teachers in an ad hoc way, without consideration of their implications as a tool for students' collaborative learning in a formative and creative way. Methodically, the study has a comparative design of various peer learning strategies and activities and how they can contribute to student-centered learning for self-directed and motivated smart higher education with resource-enriched and technology-embedded tools. Theoretically, the comparative analysis is based on socio-cultural theory by using dimensions of community of practice and the zone of proximal development for student-centered learning. The results show that peer learning activities are a key factor to reflect over the learning context, its objectives, and exchanges between the students and with different resource implications.*


## BACKGROUND

Distance education and mobile learning have several advantages comparing to traditional settings at the university when mobile activities can provide flexibility and accessibility for students learning and development. Therefore, online courses and massive open online courses, MOOC continue to increase

DOI: 10.4018/978-1-7998-4183-8.ch004

worldwide in higher education and for adult learning (Broadbent & Poon, 2015). However, many university students are networking in different ways, but frequently they use online interactions for social purposes. The often rigid format of technology-based academic courses are in conflict with the students' initiative, motivation, and self-efficacy, as well as the choice of what, when, and how to learn; and opposes greater independence in their studies, which contributes to non-conventional and informal education methods (Serdyukov & Hill, 2013). Independence in learning is directly related and is fundamental for innovation, creativity, and self-efficacy (Amhag, 2013b; 2016a; 2016b; Bandura, 2002).

This chapter enlarges the knowledge about various peer learning strategies and activities, and how students can contribute to complex types of academic works, such as reports, research papers, project productions and virtual presentations, for self-directed and motivated, smart higher education and in what ways they can be a tool for student-centered learning. The word 'smart' is an acronym for self-directed, motivated, adaptive, resource-enriched, and technology-embedded, and refers to wisdom as bounding together the ability of using and motivating self-directed learning, knowledge building, problem solving, critically reflections, collaborating and evaluating different circumstances with resource-enriched and technology-embedded tools (Hwang, 2014; Zhu, Yu & Riezebos, 2016). The following questions are addressed:

- In what way can teachers a) design and b) use different peer learning activities and wearable tools that are appropriate for student-centered learning and active participation?
- How do the students experience the peer learning activities and the wearable tools for their learning?
- In what way can the peer learning activities and tools be analyzed comparing to the students' performance?

Peer learning, PL can be defined as gaining of knowledge and skills through active helping and supporting equals or matched peers who are not professional teachers, but are helping each other to learn and learning themselves by so doing (Topping, 2007). Peer learning is a two-way, reciprocal activity, based on individuals' strengths and active participants in the learning process, as well as mutual benefits that involve sharing of knowledge, ideas and experiences among students, i.e. as a way of moving beyond independent to interdependent or mutual learning (Boud, Cohen & Sampson, 2001a;

Topping, 2007). Positive interdependence requires successful structured peer learning activities among the students in a formative and creative way. Their understandings of the course content increases more, than if they did an active learning component on their own (Coetzee, Lim, Fox, Hartmann & Hearst, 2015).

Practices of peer learning activities are often introduced by teachers in an ad hoc way, without consideration of their implications for the students (Boud, Cohen & Sampson, 2001a). Students who are unfamiliar with the approach of peer learning can be confused about what they are supposed to do, they miss opportunities for collaborative learning, and fail to develop the skills expected of them. Therefore, must university teachers design learning activities with clear instructions what emphasize peer learning activities and ensure reasons for the students and group of students to interact with and help one another. Essential is also with formally scheduled peer learning periods, and list them on timetables to acknowledge them as a part of the workload. (Amhag, 2013b; Boud, Cohen & Sampson, 2001b). Students learn in part by explaining and sharing knowledge, helping each other to learn and learning themselves by so doing (Topping, 2007). Especially, those students who do not understand or need support can have benefit from peers' explanations and support (Coetzee et al., 2015).

Therefore, higher education needs to strengthen the student-centered learning to work self-directed, motivated, constructively, collaboratively, critically and creatively. Moreover, students' need knowledge, support and training in academic reading and writing, in research inquiry, problem solving, as well as peer learning strategies to progress their learning outcomes (Amhag, 2013b; Serdyukov & Hill, 2013). Learning methods, such as project work and portfolios are considered by students as important forms of assignments and with following assessments (Flores, Veiga Simão, Barros & Pereira, 2015). Additionally, active engagement is perceived by students as a fairer assessment method and a more efficient learning process, than if they are judged by more traditional methods such as exams and written tests (ibid.).

Consequently, strategies of peer learning activities can contribute to complex types of academic works. For example, to link academic theory and practice, as well as different critical review during project work and before presentations and examinations (Topping, 2005). Other strategy of peer learning activities involves discussion seminars alt. online webinars, study groups, or counselling, peer-assessment schemes, collaborative project or laboratory work, projects in different sized groups, workplace mentoring and community activities (Boud, Cohen & Sampson, 2001a). Peer learning combines individual accountability to ensure that students work on their own with positive interdependence to ensure that all students in a learning group participate in the activities (Coetzee et al., 2015). Moreover, peer learning activities requires capability to give and receive meaningful feedback, active involvement of own and others learning, adjustment of the academic teaching and learning to take into account the results of peer learning, and effects of peer learning activities on motivation and self-efficacy, as well as the need for students to be able to self-assess and understand how to improve their learning (Amhag, 2013b; 2016a; 2016b).

In this context, peer learning activities can support and improve students' meta-cognitive, motivational and behavioural active participation on-campus and mobile learning (Amhag, 2013b). Generally, students who have high self-confidence in their ability to perform academic assignments tend to use more meta-cognitive strategies and show higher task ability, than students who have lower self-confidence levels (Zimmerman, 1989). Meta-cognitive ability is here related to a wide range of skills, such as critically reviewing, analysing, interpreting, communicating, reflecting and evaluating, specifically a learning process to create internal feedback (what you know); search and manage feedback information from peers, teachers and colleagues (what you can do); and evaluate their levels of understanding (what you know about own cognitive ability) (Amhag, 2013b; Broadbent & Poon, 2015; Puzziferro, 2008).

In spite of these benefits, success of a smart learning environment and smart education heavily relies on student's ability to actively engage in peer learning activities (Hwang, 2014; Zhu, Yu & Riezebos, 2016). Especially, when online students are required to be more independent, because of the less active role of teachers, and when the nature of online and mobile settings promotes self-directed and self-regulated learning (Wang, Shannon, & Ross, 2013). Self-regulation is concerned with students' abilities to set goals, accept strategies for meeting goals and observe the progress towards goals (Reinholz, 2016). The degree of self-regulation refers to the students' meta-cognitive, motivational and behavioural active participation in their own learning process and be able to take control over their studies and learning strategies. Learning strategies are a part of self-regulated learning process for students to put their work into a global and real world practice (Zimmerman, 1989, p. 74). These two-way, shared activity is a way of moving beyond independent to interdependent or mutual peer learning where the support to each other to learn and learning themselves by so doing is crucial for learning (Boud, Cohen & Sampson, 2001a; Topping, 2007).

## PREVIOUS RESEARCH OF PEER LEARNING ACTIVITIES

Selected articles for review of previous research were obtained from searches in databases in education and social sciences such as ERIC, Libsearch etc. and from studies cited by these authors and from previously used peer review articles published in the relevant field with keywords: peer learning and higher education. The articles displays that student engaged in teaching other students is not uncommon (Ford, Wilkins & Groccia, 2018). The origins can be drawn back to Aristotle's use of student leaders to guide younger students. From the beginning have processes of peer-assisted learning, PAL been used in the schools by giving competent students a certain responsibility for helping other students, and gain a sense of attentive and useful participation. This process has often been lacking in academic studies, because of there has been a long tradition in research of human learning to focus on individual perspectives and view meanings of dialogues only from speaker's intentions, as a kind of transfer-and-exchange model of communication (Linell, 2001). The reason for engaging students in teaching and in different peer learning activities, is mostly based on theory and research from educational- and social science (Ford et al., 2018).

During many years have many university institutions used qualified students to teach peers to reduce the professor's and the institutions work. There is a number of benefits such as the relationship between students and the ability to establish open and honest dialogues among them and an increased sense of motivation and intention (Topping, 2005). This learning process or learning tool are a part of assessment for learning, also called formative assessment by Wiliam (2011, pp. 37-39). Moreover, producing and receiving peer feedback can give extensive benefits which justify the time and effort that is required to engage and motivate students in peer learning activities. Peer learning may be particularly useful in clinical learning environments, where students are feeling marginalized, overcome, and without support, as the education often is based on the "ideal", rather than in the complex, real world (Tai, Canny, Haines & Molloy, 2017). Additionally, can peer learning activities also be an intermediated step for self-reflections, co-assessments and self-assessments (Dochy, Segers & Sluijsmans, 1999).

Therefore, peer learning covers a wide range of different activities, not a single activity or practice. Each activity can be combined with other activity in different ways to suit the needs of a particular course assignment (Boud, Cohen & Sampson, 2001a). Students require detailed explaining for the different ways of peer learning, and suggestions of how this will help them to engage in peer learning practises. These suggestions may differ depending on the peer learning strategy, the timescales and the nature of the subject. The results from peer learning experiences often develops interpersonal communication and negotiation skills, teamwork and presentation skills (Boud, Cohen & Sampson, 2001b). Wiliam (2013, p. 16) points out that peers can be very effective assessors of each other's work, especially when the focus is on activating them as learning resources for one another. Three key processes in learning activities arises between teacher, peer and student: 1) where the learner is right now, 2) where the learner needs to be, and 3) how to get there. In these learning activities the roles are independent, therefore, teachers, peers and students have their own role. In Table 1 illustrates the five "key strategies" for teacher, peer and student.

*Table 1. The five "key strategies" of formative assessment by Wiliam (2013, p. 16)*

<table>
<tr><th></th><th>Where the learner is going</th><th>Where the learner is right now</th><th>How to get there</th></tr>
<tr><td>Teacher</td><td rowspan="3">Clarifying, sharing, and understanding learning intentions</td><td>Engineering effective discussions, activities, and tasks that elicit evidence of learning</td><td>Feedback that moves learning forward</td></tr>
<tr><td>Peer</td><td colspan="2">Activating students as learning resources for one another</td></tr>
<tr><td>Student</td><td colspan="2">Activating students as owners of their own learning</td></tr>
</table>

However, teachers cannot take for granted that students have insight into the value of these peer learning activities. Therefore, they must be designed with a strategy grounded on criteria with operational terms (cf. Dochy, Segers and Sluijsmans, 1999). Topping (1998; 2005) stresses that peer learning can provide great benefits deriving from receiving other students' appreciations with aspects of other students understanding of the course content, as well as being exposed to alternative strategies and critical review based on the course literature. These benefits promote the ability to critically review different types of texts and productions, as well as to give and receive peer feedback or peer assessment.

## Trends and Forms of Peer Learning

Teachers often want to know "what works" in education, but the fact is that everything works somewhere, and nothing works everywhere (Wiliam,

2013). However, research can highlight for teachers and students what types of activities are worth exploring, and which are likely to be dead ends. This is why peer learning activities seem to be so promising, even if there is a lot of planning and thinking behind successful and effective use of peers. Most importantly, the 'peers' in peer learning do not have power over each other by virtue of their position or responsibilities (Boud, Cohen & Sampson, 2001a). Therefore, have these peer learning activities many trends and forms termed as peer teaching, peer tutoring, peer instructor, peer-assisted learning, peer leaders, peer facilitators, undergraduate teaching assistants, and so on. In the following sections describes some trends and forms of peer learning activities.

Research on *peer learning*, PL emphasizes that by assessing the work of fellow students, students learn to evaluate their own work (Dochy, Segers & Sluijsmans, 1999). For example, show the study by Hardy, Kilcoyne and Pérez-Mira (2017) that peer learning was a successful tool and could provide an opportunity to increase the content retention and engagement of the students' knowledge of key concepts and theories in the various functional areas of business. However, there is a need for training in the support for peer learning activities in order to obtain an ideal impact on the learning process, at least for beginning students (Dochy, Segers & Sluijsmans, 1999). Criteria with operational terms can provide necessary support for students who are unfamiliar with peer learning activities, and they work well if they are used jointly by teachers and students. Advantageously, students can play a role in the process of operationalizing the terms, e.g. with words from the course goals.

*Reciprocal peer learning* is easy to organize because there are fewer timetabling problems and involves students within a given class or cohort (Boud, Cohen & Sampson, 2001a). Students are by definition peers and the learning process emphasizes that students simultaneously should learn and contribute to other students' learning. The communication is based on mutual experience and the roles are less confusing, comparing to situations in which one of the 'peers' is a senior student, or is in an advanced class, or has special expertise (ibid.).

*Peer teaching* has a far more instrumental strategy in which advanced students take on a limited instructional role. They are not expected to teach and present new material (Boud, Cohen & Sampson, 2001a). Teachers must carefully consider strategies for selecting peer instructors, ideas for peer teaching, activities to facilitate learning through peer-to-peer interaction, and how the use of peers can support higher education. A critical literature review of peer teaching by Stigmar (2016) investigates 30 studies in higher education about the benefits. The potential of peer teaching is assumed to be that students are encouraging taking control of their learning and increase their engagement and responsibility for their own learning process. The result show also that university teachers do not perceive that peer teaching necessarily leads to greater academic achievement gains or deeper learning. Instead, they are favouring training of generic skills development and metacognitive training benefits from peer teaching, such as improving students' critical thinking, learning autonomy, motivation, collaborative and communicative ability. However, several of the included studies are methodologically weak and limited. Thus, it is unclear whether peer teaching stimulate students' deep level learning or generic skills development and metacognitive training that university teachers are favouring. The design of peer teaching strategy need to be implemented with a clear instructional structure (cf. Dochy, Segers & Sluijsmans, 1999; Topping, 2007) and with a focus on to foster and improve the students' metacognitive competence and learning strategies.

The longest established and most intensively researched form of peer learning is *peer tutoring,* PT (Topping, 2007). PT has also an instrumental strategy and characterised by specific role-taking as tutor or tutee, with high focus on curriculum content and usually also on clear procedures for interactions between students from similar social groupings. The tutor or tutee are not professional teachers, they are helping each other to learn, and learning themselves by teaching. De Wever, Van Keer, Schellens and Valcke (2010) found in their study among 15 asynchronous discussion groups of nine student beginners in each (N=135) that the peer tutor-supported group reached significantly higher levels of knowledge construction, comparing to student beginners in the role-supported group. Four roles were assigned to the students in the study:

1. *Moderator* is starting off the discussion, monitoring the discussion, asking critical questions, inquiring for others' opinions, adding new points upon which other students can build, and giving new impulses every time the discussion slacks off.
2. *Summariser* is expected to post interim summaries during the discussion and a final synopsis at the end.
3. *Theoretician* is introducing theoretical information and ensure that all relevant theoretical concepts are used in the discussions.
4. *Source searcher* is seeking external information on the discussion topics in order to stimulate other students to go beyond the scope of the course reader.

The analysis of peer tutoring strategy was based on the model of Gunawardena, Lowe and Anderson (1997) who are distinguishing five different levels of knowledge construction activities: (a) sharing and comparing information, (b) identifying areas of disagreement, (c) negotiating meaning and co-construction of knowledge, (d) evaluation and modification of new schemas that result from co-construction, and (e) reaching and stating agreement and application of co-constructed knowledge. The findings emphasise the value of instructions by cross-age peer tutors with different experience levels to stimulate student beginners to improve collaborative knowledge construction through social negotiation in online asynchronous discussions (De Wever, et al., 2010).

Another strategy, used by Ford et al. (2018), is *undergraduate peer instructor*, UPI, which refers to an undergraduate who is given responsibility by the faculty to support their fellow undergraduates' learning. The implementation of UPI is based on the idea that learning occurs best when students are actively engaged with the course content and with each other, as well as the opportunity to capitalize each other's ability to be powerful role models and change agents in the classroom. The degree of responsibility can vary from incidental assistance on a specific in-class learning activity, to full control over content selection, delivery, and assessment. Research about UPI has reported following results (Ford et al., 2018):

- Increased confidence in communication and teaching that contributes to the development of interpersonal, group facilitation and organizational ability;
- The roles contribute to more in depth learning as they receive the material earlier and with more regularity;
- The roles encourage more collaboration with their peers and the importance of academic integrity;
- As peers, UPIs often understand the problems and challenges that students face, resulting in improved problem-solving ability;
- The relationship between UPI and teachers makes them feel better prepared to deal with class challenges and their role in that environment.

*Peer-assisted learning,* PAL, has also an instrumental strategy and commonly used in medical education as in the study of Tai, Canny, Haines and Molloy (2017) with problem-based learning, PBL activities. The students PBL activities included creating learning objectives and developing learning resources in response to a case or a problem. The empirical findings from three research phases, a survey among medical students, an observational study of their PAL activities on clinical assignments and the final phase, semi-structured interviews with thematic analysis. The aim was to generate triggering discussions with experienced educators about the perceived treatment and the support of PAL. The result identified a number of treatment barriers and facilitators for PAL in clinical settings by developing a framework. Culture, perceived epistemic authority, and the patient-centered environment were found to be important considerations for a range of proposed strategies for the implementation of PAL.

Peer teaching and peer tutoring is also termed *supplemental instruction*, SI, even known as peer-assisted learning, PAL or peer-assisted study session, all of them with an instrumental strategy. The result from a review of 29 articles from 2001 to 2010 about SI by Dawson, van der Meer, Skalicky and Cowley (2014) show that none study had sufficient details about methodology and participants, and the SI intervention in practice were not well grounded in any learning theory. Therefore, the result could not fully answer the research questions about the effectiveness of SI. During a SI session, an academically, successful senior student leads and facilitate the peer learning activities to undergraduates. Especially, students who are studying a high-risk course with a large amounts of weekly readings from both difficult textbooks and secondary library reference works, uncommon examinations, voluntary and unrecorded class attendance, as well as large classes in which each student has little opportunity for interaction with the professor or other students. The isolated individual work attitude without peer contacts is similar to the context of massive open online courses, MOOCs attitude where most students learn in isolation (Coetzee et al., 2015).

## Online Peer Learning

In the nature of the Web as a medium, peer learning activities appear to be most effective when there are direct interactions between teachers and students and among students themselves (Boud, Cohen & Sampson, 2001a). Peer learning provides a key solution for online interactions reconciled with the limitations on the capacity of teaching staff. It is possible for teachers to deal with the volume of interactions emerging from groups of students working together in different ways, which is not realistic with individuals.

In an online context uses frequently the strategy of *self-regulated learning*, SRL which is common in academic achievement and as a learning activity in online higher education learning environments. The relationship between self-regulated learning and academic achievement has been theorised based on the social cognitive view that self-regulated learning is acquired through a triadic interaction between three important characteristics (Broadbent & Poon, 2015): a) self-observation, monitoring one's actions which is most important; b) self-assessment of one's performance, and c) self-reactions, one's response to performance outcomes (Zimmerman, 1989). A review by Broadbent and Poon (2015) of 12 studies, published from 2004 to December 2014, show that peer learning had a moderate positive effect, but its confidence intervals crossed zero. Positively correlated with academic outcomes of teachers' strategies of time management and effort regulation, as well as students' metacognitive ability, and critical thinking. The least empirical support had practise, explanation, and organisation. However, online webinars face-to-face, F2F activities seem to contribute to the online context, but the effects were weaker and may be due to the lack of design in the learning environment and unexpected social factors, which are important in an online context. But it is problematic to isolate factors in an academic context and then comment on causal relationships, in order to distinguish how didactic efforts affect learning when certain results are positive (+), some neutral (+/-) and other negative (-).

Another study by Puzziferro (2008) among 163 course sections how students best could apply *self-regulated learning* strategy to achieve academic success in the online learning environment, show the two surveys that time, learning environment and work instructions were significantly related to performance and higher final grades. In addition, practises, explanations and metacognitive ability were significantly positively correlated with the levels of satisfaction. Peer learning and help-seeking had the lowest comparative scale with other scales, which show that teachers do not integrate the students in collaborative learning strategies that are peer-based or involve seeking help from others.

To measure the use of *self-regulated learning* strategy and the development of numerous instruments, have Roth, Ogrin and Schmitz (2016) conducted a systematic literature review of self-report instruments that measure SRL in higher education to highlight their main characteristics. This research field has diverse types of assessment methods due to the complexity of SRL. The systematic literature review included identifying SRL-studies between 1988 and 2013, further secondary searches, filtering of the instruments based on academic presence, and finally analysing the instruments into two categories: self-efficacy for SRL and behavioural strategies. The comprehensive characteristics of SRL included: (a) the intended measurement focus, (b) the degree of situational specificity, and (c) measurement standards (quantitative vs. qualitative, online vs. offline). The analysis of 211 studies show that the vast majority of the 225 instruments were questionnaires (87.11%). Considerably fewer authors used think-aloud techniques (4.89%), diaries (4.00%), and interviews (4.00%). Consequently, there is an apparent gap between assessing SRL close to real behaviour and actual research practices (cf. Zimmerman, 2008).

Two sets of MOOC experiments with *peer learning activities* in synchronous group wise tasks, by Coetzee et al. (2015) show that these processes can expand students learning in higher education and in MOOCs. The first experiment tested unstructured discussions, comparing different size groups and the effects of a bonus condition. The second experiment tested the effects of adding more dialogical structure to the interactions between the students. Both studies followed the pedagogy of peer instruction. The result display that many students prefer the social nature of interacting with others while studying. Even adding progressively more structure and more opportunities for discussions to the learning tasks were leading to better outcomes.

Jones and Gallen (2016) were studying whether *peer observation of teaching* can play a useful role in developing university staff (N=20) for online and technology-embedded higher education. The method of peer observation of teaching is an established developmental tool in face-to-face settings, but not online. Jones and Gallen used in this study a student-centred approach and a collaborative model with three stages: pre-observation meeting, the observation itself and a feedback meeting, based on that shared perceptions and peer relationships are genuine. In such online environment, a process of dialogue exchanges about practice may lead to mutually and beneficial development. Methodically, the participants were engaged in a series of online peer-observed tutorials, and evaluated them afterwards by using synchronous conferencing tools to facilitate learning. The result show that the peer observation process had some effect, but the process of development through reflection and shared understanding of practice requires that participants have relevant skills in observing, filed notes and providing formative feedback. This was lacking in the study. Peer relationships seems to be more a valuable collegial way of learning in higher education.

Tsuei (2014) was studying the impact of a synchronous *peer tutoring* system among fourth-grade students with learning disabilities, LD. The system integrated an instrumental strategy with modules for teachers to manage peer tutoring activities, including various math representation objects, communication tools, and reward schema for facilitating online peer learning activities. The face-to-face online peer tutoring was implemented with one lesson per week (40 minutes) during two semesters teaching (one year). The results indicated that the peer tutoring system was effective to enhance the mathematics learning of students with LD, especially the learning of conceptual skills and application of math problems. The findings in the online activities also supported the communication among the students and their understanding of math concepts.

The study by Serdyukov and Hill (2013) provides some insight on *autonomous students* by a questionnaire among 57 research students if they prefer organized on-campus studies, independent online learning, or will be comfortable in either format of learning. The principle of autonomous students is correlated with student centered education, social constructivism, and collaborative approach. Autonomy means: 1) moving the focus from teaching to learning, 2) empowering students and 3) encourages needs for peer support and collaboration. In other words, take responsibility for their own learning and learn to learn, which is involving an interactive process with a set of short and long term learning objectives, reflections on and evaluations of the learning progress. The result show that the majority of the students (56.7%) preferred to choose organized on-campus studies, only 37.8% favoured independent online learning, and 5.4% should be comfortable in either format of learning. The major factors ensuring the students success in independent learning were; time management (32.4%), structure, organization, and guidance (29.7), and motivation and support (10.9% each).

## DESIGN OF PEER LEARNING ACTIVITIES

The main goal of higher education has changed, it is not enough for students to learn scientific knowledge, they must also develop theoretically and professionally skills, as well as in different contexts (Dochy, Segers & Sluijsmans, 1999; Zhu, Yu & Riezebos, 2016). University teachers are responsible for the transformation of the learning environment to be SMART for student-centered learning through blended course design with peer learning activities to improve students' preparations for academic success and for their future careers (Amhag, 2013b; 2016a; 2016b; 2017; Serdyukov & Hill, 2013). Therefore, online courses need a higher degree of peer learning activities and group wise interactions, which requires more motivated, adaptive, resource-enriched and technology-embedded learning activities for self-regulated and self-directed participation. Independently, students should be possible to access the course materials and structure their time, space, and place of their own learning process, as well as to have dialogical exchanges with other students (Amhag, 2016a; 2016b; 2017).

Usually, peer learning are added for a particular purpose or course in an ad hoc way, and the development of peer activities tends to take place "on the go" (Boud, Cohen & Sampson, 2001b). Cohen and Sampson (ibid.) highlight the importance of formalizing peer learning activities within academic courses and explicitly designing them to meet desired learning outcomes. When the students start a course, it is important that the contact with the peers increases, while also exploring the subject's content area that prepare them to deal with more complex types of academic works for later peer learning experiences. But also help them to mix with a greater number of students from the beginning of the education. In teacher training courses, the peer learning strategy should be structured to encourage students to reflect on their learning experiences to consider how they can use similar strategies with their pupils during their teaching practice.

## Implementation of Peer Learning Activities

A number of issues need to be addressed in the implementation of the peer learning activities. Following design features and necessary implementation aspects are needed (revised from Boud, Cohen & Sampson, 2001b, p. 22):

- Considering the context into which peer learning activities is to be introduced, recognize the expectations, experiences and beliefs about learning to ensure that the activities are challenging, creative, exciting, and supportive. Justify also whether the course is student centered or oriented around the needs of the discipline or profession.
- Focusing on course goals and learning outcomes, as well as the more specific desired learning outcomes which are necessary for the group of students and their future learning.
- Ensuring the collaborative dialogues between the students, their roles and responsibilities. The processes are personally and intellectually demanding, therefore, important for students to feel that the effort they are contributing to will be appreciated.
- Considering resource implications to manage the process, from the introduction and support to the evaluation of the peer learning process. For some teachers, peer learning activities will contribute to their assessment and feedback; for others, the approach will be a major

change – from teacher-directed and controlled learning – to student-negotiated and peer active learning.

Topping (2007, p. 634) suggests similar design features and necessary implementation with following 12 aspects to be considered in peer learning activities:

1. Context – specific problems and opportunities to the local practice.
2. Objectives – consider achievements and in what domains.
3. Curriculum area – learning goals and learning outcomes.
4. Participants – strategy for peer learning; who, why, when and how? There is need for training and quality assurance.
5. Helping technique – which method, design and technology-embedded activities?
6. Contact – how frequent, how long, and where will the communication occur?
7. Materials – consider and describe the necessary resources.
8. Training – first for staff, then for students and peers.
9. Process monitoring – consider the quality assurance of the process.
10. Assessment of students – assess the product and the process; or self and/or peer assessment.
11. Evaluation – what worked or not?
12. Feedback – should be provided to all participants to improve future efforts.

## Strategies for Peer Learning Activities

Strategies for peer learning activities are necessary to consider in order to adapt the courses special features, its learning goals and outcomes, and the educational environment in which it takes place, on campus or online or both. Some of these strategies might be (revised from Boud, Cohen & Sampson, 2001c, p. 35):

- as a series of alternative teaching methods - for example as a substitute for certain types of lessons to develop formal learning – for example, to give students more practice in critical review and higher-order thinking;
- as part of a constellation of learning strategies - for example, to ensure that all students are experiencing informal peer learning;

- as a strategy to address specific problems - for example, to give students more practice in verbal presentation or in inquiry questioning about a case;
- as the central organizing element of learning - for example, as an integral part of student-centered learning;
- as part of a holistic view of teaching and learning - for example, by explicitly acknowledging the role of peers in the overall repertoire of learning and learning experiences.

There are a number of different elements used in various ways in peer learning activities, for example preparatory activities, ways of working in groups, communication skills such as presenting, listening, arguing and explaining, dealing with conflicts, problem solving, planning and negotiation, facilitation, reflection and self-assessment. Some common approaches of peer learning activities include the following (revised from Boud, Cohen &Sampson, 2001c, p. 37):

- Seminar presentations in small groups of 3-4 students or pairs after completing a shared project or assignment.
- Work-in-progress reports by individuals or groups working together on a project or assignment, followed by questions and discussion sessions.
- Debriefing sessions (in pairs, small groups or larger plenary sessions) after practical education training, field study or work experience.
- Peer feedback where assignments are first critical reviewed by fellow students and then the feedback or comments are discussed. The justification of peer feedback is a valuable learning experience for both parties.

The most common strategies are (revised from Boud, Cohen and Sampson, 2001c, p. 40):

- *Learning partnerships:* one-to-one learning relationships involving regular contact at mutually selected times where students negotiate and support each other's learning. Partners are self-chosen and characterized by openness and reflective discussions about ideas, give reciprocal feedback based on relevant experiences and evaluate for continuing professional development.
- *Study groups:* five to seven students chosen by the groups themselves, staff and/or of a larger class, with either a formal (staff-facilitated)

or informal (student directed) strategy, scheduled when everyone is available to attend to explore course-related matters collaboratively for exchanging learning and providing peer support during the course.

- *Student-led workshops:* three to eight students work together to plan and conduct a workshop for a wider student group, thus learning about working as a team member while researching and preparing the workshop content, and presenting and evaluating the workshop. Staff will receive written report on the development.
- *Learning exchanges:* five to eight students learn about a topic directly from their peers, whilst learning from the experience of delivering with limited time presentation and observing each other's presentation approaches, and learning to giving and receiving critical feedback. Staff facilitate group reflection and debriefing of the overall activity.

*Table 2. Illustration of which peer learning strategies contribute to the learning outcomes*

| Learning outcomes of each peer learning strategy | | | | |
|---|---|---|---|---|
| | **Learning partnerships** | **Study groups** | **Student-led workshops** | **Learning exchanges** |
| Working in groups | One-to-one | 5-7 | 3-8 | 5-8 |
| Planning | X | X | X | X |
| Presenting | | | X | X |
| Negotiating learning | X | X | | |
| Reflection | X | | | X |
| Articulating understanding | X | X | X | X |
| Peer support | X | X | X | |
| Giving feedback | X | | | X |
| Evaluating | X | | X | X |

Table 2 illustrates the four groups' peer learning strategy with different activities and emphasis, e.g. group size, planning, presenting, negotiating learning, reflecting and evaluating peer learning, as well as providing peer support, and providing and receiving critical feedback (revised from Boud, Cohen & Sampson, 2001c, p. 47).

## METHOD OF PEER LEARNING ACTIVITIES

Methodically, the study has a comparative design which involves a comparison between various peer learning strategies in previous research in order to illustrate existing activities as a result of the opposite results based on this comparison (Bryman, 2016) and how they can contribute to student-centered learning for self-directed and motivated smart higher education with resource-enriched, and technology-embedded tools (Hwang, 2014; Zhu, Yu & Riezebos, 2016). The research studies selected for the comparison were obtained from databases in education and social sciences from Libsearch that allow searching at almost all library databases, such as Web of Knowledge, ERIC, Scopus and Google Scholar, as well as from studies and from studies cited by these authors of the articles and from previous used peer review articles published in the current field with the keywords: peer learning in higher education.

Table 3 gives an overview of five different design features and necessary implementation aspects of peer learning activities in higher education from previous research.

*Table 3. Overview of five different design features and necessary implementation aspects of peer learning activities*

| Participant | Reciprocal peer learning | Peer teaching | Peer tutoring | Supplemental instruction, SI | Peer-assisted learning, PAL |
|---|---|---|---|---|---|
| **Teacher team** Considering the context & objectives of peer learning activities based on goals and outcomes. | Collaborative strategy. Easy to organize within a given class or cohort, on-campus or online, or both. | Instrumental strategy. Selects advanced students as peer instructors and designs peer teaching. | Instrumental strategy. Specific role-taking as tutor or tutee with focus on curriculum and tutoring. | Instrumental strategy. Role models of agents who are changing in the classroom as moderator, summarizer, theoretician or source searcher. | Instrumental strategy where experienced teachers have a responsible role in creating learning objectives and resources for a case. |
| **Experienced teacher** (after peer learning give feedback that moves learning forward) | Clarifying course content, ensuring the communication, sharing's and learning intentions. | Activate and facilitate learning through peer-to-peer interaction. | Activate interactions between students from similar social groupings. | Engage and activate the students with the opportunity to capitalize each other's abilities to be powerful. | Generate triggering discussions about the perceived treatment and the support of PAL. |
| **Peer** | The role is equal. Contributing to other students' learning with communication about mutual experiences and theories. | Limited instructional role. Activate students as learning resources for one another. | Role as tutor or tutee. Helping each other to learn and learning themselves by teaching. | Undergraduate peer has responsibility to support their fellow undergraduates' learning. | Active and constructive discussions among students with elicit evidence of learning. |
| **Student** | Activating students as owners of their own learning and development. | | | | |

The overview in Table 3 show that many of the strategies and activities practised in peer learning are not new or unique. What is new is to illustrate how a systematic design of peer learning activities are implemented in the course and how the chosen strategy, such as reciprocal peer learning, peer teaching, peer tutoring, supplemental instruction and peer-assisted learning, and how the process of the activities are monitored, and the outcomes are evaluated. The difference between a more traditional teacher directed approach and peer learning approach is that students take a more active and self-directed role in planning and managing their own learning during the peer learning activities. Immediate contextual factors that may influence students' acceptance of peer learning activities are the learning outcomes that students expect from the course, previous experience of working in a group with peers, and collaborative activities.

As with all teaching and learning strategies, the most important purpose of a smart higher education is that the peer learning strategy more or less should be self-directed, motivated, adaptive, resource-enriched, and technology-embedded. Therefore, be designed to the specific context, on-campus or online or both, based on the specific learning objectives and the numerous of students and teachers that will be involved. The challenge of using peer learning activities is to adapt the approach to the context which shall be resource-enriched and technology-embedded, as well as with motivated and self-directed learning needs. This smart approach is the central key function to preserving the success of each peer learning strategy.

Practical factors that also influence the acceptance of peer learning are the workload and access to time and place and how the activities are to be implemented and assessed. For teacher staff, previous experience of using peer learning activities is a critical factor, as well as the expectations of the role as a teacher and expert, but also appropriate course assessment and evaluation (Boud, Cohen & Sampson, 2001d). Useful for students is a guide for the peer learning activities, which should be integrated in a resource-enriched higher education. The main purpose of the guide is to clarify what is expected of the students and give some concrete examples of how peer learning activities works and how the activities are supplementing the workload, the learning relationship and their mutual and collaborative learning. The concrete examples in Table 3 are describing the role or roles in the group, how they should share the task and time, listening and questioning skills, feedback suggestions and some reflection and self-evaluation strategies (revised from Boud, Cohen & Sampson, 2001d, p. 55). Conditions that should be discussed to promote peer learning activities are:

- the value of collaboration and the roles involved;
- students' trust in each other;
- the basic peer learning activity, decided by the group;
- practical suggestions on what the collaboration contributes to;
- self-directed and reflective discussions;
- it is acceptable to make mistakes and seek help.

Assessment practices in higher education institutions tend not to prepare students well for the processes of peer learning. Sustainable peer assessment should be promoted which includes the abilities required to undertake peer learning activities that necessarily accompany learning throughout life in formal and informal settings. Assessment practice need both to meet the specific and immediate goals of a course, as well as establishing a basis for students to undertake their own peer assessment activities in the future (Boud, 2000).

## Evaluations of Peer Learning Activities

There are a number of ways to evaluate the results of peer learning, such as self-evaluation of the performances, but the timing is crucial (Boud, Cohen & Sampson, 2001d). Evaluation is an ongoing process, therefore, important that the evaluation is done both during the course after the first peer learning activity in order to make appropriate adjustments, and at the end of the course to increase the quality of the peer learning activities for future development. As with assessment, the form of evaluation must be consistent with the peer learning philosophy. The following evaluation methods are in line with peer learning objectives (revised from Boud, Cohen & Sampson, 2001d, p. 60):

- Self-evaluations: Critical review of students own learning, based on the learning goals and the specific criteria for the selected peer learning activity (see Table 2 and 3). The most common method is to use a reflective log journal where students are encouraged to self-assess during the course, e.g. a critical incident, situation, or a problem that they wish to share with others and discuss. Or may they choose to discuss some of the highlights and problems with a peer member. Other useful methods may be to use a metaphor for the process to discuss and analyse its results.
- Evaluations of peers about their joint performance: Critical review of their joint performance, based on the learning goals and specific criteria to the selected peer learning activity. The discussion preceding

of the evaluation is the most important part of the process, either in small feedback group sessions or in the whole group, depending on the number of participants. It is advisable that the students answer anonymously to both specific questions based on the course objectives and about the learning outcomes of the peer learning strategy (see Table 2 and 3).

- Staff evaluations: Critical review based on the student's self-evaluation and the peer's evaluation as a part of the whole evaluation process where the results are compiled based on the course's learning objectives and the specific criteria for the selected peer learning activity (see Table 2 and 3). Interviews with interested students also provide valuable data. The answers are compiled and reported for further discussion in the whole group on future improvement and development or technology-embedded in the students learning management system, LMS.

The results of the evaluation must be made visible for all participants. Especially, the students want evidence of how their comments have been used to develop and / or change the peer-learning activities. Moreover, positive evaluations can help other teachers to choose the use of peer learning activities in their courses. Teachers can also use staff seminars, conferences and research publishing where their peer learning strategies can be described, discussed and analysed based on the evidence of the results.

## ANALYSIS OF PEER LEARNING ACTIVITIES

The analysis of peer learning activities is based on socio-cultural theory when the focus in peer learning activities is on students' interactions and interplay which constitute a determining factor for the peers', as well as the groups' metacognitive ability, critical thinking and collaborative knowledge development. According to a socio-cultural perspective, one of the basic principles is that learning has to do with relationships and always arises as a product of a situated perspective in a social community of practice where people are involved in different forms of processes to create meaning. Thus, learning is a social and collective process in which the person who writes or speaks is dependent on one another, as well as the one who reads or listens as co-authors in a collaborative construction of meaning. In this way, a parallel development of languages and concepts takes place since the peers in the group use communication and negotiate learning with each other, and were a mutual development of understanding and problem solving takes place (Amhag & Jakobsson, 2009; Kozulin, 1997; Wertsch, 1998).

According to Wenger (1998), the *community of practice,* CoP is designed for situated learning maintained by the participants' mutual engagement and common interests which offers opportunities for imagination and alignment to create a common focus. Learning is described as taking place in a specific situation and the situation has significance for the nature and results of the learning. The focus shifts from the individual to the collective, and that learning is a fundamental social / collective phenomenon, is done primarily by participating in a community of practice. As in peer learning strategies with a set of roles, means and working methods (see Table 2 and 3). The students are engaging in their group, as a kind of a community of practice, situated within a proscribed time to produce something that they are sharing together in the group, which can be based on a critical incident, situation, dilemma or different viewpoints. Afterwards they are sharing their work with others for further critical review and evaluation.

The concept of the *zone of proximal development*, ZPD, is also used to analyses the peer learning activities to highlight the difference or development zone between what students already can and what they can achieve with support from others. The form of teaching that Vygotsky (1978) emphasizes requires both consultations between students and teacher and the guidance of a more knowledgeable person, both of which add activity and creativity. For example, the student should have a slightly more difficult problem to solve than he / she can solve on their own. Through the guidance of a more knowledgeable person or teacher, the student is guided through the development of learning. Thus, new understanding and new achievements arise. Del Rio and Alvarez (2007, p. 281) describe the concept of ZPD as a Vygotskian leading window that opens for the following questions: *Who?* That we learn ourselves. *With whom?* That we learn together with others and by those who know more. *What is developed?* That our higher functions are developing, changing, and enabling new actions. *With what? How?* That we, through communications and negotiations, can have benefit from each other's different knowledge and experiences. *Where?* That we can do things that we otherwise would not have been able to do. Thus, the development zone forms a basis for individual and collective learning.

However, there is a difference between being *outside* and *inside* the ZPD (Del Rio & Alvarez, 2007). Confirmatory statements are outside the ZPD, e.g. "You describe it well and clearly!", "I agree with you!", "I think you grabbed it well!", "I got the same idea as you!" These confirmations do not contribute to any clarifying's or understandings, thus, do not lead to any further development. Being inside the ZPD is when you can have benefit and support from other's different knowledge and clarifying's. One way is to ask inquiring questions: "I respond to that you write about the dilemma between...?", "How do you mean this theory works...?", "Does that mean that this viewpoint clarify...?" But it can also consist of counterproposals, alternative solutions, advice or problematics. Here follows a short example with a dialogue exchange between two students about source reference:

*Student 1 writes:*

*It is a bit confusing with two different ways to specify your source references in the text. Was there any thought behind it?*

*Student 2 answers:*

*I agree that the source references are a bit messy. When I first wrote the text I had them in parentheses, but then I thought it looked better with underlining. It was easier to understand. Then I forgot to correct it throughout the text. So it is pure carelessness on my part.*

Student 1 has made Student 2 aware of that he must refer to the sources in a correct and uniform way and make him reflect on his writings. The comment from student 1 turned out to be within the students' inside-zone of ZPD, because he was receptive to the observation and support from a more competent student (Del Rio & Alvarez, 2007). This comment creates new understanding that leads to new actions, such as correcting the source references in a uniform way.

## CONCLUSION

The results of peer learning activities based on comparing's of peer learning strategies in previous research, with a focus on the students' interactions and interplay, show that the activities were a decisive factor for the peers, as well as the groups' critical thinking and collaborative knowledge development. The strategies of peer learning activities highlight that it is necessary to consider the context, its learning goals and outcomes, ensure the collaborative dialogues between the students and resource implications to manage the process, from the introduction and support to the evaluation of the peer learning processes. Likewise, the smart educational environment in which the peer learning activities takes place, on campus, or in a mobile setting, or both is central (Hwang, 2014; Zhu, Yu & Riezebos, 2016). There are a number of various peer learning strategies and designs that can be used (see Table 2 and 3), for example preparatory activities, ways of group working, communication skills such as planning and presenting a project, explaining and questioning over a case, dealing with conflicts, discuss problem solving, negotiating a concrete solution or dilemma, facilitate and develop each other's work, and reflect and evaluate the peer learning activities.

However, university courses need a higher degree of peer learning activities which is a key solution for smart mobile settings with interactions and interplay in discussions fora and other mobile e-meeting system about different issues for their peer learning and collaborative development. Positively correlated with academic learning outcomes in a mobile setting have teachers' strategies of time and place, e.g. with online webinars face-to-face, F2F and chat communications for students' metacognitive ability, and critical thinking.

## REFERENCES

Amhag, L. (2013b). *Creativity in and between Collaborative Peer Assessment Processes in Higher Distance Education. Creative Education, 4(7A2)*, 94–104. doi:10.4236/ce.2013.47A2011

Amhag, L. (2016a). Mobile technologies for student-centered learning in a distance higher education program. In *Wearable Technology and Mobile Innovations for Next-Generation Education,* (pp. 184-199). IGI Global. https://www.igi-global.com/book/wearable-technology-mobile-innovations-next/142108

Amhag, L. (2016b). Mobile technologies for student-centered learning in a distance higher education program. *Blended Learning: Concepts, Methodologies, Tools, and Applications*, *4*, 802–817. doi:10.4018/978-1-5225-0069-8.ch010

Amhag, L. (2017). Mobile-Assisted Seamless Learning Activities in Higher Distance Education. *International Journal of Higher Education*, *6*(3), 2017. doi:10.5430/ijhe.v6n3p70

Amhag, L., & Jakobsson, A. (2009). Collaborative Learning as a Collective Competence when Students Use the Potential of Meaning in Asynchronous Dialogues. *Computers & Education*, *52*(3), 656–667. doi:10.1016/j.compedu.2008.11.012

Bandura, A. (2002). Growing primacy of human agency in adaption and change in the electronic era. *European Psychologist*, *7*(1), 2–16. doi:10.1027//1016-9040.7.1.2

Boud, D. (2000). Sustainable assessment: Rethinking assessment for the learning society. *Studies in Continuing Education*, *22*(2), 151–167. doi:10.1080/713695728

Boud, D., Cohen, R., & Sampson, J. (2001a). Peer learning in higher education: Learning from and with each other. In Introduction: Making the move to peer learning. Routledge.

Boud, D., Cohen, R., & Sampson, J. (2001b). Peer learning in higher education: Learning from and with each other. In Designing peer learning. Routledge.

Boud, D., Cohen, R., & Sampson, J. (2001c). Peer learning in higher education: Learning from and with each other. In Strategies for peer learning: some examples. Routledge.

Boud, D., Cohen, R., & Sampson, J. (2001d). Peer learning in higher education: Learning from and with each other. In Implementing and managing peer learning. Routledge.

Broadbent, J., & Poon, W. L. (2015). Self-Regulated Learning Strategies & Academic Achievement in Online Higher Education Learning Environments: A Systematic Review. *The Internet and Higher Education*, *27*, 1–13. doi:10.1016/j.iheduc.2015.04.007

Bryman, A. (2016). *Social research methods*. Oxford University Press.

Coetzee, D., Lim, S., Fox, A., Hartmann, B., & Hearst, M. A. (2015, February). Structuring interactions for large-scale synchronous peer learning. In *Proceedings of the 18th ACM Conference on Computer Supported Cooperative Work & Social Computing* (pp. 1139-1152). ACM. 10.1145/2675133.2675251

Dawson, P., van der Meer, J., Skalicky, J., & Cowley, K. (2014). On the effectiveness of supplemental instruction: A systematic review of supplemental instruction and peer-assisted study sessions literature between 2001 and 2010. *Review of Educational Research, 84*(4), 609–639. doi:10.3102/0034654314540007

De Wever, B., Van Keer, H., Schellens, T., & Valcke, M. (2010). Structuring asynchronous discussion groups: Comparing scripting by assigning roles with regulation by cross-age peer tutors. *Learning and Instruction, 20*(5), 349–360. doi:10.1016/j.learninstruc.2009.03.001

Del Rio, P., & Alvarez, A. (2007). Inside and Outside the Zone of Proximal Development. An Ecofunctional Reading of Vygotsky. In The Cambridge Companion to Vygotsky (pp. 276-303). Cambridge: Cambridge University Press.

Dochy, F., Segers, M., & Sluijsmans, D. (1999). The use of self-, peer- and co-assessment in higher education: A review. *Studies in Higher Education, 24*(3), 331–350. doi:10.1080/03075079912331379935

Ford, C. R., Wilkins, E. B., & Groccia, J. E. (2018). Students Engaged in Teaching. *New Directions for Teaching and Learning, 2018*(154), 33–43. https://doi-org.proxy.mau.se/10.1002/tl.20289. doi:10.1002/tl.20289

Gunawardena, C. N., Lowe, C. A., & Anderson, T. (1997). Analysis of a global online debate and the development of an interaction analysis model for examining social construction of knowledge in computer conferencing. *Journal of Educational Computing Research, 17*, 397-431.

Hardy, M., Kilcoyne, M., & Pérez-Mira, B. (2017). A Pilot Study on Subject Matter Expert-Peer Learning in Higher Education: A Continuous Improvement Process. *Federation of Business Disciplines, 5*, 1–10.

Hwang, G. J. (2014). Definition, framework and research issues of smart learning environments – a context-aware ubiquitous learning perspective. *Smart Learning Environments, 1*(1), 4. doi:10.118640561-014-0004-5

Jones, M. H., & Gallen, A. M. (2016). Peer observation, feedback and reflection for development of practice in synchronous online teaching. *Innovations in Education and Teaching International, 53*(6), 616–626. doi:10.1080/14703297.2015.1025808

Kozulin, A. (1997). *Thought and Language Lev Vygotsky*. London: Cambridge University Press.

Linell, P. (1998). *Approaching dialogue: Talk, interaction and contexts in dialogical perspectives* (Vol. 3). John Benjamins Publishing. doi:10.1075/impact.3

Puzziferro, M. (2008). Online technologies self-efficacy and self-regulated learning as predictors of final grade and satisfaction in college-level online courses. *American Journal of Distance Education, 22*(2), 72–89. doi:10.1080/08923640802039024

Reinholz, D. (2016). The assessment cycle: A model for learning through peer assessment. *Assessment & Evaluation in Higher Education, 41*(2), 301–315. doi:10.1080/02602938.2015.1008982

Serdyukov, P., & Hill, R. (2013). Flying with clipped wings: Are students independent in online college classes? *Journal of Research in Innovative Teaching, 6*(1), 54–67.

Stigmar, M. (2016). Peer-to-peer Teaching in Higher Education: A Critical Literature Review. *Mentoring & Tutoring, 24*(2), 124–136. doi:10.1080/13611267.2016.1178963

Struyven, K., Dochy, F., & Janssens, S. (2005). Students' perceptions about evaluation and assessment in higher education: A review. *Assessment & Evaluation in Higher Education, 30*(4), 325–341. doi:10.1080/02602930500099102

Tai, J. H. M., Canny, B. J., Haines, T. P., & Molloy, E. K. (2017). Implementing peer learning in clinical education: A framework to address challenges in the "real world". *Teaching and Learning in Medicine, 29*(2), 162–172. doi:10.1080/10401334.2016.1247000 PMID:27997224

Topping, K. J. (2005). Trends in peer learning. *Educational Psychology, 25*(6), 631–645. doi:10.1080/01443410500345172

Vygotsky, L. S. (1978). *Mind in Society: Development of Higher Psychological Processes* (M. Cole, Trans.). Academic Press.

Wang, J., Shannon, D., & Ross, M. (2013). Students' characteristics, self-regulated learning, technology self-efficacy, and course outcomes in online learning. *Distance Education, 34*(3), 302–323.

Wenger, E. (1998). *Communities of Practice - Learning, meaning and Identity*. New York: Cambridge University Press. doi:10.1017/CBO9780511803932

Wertsch, J. V. (1998). *Mind as Action*. Oxford: Oxford University Press.

Wiliam, D. (2011). What is assessment for learning? *Studies in Educational Evaluation, 37*(1), 3–14. doi:10.1016/j.stueduc.2011.03.001 PMID:22114905

Wiliam, D. (2013). Assessment: The bridge between teaching and learning. *Voices from the Middle, 21*(2), 15.

Zhu, Z. T., Yu, M. H. & Riezebos, P. (2016). A research framework of smart education. *Smart Learning Environments, 3*(1), 4.

Zimmerman, B. J. (2008). Investigation self-regulation and motivation: Historical background, methodological developments, and future prospects. *American Educational Research Journal, 45*(1), 166–183. doi:10.3102/0002831207312909

# Chapter 5
# Peer Feedback Activities in Smart Education


## ABSTRACT

*New ways of communication and peer feedback activities provide several opportunities for student-centered collaborative learning in smart higher education. This chapter increases the knowledge about how collaborative peer feedback processes can support student-centered learning toward higher-order thinking and critical ability in smart higher education. Methodically, various types of feedback are illustrated based on review of selected articles from previous research. The qualitative empirical data of feedback processes (N=155) among 22 students was grounded on criteria and guidance on feedback for collaborative learning. Theoretically, the analysis of excerpts is based on a feedback model and an assessment cycle to identify the gap between the main process, self-regulated and self-directed actions, and the self as a person (i.e., what is understood and what is aimed to be understood). The results demonstrate that peer feedback provides one of the most critical and self-directed impacts on student-centered collaborative learning and higher-order thinking.*


DOI: 10.4018/978-1-7998-4183-8.ch005

## BACKGROUND

Peer feedback between students and feedback from teachers is one of the most important skills in teaching that improves students' collaborative learning and outcomes (Hattie & Timperley, 2007). In a broad sense the whole process is including how students receive and use the feedback for their reflecting back on their own work and future process, but also give other students concrete peer feedback. Thus, it is not just about the formal response-giving activity (Dysthe, Lillejord, Vines & Wasson, 2010), instead more knowledge that leads to greater opportunities for learning, improved challenges, more self-directed and self-regulated learning processes about what exists and what is not understood (Hattie & Timperley, 2007).

This chapter increases the knowledge about in what way collaborative peer feedback processes can be a tool for self-directed and motivated student-centered learning in a resource-enriched learning environment with technology-embedded tools in smart higher education. The following questions are addressed:

- In what way can teachers a) design and b) use different feedback activities and wearable tools that are appropriate for student-centered learning and active participation?
- How do the students experience the feedback activities and the wearable tools for their learning?
- In what way can the feedback activities and tools be analyzed comparing to the students' performance?

'Smart learning' refers to wisdom bounding together the ability of using and motivating self-directed learning, knowledge building, problem-solving, critically reflecting, collaborating and evaluating different circumstances with resource-enriched, and technology-embedded tools, as with written e-feedback or in face-to-face, F2F-webinars / conferencing in a mobile setting at distance (Hwang, 2014; Spector, 2014; Zhu, Yu & Riezebos, 2016).

Feedback ability is related to a dialogic interaction with responses to a specific written text, production or presentation in order for the recipient to become a more conscious writer, producer or presenter (Alvarez, Espasa, A. & Guasch, 2011). Specifically, makes feedback online (e-feedback) the interaction process transparent for students and teachers, as well as acts as a mediated artifact or a tool for the joint activities between the groups of students. Another practical benefit of implementing peer feedback between students is that the feedback becomes available faster during the course, and that more strengths and weaknesses, or alternative strategies for improvement are available earlier than the teachers could ever provide alone (van der Pol, van den Berg & Admiraal, 2008). Moreover, peer feedback can also help students to understand the work in another way, thus, perceive peer feedback as more useful and understandable, than teachers' feedback due to a more available language (Nicol, Thomson & Breslin, 2014). The feedback process can either be done face-to-face, F2F on campus or technology embedded as written e-feedback or in oral F2F-webinars / conferencing in a mobile setting at distance (Amhag, 2013b).

The term assessment feedback or peer assessment is used in research as an umbrella concept with a set of activities for formative or summative purposes in which students comment on the quality of their fellow students' work and have feedback exchanges about conceptual understandings, communication and self-assessment skills, generally between students in the same course (Dochy, Segers, & Sluijsmans, 1999; Evans, 2013; Topping, 1998). Collaborative peer feedback is defined as a joint activity that requires interactions between actively participating students and teachers (Dysthe et al., 2010). Formative feedback is defined as conceptualized information in terms of *feed-up*, *feed-back* and *feed-forward*, provided by an agent for self-directed learning e.g. by teacher, peer, book, parent or self, regarding different aspects of one's work (Hattie & Timperley, 2007, p. 81). A teacher usually provides corrective directions, a peer can ask questions and suggest an alternative solution, a book has facts and information about concepts and theories, a parent can provide encouragement and motivation, and the self can value and reflect over the feedback.

Thus, this resource-enriched feedback is a "consequence" of various contributions with details of how to improve. However, there is a clear distinction between providing instruction and providing feedback. Feedback shall provide information specifically relating to the assignment or process of learning that fills a gap between what is understood and what is aimed to be understood (Sadler, 1989), and the process can be done in different ways. When feedback is combined with more a correctional review, the feedback and instruction become intertwined to a new instruction, not only about correctness.

Broad research show that writing is a central activity in higher education across disciplines and is often referred to a 'skill' or a 'competence' which involves much more than being able to communicate what the students already know (Dysthe, 2007; Sadler, 1989). It is argued that this type of creativity is a central characteristic of academic studies and an important tool for thinking, learning and knowledge building. Peer feedback processes includes creativity as "higher order thinking skills" to develop awareness of resource-enriched contributions through communication with each other, and perceive the various qualities that make the contributions relevant (Richardson & Ice, 2010; Wegerif, 2007). Moreover, the peer feedback process requires provision of active involvement of own learning, adjustment of the teaching to take into account the result of peer feedback that influence motivation and self-esteem, and the need for students to be able to assess themselves and understand how to improve. These elements, not only help students to make judgments about their own learning outcomes, but also allow them to consider the characteristics of competent work, and learn how to apply these criteria, both on their own and others´ work (De Wever, Van Keer, Schellens & Valcke, 2009).

However, evidence of progress in improving feedback practices have not higher education been as attentive to as they should have been, based on the emerging research and findings from schools that these activities enhance assessment feedback and the formative approach (Evans, 2013). Traditionally, has teachers' feedback to students' written draft in progress or completed assignment either been orally face-to-face, F2F or with short written corrections, often based on own expert models aimed to give content information, and ideally, also foster generative skills (Dijks, Brummer & Kostons, 2018). Generative skills are providing information alongside complex content-related information and can be too complicated for students to understand how to proceed. On the other hand, students tend to be more satisfied with teaching quality and intellectual stimulation, than by feedback from teachers and students (ibid.). One reason may be that teachers' competence differs on how formative- and peer feedback processes can be implemented in an academic context and what types of feedback have impact on students' knowledge building in a digitized higher education (Amhag, Hellström & Stigmar, 2019).

In spite of the increased popularity of peer feedback activities in higher educational settings, researchers point out that more studies are needed to shed light on best practices for teachers to design the activities (Dijks, Brummer & Kostons, 2018; Raes, Vanderhoven & Schellens, 2015). In a collaborative context, peer feedback enables reflections on the eminence of own and others contributions and the input of others, and develops awareness of high quality contributions to the discussions. In these respects, peer feedback processes, conducted individually and in group, can promote students' learning and development; together with other forms of reflective interactions that support students' creative and critical ability to collaborate, reflect and self-assess in a meaningful way (Amhag, 2013b; Amhag & Jakobsson, 2009).

## PREVIOUS RESEARCH OF PEER FEEDBACK ACTIVITIES

The value of implementing formative assessment approaches in higher education and peer feedback processes between students have been highlighted widely in the research (e.g. Amhag, 2013b; Dysthe, Lillejord, Vines & Wasson, 2010; Sadler, 1989; Struyven, Dochy & Janssen, 2005; Topping, Smith, Swanson & Elliot, 2000; Wiliam, 2011; 2013). Selected articles for review of previous research were obtained from searches in databases in education and social sciences such as ERIC, Libsearch etc. and from studies cited by these authors and from previously used peer review articles published in the relevant field with keywords: peer feedback and higher education. Overall, show the review that providing feedback promotes students' ability to give and receive peer feedback, and are an intermediate step for self-assessment when they evaluate their own work (Dochy, Segers, & Sluijsmans, 1999; Topping, 1998). Therefore, the usefulness of feedback depends both on the content of the feedback, as well as on the mediator of the feedback with the perceived added value of argumentation in oral and written feedback.

In the following sections, describes various types of feedback and gap between the processes, themes and discourses, as well research and practice. Overall, it is crucial to integrate cognitivist and constructivist approaches to the feedback processes based on the requirements of the task, topic, and context to develop the feedback research agenda forward (Evans, 2013). Within a constructivist paradigm, students not only construct meaning from feedback from others, they also learn by constructing meanings to themselves in the use of cognitive- and meta-cognitive abilities that are stimulated when students are engaging in reviewing activities. A literature review of feedback in higher education by Evans (2013) is based on an analysis of 460 articles published during year 2000 to 2012 about how students receive feedback within their coursework. The result show that the universities need to provide a pragmatic action plan for students with a clear guidance on how they can improve their works and how they address feedback practices at a micro-level, and at a macro-level, clarifying the students role in the feedback process, and also ensuring that the staff have the opportunities to share best practice.

## The Nature of Feedback

The nature of teacher feedback is investigated by Alvarez, Espasa and Guasch (2011) during a collaborative writing assignment among 83 university students, divided into 16 work groups. The aim was to identify the possible effects of e-feedback on the revision of the written texts in an asynchronous online learning environment. The result show four types of feedback: corrective feedback, epistemic feedback, suggestive feedback, and epistemic + suggestive feedback:

- *Corrective feedback* refers to the learning objectives and the requirements of the assignment, e.g. "The content is not sufficient"; "This is not included in the task"; "More is needed about ..."; "The right answer is ..."
- *Epistemic feedback* refers to knowledge building with questions about explanations and / or clarifications in a critical way, e.g. "Do you think this statement reflects what the author highlights in the study?"; "Why do you think A is an example of what the author is referring to?"
- *Suggestive feedback* contains advice on how to proceed or move forward and invites descriptions, expansion or improvement of a problem, e.g. "Please, give examples at the end of the argument that clarify some solutions to the problem".
- *Epistemic + suggestive feedback* is the combination of both, e.g. "Do you think this sentence is convincing enough?"; "You should read the article again and identify similarities and differences between the theories"; "It can help if you perform the task more adequately".

The result show that epistemic feedback or epistemic + suggestive feedback contributed best to a higher level of interaction to the students' work groups, since they are questioned about their knowledge building, and they must make decisions together how to proceed.

These four types of feedback are investigated further by Guasch, Espasa, Alvarez and Kirschner (2013) among 201 students on which of them can best improve the quality of collaborative writing of an essay, and what effects teachers' feedback and peer feedback among students have on their learning in an online learning environment based on asynchronous written communication. The result show that the quality of collaborative writing performance was most improved by providing the students with epistemic or epistemic + suggestive feedback. These two types affected the quality of the collaborative writing product more than corrective feedback with instruction on what could be done better or, more importantly, only receiving suggestive feedback how to proceed. Dealing with epistemic knowledge building questions, require the students to be more active in reviewing and rewriting their work, and self-assess what they had done and what they need to do more.

Differences of peer feedback and the proportional content between; no structure; basic structure; and elaborate structure conditions in particular is investigated by Gielen and De Wever (2015). The study illustrates how a practical instructional intervention in the peer feedback process can increase the impact of peer assessment and the students' learning in higher education. The result show that a higher structuring degree in a peer feedback template during the peer assessment process have an impact on the peer feedback content. But, there was a significant difference between the three categories of conditions of the peer feedback content; (a) feedback on content and the relevance of information, clarity of the problem, argumentation and conceptual explanations; (b) feedback on the structure of the text e.g. on the relationships between problems, purpose and research questions, etc., and (c) feedback on style: language, grammar, style rules, source references etc. All peer feedback categories had balanced proportion of verifications and elaborations in the messages, usually with positive and general verifications, but with more and less on the specific criteria of content (a) and structure (b).

Additional study by Chaqmaqchee (2015) among academic staff (N = 20) makes a comparison between a novel approach with teachers e-feedback, and a traditional approach with teachers written corrective feedback. The novel approach had focus on enhancing students' learning outcomes through participating, cooperating, observing, achieving an activity or an assignment, and exchanging ideas. The traditional approach had focus on teachers' written and corrective feedback with correcting errors, either directly in the text without identifying the errors, or indirectly by referring to the errors in order to be corrected by the students. The result show that the majority of academic staff were using the traditional approach with teachers written corrective feedback, while only a few reported they were using the novel approach with e-feedback. In the result suggests for academic staff to use the novel approach with focus on online feedback for enhancing students' learning outcomes and encourage them to be more proactive in their learning, than using the traditional written corrective feedback.

## Anonymous Peer Feedback

Anonymous peer feedback and peer observation to enhance learning are studied by Chun-Yi and Zhi-Feng (2013) among 12 graduate students. During the reciprocal and anonymous peer assessment activities, the students had to complete their work, review the work of others, provide others with feedback, reflect on the feedback they received and adjust their work according to the feedback. The result show that the students adapted their work to some extent according to the feedback from their peers, but they did not fully accept them. Nevertheless, they condemned holistic feedback or scores and valued higher specific and detailed feedback on the content with more suggestions to be a guide in the process of revision. Overall, the students reported positive attitudes toward the peer feedback activities and the expectations regarding the amount and quality of feedback they received.

Anonymous peer feedback is also examined by Dijks, Brummer and Kostons (2018) among 51 students, divided into 14 groups of two to four students, but also the relationship between perceived expertise of the reviewer and the perceptions of anonymous peer feedback. Students collaboratively had to write a short paper (500 words) and arguing academically for or against a statement. Students provided peer feedback through a standardised feedback form with seven criteria, rated in a five-point Likert-scale, about: clarity of the text, relevance of the text, clear argumentation within the text, quality of the English text, size of the text, adequate proposition, clear referencing and sufficient academic use of language in terms of spelling etc. In the analysis, three dimensions of perceptions of peer feedback are used: 1) the adequacy of feedback (usefulness, fairness and acceptance), (2) willingness to improve, and (3) affect. The reviewing student was also asked to fill in their self-perceived expertise by grading their expertise from 1 (very poor) to 10 (very good), based on their own subjective judgement without criteria. The result confirms that students with a higher perceived expertise can be more truthful, comprehensive and motivating in reviewing due to their better underlying skills in observing and identifying the problems that can lead to a higher level of willingness to improve.

Nicol, Thomson and Breslin (2014) were also specifically focused on anonymous peer review and feedback, rather than on peer assessment with markings or rating others work. The aim was to identify the different learning benefits resulting from receiving feedback reviews from peers, and from producing feedback reviews for peers to gain a deeper insight into the cognitive processes that are activated when students engage in reviewing activities. The participation was a stated course requirement for the 82 students when they individually produce a Product Design Specification, PDS. The main result of the study was that the students were positive to participate in peer review. The majority of them (55%) had not participated in a peer review exercise before, but most of them (76%) would choose it in the future. Importantly, the majority of students (68%) reported that the review process resulted in their reflecting back on their own work and / or in their transmission of ideas, and new ones were generated through the review process. In the focus group interviews, the students stated that giving feedback was the most beneficial and gave them more control over, or more responsibility for the feedback processes. This result highlights the importance of the *inner* feedback process. External feedback does not work alone, it triggers and adds student-generated feedback that confirms, complements or contradicts the inner feedback. Feedback production is recognized by the students as just as valuable for learning as receiving feedback.

Anonymous peer assessment processes in a face-to-face, F2F authentic classroom setting in higher education is investigated by Raes, Vanderhoven and Schellens (2015) among 51 third-year Bachelor students in Educational Studies during 12-week intensive mandatory course with various instructional design strategies based on a social constructivist learning approach. A mixed methods approach was used with quantitative and qualitative triangulated data between classroom response technology, CRT which is a system with individual infrared handset transmitters used in a face-to-face setting, followed by additional oral feedback or anonymous written feedback. The aggregated CRT-totals of votes are subsequently displayed as a graph on the screen as immediate and anonymity feedback. A voting system, only gives points (1 to 5 points), not comments, suggestions or justifications for those points that are emphasized in both summative and formative assessment methods. The students were divided in two groups (group A = anonymous written feedback, group B = non-anonymous oral feedback), first they gave anonymous feedback using CRT, and afterwards anonymous written feedback or oral feedback. The interactive variables in the analysis included perceived peer pressure, feelings of comfort, and positive attitudes, all with regard to assessing their peers. The results show that the students felt that the various peer assessments activities were valuable. CRT enables anonymous scoring with immediate visual feedback in the face-to-face setting, and the oral and written feedback provides the necessary comments, suggestions and motivations. Students were less comfortable with the non-anonymous oral feedback, while the written anonymous feedback were perceived as the most valuable.

## Mindset of Feedback

The relationship between two mindsets and feedback are examined by Forsythe and Johnson (2017) with a focus on to which extent the students are appreciating, engaging, and acting on the feedback they receive. Those with a growth mindset are motivated to learn and their ability can be educated through knowledge and experience. Those with a fixed mindset believe they have a certain amount of intelligence that cannot be significantly developed through effort and knowledge. Theories of self-efficacy were used to analyze students believes about their abilities (Bandura, 1977, p. 194). The more self-efficacious a student is, the more persistent they are, and those who discontinue their efforts prematurely will retain their self-debilitating and defensive performance. That is, as a student becomes increasingly defensive, they do not perceive and integrate the feedback they receive. Instead, they will spend more time and energy blaming others, e.g. the information or teacher, and sometimes the behavior is self-destructive. 222 students initially responded the questionnaires, but only 151 completed the questions (68%) from the following disciplines: social sciences (94), science (24), mathematics and engineering (15), arts and languages (9) and business (9). The mindset was measured with a combination of two questionnaires consisting of a total of 20 questions. The result show that 86 students (57%) were identified as having a fixed mindset with significant levels of motivation such as thoughts and feelings about their feedback as either all-good or all-bad. 65 students (43%) were identified as having a growth mindset and their motivation was higher to act on their feedback and engage in peer feedback activities. The conclusion is that the students need support in exploring the underlying motivational factors and in developing their self-esteem.

## Peer Feedback Online

The use of online interactive peer feedback in higher education are investigated by van der Pol, van den Berg and Admiraal (2008) between the natures of students' feedback, the way it is evaluated by the receiver, and its consecutive use for the revision of students' works across different educational contexts and tools. A total of 335 feedback postings were produced, 200 by the four groups of students in the Annotation system and 135 by the two groups of students in Blackboard. The analysis of peer feedback was coded from two major perspectives: feedback function and feedback aspect. Feedback function refers to analysis, evaluation, explanation and revision, and feedback aspect refers to the subject of feedback: content, structure or style. The result has shown significant relationships between elements of both the nature and the reception of feedback on the one hand, and the use of this feedback by the receiver on the other hand. In addition, the more students agreed to the received feedback, the more the feedback was evaluated as useful; and the more students who agreed to the provided feedback, the more they revised the corresponding parts of their texts.

The impact of the role of feedback assigned to students (N = 273) in online asynchronous discussion groups of 10 students, added with weekly face-to-face working sessions during 12 weeks, is evaluated by De Wever, Schellens, Valcke and Van Keer (2006). Specific students of a group were assigned one of the following five roles in rotation: the role of starter, moderator, theoretician, source searcher and summarizer, in order to promote knowledge construction through social negotiation and the surplus value of self-assessment based on an online questionnaire in which students had to rate their knowledge construction after each discussion assignment. The model of Gunawardena et al. (1997) was used to analyse the written discussions based on five different levels of knowledge construction activities: (1) sharing and comparing information, (2) identifying areas of disagreement, (3) negotiating meaning and co-construction of knowledge, (4) evaluation and modification of new schemas that result from co-construction, and (5) reaching and stating agreement and application of co-constructed knowledge. The result demonstrated that the time when the roles were introduced appeared to be important, also the moment of introduction of these roles. However, they worked at the start of the discussions, but faded out towards the end. The findings also show that students make fewer contributions focusing on identifying differences of opinion, negotiating meaning, evaluating co-constructed meaning and agreeing and applying the co-constructed knowledge, than they actually think they do. This results indicate that self-assessment has no significant added value as the students are not capable of judging themselves. It may be due to that teachers often take for granted that students can realize the benefits of self-assessment, and know how to use various peer assessment processes.

These examples of previous research on peer feedback activities in higher education show the impact of feedback processes to integrate in the courses collaborative peer feedback regularly, both individually and in groups, to promote students' learning and development, supported by criteria, and analyse and discuss illustrating excerpts how to provide each other with concrete suggestions and ask inquiry questions for developing further the tasks, and afterwards reflect and self-assess in a meaningful way.

## DESIGN OF PEER FEEDBACK ACTIVITIES

Regarding to the research described in the previous chapter, there is a need for a common terminology and generally accepted theoretical and practical model for how formative assessment approaches and peer feedback processes and activities for students learning in higher education can be designed and analysed. I have chosen an assessment cycle and a feedback model how university teachers can design and analyse peer feedback processes.

### An Assessment Cycle

A theoretical and practical model to design peer assessment as an umbrella concept with peer feedback activities and how it supports self-assessment is demonstrated by Reinholz (2016) in an assessment cycle. The focus is on the role of peer assessment and how it supports self-assessment with the same learning mechanisms, e.g. explanation, collaboration and content understanding. The learning effects of peer- and self-assessment are generally considered to be independent of each other, therefore, needs more studies on how peer assessment supports self-assessment. Self-assessment refers to the involvement of learners in making judgements about their own learning in different achievements with a desired goal to adapt and improve the outcomes (Sadler, 1989). Self-assessment is concretized by Sadler (1989) in three components: (1) *goal awareness* of desired performance, (2) *performance awareness* of actual performance and (3) *gap closure* between desired and actual performance. The assessment cycle, summarized in Table 5.1, is based on Sadler's (1989) three components of self-assessment, and illustrates how peer assessment supports self-assessment and how the most beneficial activities are implemented to support *goal awareness*, *performance awareness* and *gap closure*.

The assessment cycle by Reinholz (2016) is based on these three components of self-assessment (Sadler, 1989) to examine which connections there are between peer- and self-assessment in a domain-general way, contrasting

*Figure 1. The assessment cycle, revised from Reinholz (2016, p. 305)*

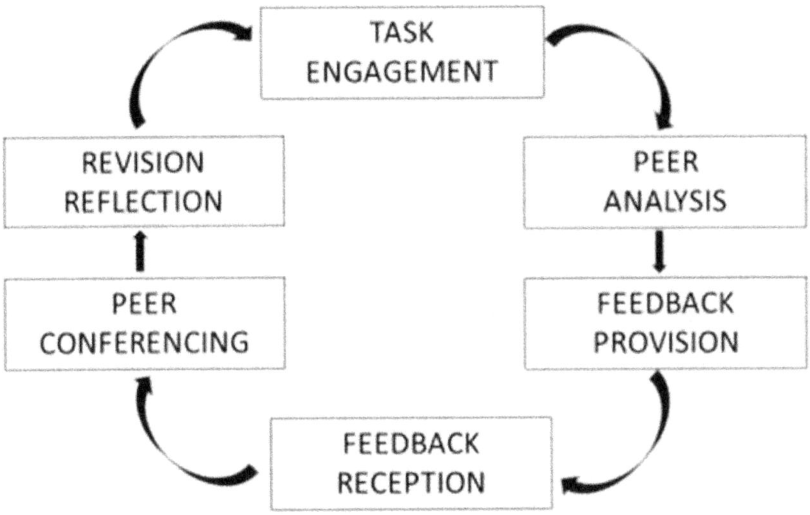


with domain-specific models. In Figure 1 illustrates the six activities in an assessment cycle (Reinholz, 2016).

1. **Task engagement** begins with the work of a task with a *goal awareness* of desired performance, similar to the one the students will give and receive feedback from. This allows students to support their peer analysis through the insights from their own work on the task. Self-assessment can help students to reflect on the quality of their work, which is developing greater *performance awareness*. Likewise, to work towards the *gap closure* in reviewing the quality of their work and self-assess their engagement processes for further developing the self-regulation skills.
2. **Peer analysis** involves judgements about the quality of a work to generate feedback and give constructive feedback. When students are able to compare different solutions to a similar task, they progress their *goal awareness*. It is easier to see the strengths and weaknesses in the content which are progressing the *gap closure* in reviewing the quality. Such experience help students develop deeper conceptual understanding and *performance awareness*.

3. **Feedback provision** involves students providing written and / or verbal feedback about their analyses to their peers. Written feedback can be provided efficiently from a number of students. Verbal feedback provides opportunities to practice explaining's and to receive immediate feedback if the analyses are understood or not. This process is progressing further *goal awareness* of desired performance, *performance awareness* of deeper understanding and *gap closure* in reviewing the quality.
4. **Feedback reception** expands students' understandings to see their work from another's perspective that helps them to learn independently, analyses critique and improve their own work, based on additional *goal awareness* of desired performance. This process forms an objective lens for self-assessment and promote deeper *performance awareness* and *gap closure* in improving their work.
5. **Peer conferencing** or peer webinars online face-to-face, F2F allows students to discuss their feedback and analyses, as well as explaining their understandings verbally and also have knowledge exchanges about strengths and weakness. This process support *goal awareness, performance awareness* and *gap closure* by improving the benefits of peer analysis, feedback provision and feedback reception.
6. **Revision and reflection** allows students to close the assessment cycle (Sadler 1989). Peer assessment should be conducted formatively, and as a result, the process is influencing the feedback provision and the feedback reception. Students can revise and reflect over their work before submitting the final version to practice *gap closure* as they revised their work. Feedback after an assignment is already submitted, give no opportunity to use the feedback and is detrimental because they cannot do any revision.

The assessment cycle, revised from Reinholz (2016) in Figure 1 is useful for university teachers when they are designing what should be included in peer feedback activities between students. Peer assessment should include all six activities or most of them. The order between them can vary, e.g. feedback reception and feedback provision can be done in the opposite order. The size of the group is also important, according to Tolmie and Boyle (2000) works communication better in groups of six students. In smaller groups, a power relationship often occurs, in larger groups subgroups are often formed. However, discussing the provision of feedback and the reception of feedback during peer conferencing or webinar online F2F without the possibility of revision and reflection, limits the value of feedback (Amhag, 2013b). The study by Reinholz (2016) was designed on all components in the assessment cycle. The result show that the students developed *goal awareness* by regularly analysing the work of their peers, *performance awareness* by receiving and integrating peer feedback, as well as discuss their work during the peer conferences or webinars online F2F, and finally, revising and reflecting their own work to practice the *gap closure* as they revised their work.

## A Model of Feedback

Hattie's (2009) synthesis of over 800 meta-analyses based on over 50.000 studies relating to achievement, show at the top that feedback was powerful as follows: direct instruction (0.93), mutual instruction (0.86), students' prior cognitive ability (0.71), socio-economic impacts (0.44), homework (0.41), use of calculators (0.24), reduce class size (0.12), and retention 1 year back (–0.12). The most effective form of feedback consists of information about the progress related to goals, and/or about how to proceed with signals or support by using video, audio or computer-assisted instruction. Programmed instruction, praise, punishment and outer rewards are the least effective in improving performance. Thus, rewards and punishment should not be considered as feedback.

The model of feedback to enhance learning by Hattie and Timperley (2007, p. 87) is illustrating how the discrepancies can be reduced between increased effort, understandings and engagement, performances and goals. Active / effective feedback include three major questions asked by a teacher and/or by a student: Where am I going? (What are the goals?), How am I going? (What progress is being made toward the goal?), and Where to next? (What activities need to be undertaken to make better progress?). These questions correspond to the concept of Feed Up, Feed Back, and Feed Forward, illustrated in Figure 2.

An ideal learning environment or learning experiences occurs when both teachers and students pursue answers to each of the three questions – Where am I going? How am I going? Where to next? – rather than limiting students' opportunities to receive feedback on their performance (Hattie & Timperley, 2007). How creatively the student answers them gives both an increased opportunity to reduce the gap between them, and at what level the feedback operates (Amhag, 2013b; Zimmerman, 2008). Feedback has different effects at the four levels about the task, the process, the self-regulation and the self (Hattie & Timperley, 2007).

*Figure 2. A model of feedback to enhance learning, revised from Hattie and Timperley (2007, p. 87)*

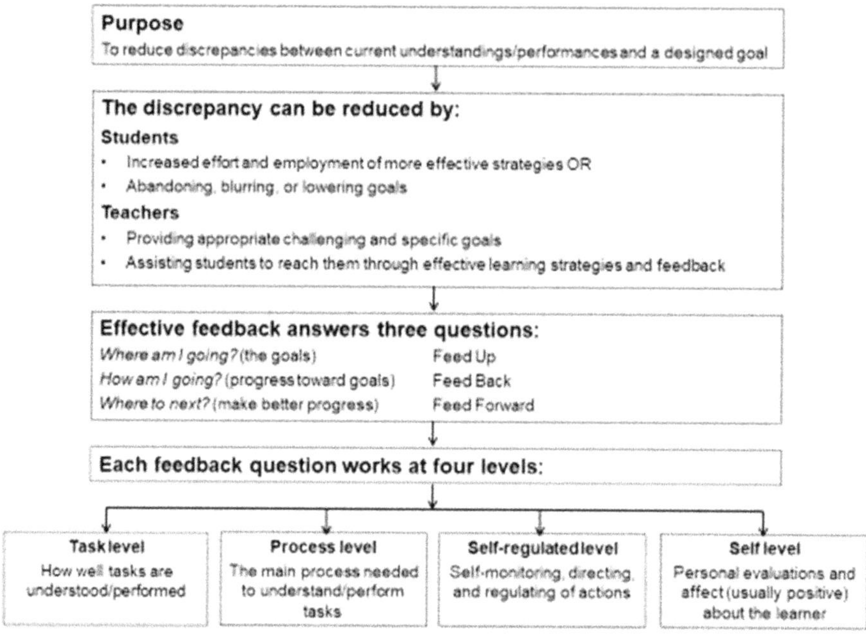


- **The task level** refers to the basic feedback about how well a task is being understood and carried out based on curriculum and learning goals with the aim of clarifying and reinforcing different aspects of the learning task, e.g. dimensions of high to low complexity, correct or incorrect answers, as well developing more or different information. This type of feedback is most common and is often called corrective feedback relating to correctness, preciseness, behaviour, or other criteria of the task.
- **The process level** refers specific to the main cognitive processes concerning deeper understanding of learning and construction of meaning and relationships between performing or relating and extending task, and the transference to other more difficult task to improve students' confidence and self-efficacy, which in turn provides resources for more effective and innovative information and strategy searching.
- **The self-regulated level** or metacognitive process level has cognitive impact and relates to self-monitoring, control / guidance and regulation

of measures towards the learning goals. It means independence, self-control, self-direction and self-discipline, which involves thoughts, feelings of self-efficacy and mediated actions that are planned and adapted to achieve personal goals. The capability to create internal feedback and to self-assess, include the willingness to seeking help and dealing with feedback information.

- **The self-level** refers to personal evaluations and how the evaluations affects them if it leads to changes in students' effort, engagement, or feelings of self-efficacy in relation to the learning or to the strategies they use when attempting to understand tasks. The effects have too little value to result in learning gains and are often diluted, un-informative about performing the task, and influenced by students' self-concept to be effective in increasing engagement or understanding of tasks.

Most effective feedback is to move students from task to processing and then from processing to self-regulation. Students need feedback that they can confirm, add, rewrite, reformulate, rearrange, or use cognitive tactics and strategies as tackling more challenging tasks or appreciating higher quality experiences, rather than just doing more, whether it be domain knowledge, task knowledge, metacognitive knowledge and / or beliefs about the self to use self-regulatory abilities (Hattie & Timperley, 2007). Teachers often assume that students are motivated and share a commitment to their academic studies, but to develop shared commitment must be supported by teachers and built in peer groups, on peer feedback, on role models and joint collaboration with different meanings and understandings (Amhag, 2013b; Amhag & Jakobsson, 2009).

However, the relationship between feedback and goal-related challenge is complex. If the task is unknown or abstract, feedback has little effect on the requirements, since there is nothing to relate to what already is known. Likewise, if the goal is poorly defined, feedback cannot reduce the current understanding and the goal between them. Instead, the gap is closing by the students exaggerating their knowledge or blaming on unclear goals that reduce the effort and engagement (Hattie & Timperley, 2007). Furthermore, feedback can lead to not engaging students in the pursuit of further goals or ignoring them, instead accepting their performance far below their capacity as satisfactory (Bandura, 1982).

Instead, the gap between the four levels of feedback can be reduced through a number of different cognitive processes, such as confirming the student that the work follows the task's goals and guidelines correctly or incorrectly, but also clarifying what needs to be corrected and why. The power of feedback should specifically address "where to next?" by using development issues that have the most powerful effects on learning, e.g. providing information that leads to greater opportunities for learning, improved challenges, more self-regulation of the learning process, greater flow and critical review, more strategies and processes for working with tasks, deeper understanding and more information about what exists and what is not understood (Hattie & Timperley, 2007). Moreover, feedback is most powerful when it comes to incorrect interpretations, not when a complete lack of understanding occurs. Thus, if the goals are challenging and creative, and teachers and students are engaged in these goals, a clearer understanding of the task is created. There must also be a learning context to which feedback is addressed. Feedback is a central part of the teaching process, but reactions occur quickly after the students have been given the first instruction on the assignment or when the study guide is handed out with one or more aspects. Therefore, the feedback must add up the task with more information on what support is available or needed, point to directions to be followed or indicating what alternative strategies exist to reach the student's understanding (Amhag, 2013b).

## METHOD OF PEER FEEDBACK ACTIVITIES

Methodically, the qualitative empirical data (N=155) from 22 students is based on criteria and guidance of feedback for collaborative learning. At the start of the first course the students had trained how to provide peer feedback in their groups. The exercise was based on course goals and guidance of peer feedback inspired from Dysthe, Hertzberg and Løkensgard Hoel (2011) as follows:

*When reading other students assignments, start by capturing its text focus or purpose, then indicate clear or unclear content and formulate briefly in your own words what you consider most important, ask inquire questions about unclear content and provide explanations and clarifications or suggest alternative solutions and/or advice, and finally discuss strength and weakness based on the course goal and guidelines of the assignment.*

The students are not asked to grade the meaning content in the course assignments. It is the teacher's responsibility to put equal and fair grades on the course at the end.

The empirical data (N=155) was collected from 22 student teachers' (15 women, 7 men) peer feedback processes during twenty weeks of participation in the first two consecutive 15 credit courses with blended learning activities in Teacher Education, 90 credits. Blended learning includes that students can learn anywhere and anytime, and can easily switch learning contexts to another or a variety of settings in school and out of school, both mobile and mixed (Wong, Chai, Aw & King, 2015). One assignment in each course was implemented in an online learning management system LMS, where students could share their course assignments, give peer feedback / feedback provision and receive peer feedback / get feedback reception and evaluate their peer feedback both directly and retrospectively. In both courses the students were divided into the same six groups, with five to seven students in each, mixed with both women and men. Group wise, they provided peer feedback on each other's case in a chain, e.g. student 1 on student 2, student 2 on student 3, student 3 on student 4, student 4 on student 5 and student 5 on student 1.

In the both courses the same rules and procedure were followed in two steps. In the first step, the students were asked to submit their own particular written contribution to the course assignment in their groups' discussion forum within a specified deadline, where they could either download or carefully read their fellow students assignments online. In the second step, students were requested to read carefully and critically analyse the content of a fellow students' contribution, as specified in the course goals and guidance for feedback inspired by Dysthe et al. (2011), and formulate a written peer feedback in which they express their own perspective on the presented initial content in the selected case, based on course goals, guidelines of the assignment and course literature. These written peer feedbacks were submitted to their groups' discussion forum, also within a specified deadline. Thereafter, the assignments were assessed by the teachers along with the peers' feedback to which they provided feedback to the students on what progress was made towards the goals and what content should be improved / developed to achieve better progress.

## ANALYSIS OF PEER FEEDBACK ACTIVITIES

The analysis of the peer feedback activities is based on the assessment cycle by Reinholz (2016) and the model of feedback from Hattie and Timperley (2007) which have focus on how formative evaluation method and peer feedback processes with activities promotes student-centered learning in higher education and how they can be analysed and assessed.

The first analysis focuses on the second course assignment in course 1, where the students worked both individually and collaboratively in groups with different cases of teacher leadership. One concerned an official case about a pupil who was exposed for humiliating treatment at school, while the other was the students own case – a story that illustrates a situation in which pupils, parents and / or teachers, felt that they had been badly treated. The second analysis is from course 2, where the students worked both individually and collaboratively in groups with their own cases of bilingualism and second language learning. They had individually observed a teaching situation at a school, and in the assignment they were requested to describe and analyse the situations they had observed, and explaining the circumstances, and finally providing their own didactic suggestions on how to manage the teaching situations.

## Excerpt 1

The first excerpt, gives a picture of the *task level* from course 1, where the students worked both individually and collaboratively in groups with cases of teacher leadership that illustrates a situation in which pupils, parents and / or teachers, felt that they had been badly treated. Student 1 receives written feedback from a fellow student on her case about a boy who was accused by the teacher of a situation in the school dining room in front of the classmates.

**Fellow student***: You must as a teacher be careful with the position of power you [student 1] have over the pupils. In this case, the teacher also brought group of pupils with her on side, because, they promised to be a witness to the situation for which the boy was accused of. She puts the boy for "more-against-one" situation. That the boy has his classmates around him, may find it difficult to be himself, and is violating him even more [...]*

*In this case, there has been an unfair treatment of the boy, and gives an example of abusive treatment. In addition, teachers must also be careful of the pupils' intrinsic value (ref. course literature). The teacher also makes mistakes when she discloses information others, who may contribute to contempt, as in this case, among all his classmates. She is pointing out the reprehensibility of the pupil, which is a crime (ref. course literature). It is contrary to the Education Law paragraphs' that a teacher offends a pupil (ref. course literature).*

This excerpt identifies the meaning content of the peer feedback on the *task level* (Hattie & Timperley, 2007) as the fellow student's peer feedback follows the aspects of the task on a leadership case with a *goal awareness* of desired performance (Reinholz, 2016; Sadler, 1989). The feedback starts with a claim that "you must as a teachers be careful with the position of power you have over the pupils" and continues further over the teachers' witness arrangement by using "more-against-one" situation which is violating the boy even more. This feedback is a type of *corrective feedback* because the content confirms the teacher's lack of correctness and behaviour (Alvarez, Espasa & Guasch, 2011; Hattie & Timperley, 2007), but without evidence of deeper knowledge from course literature and her teaching practice at a school.

In the following peer feedback, shows more *task engagement* (Reinholz, 2016) when there is evidence from the course literature on the pupils' intrinsic value and that the teacher is pointing out the reprehensibility of the boy in front of the classmates, which is a crime and morally wrong. The fellow student may have reflected more over "what I write is highlighted in the literature and therefore, I write it in my post" and on the quality of the case, when she is developing more information and reproductions from course literature (Hattie & Timperley, 2007), which promotes greater *performance awareness* (Reinholz, 2016; Sadler, 1989). Likewise, when she ends with the behavior is contrary to the Swedish Education Law paragraphs' that a teacher offends a pupil. However, the fellow student is now using more knowledge in her peer feedback with statements and reproductions from course literature, but there is a need for broader and deeper construction of meaning with critical thinking and reflections on own learning.

A summary description of the *task level* (Hattie & Timperley, 2007) with *task engagement* (Reinholz, 2016) in the peer feedback in Excerpt 1 is given in Table 1.

## Excerpt 2

The second excerpt, gives a picture of the *process level* with *feedback reception* from course 2, where the students worked both individually and collaboratively in groups with cases on bilingualism and second language learning, based on an observed teaching situation at a school, and explain the circumstances and give own didactic suggestions on how to manage the

*Table 1. Summary description of the task level with task engagement*

| Level of feedback | Criteria displayed from the peer feedback activities |
|---|---|
| Feedback on the task level with task engagement | • how well a task is understood and carried out<br>• based on goals awareness of desired performance<br>• corrective feedback with use of others knowledge<br>• information and reproductions from course literature<br>• reflecting on the quality and developing performance awareness<br>• lack of own critical thinking and reflections on own learning |

teaching situation. Student 2 summarizes the fellow students´ peer feedback with didactic suggestions on her case.

**Student 2***: I described in my statement of didactic proposal, that the pupils with Swedish as a second language would be able to read Swedish literature in their native language. Of course, I agree with you all [comments from three fellow students] that it is important that the pupils read literature for the most part in Swedish since the purpose of literature reading is on the Swedish language. However, I believe that the pupils could take part of the literature also in their native language as the purpose of fiction is to gain a deeper understanding of how people have lived and thought in different cultures at different times (course literature). The writing itself is important for all pupils, I completely agree with that [comments from three fellow students]. But I do believe that teachers can create various opportunities for them where there is more or less appropriate to write. If you have pupils in the class with Swedish as a second language, I maintain that it may be too difficult for them to focus on both languages on what is said and what should be written (course literature). It is important that all pupils get the same opportunities and include them, not exclude anyone. There are so many other situations where the writing comes in focus, especially in the design of teaching that teachers use today.*

In excerpt 2, identifies the meaning content of the peer feedback on the *process level* (Hattie & Timperley, 2007) when Student 2 gets *feedback reception* (Reinholz, 2016) from fellow students with comments on her didactic proposal on the case of bilingualism and second language learning at a school. She begins with her construction of meaning by her claim that pupils might be able to read Swedish literature in their native language to gain a deeper understanding of how people have lived and thought in different cultures, and at different times, based on additional *goal awareness* (Reinholz, 2016; Sadler, 1989), as the course literature illustrate.

Furthermore, she is extending her understanding when she is agreeing with the three fellow students about the importance that the pupils should read literature for the most part in Swedish since the purpose of literature reading is on the Swedish language. She also discusses the relationship between the importance that pupils are writing in both languages and her beliefs that teachers can create various opportunities where there it is appropriate to write, which can be interpreted as a transference to an alternative strategy in teaching (Hattie & Timperley, 2007) and as a lens to promote deeper *performance awareness* (Reinholz, 2016; Sadler, 1989). Finally, she expands the meaning content on pupils' difficulty in focusing on both languages, and therefore, include all pupils in the design of teaching with the same opportunities, not exclude anyone, by having the writing in focus as a *gap closer* in improving her feedback reception (Reinholz, 2016; Sadler, 1989). However, there is a need for broader use of course literature and deeper construction of meaning with critical thinking and reflections on own learning.

A summary description of the *process level* (Hattie & Timperley, 2007) with *feedback reception* (Reinholz, 2016) in the peer feedback in Excerpt 2 is given in Table 2.

*Table 2. Summary description of the process level with feedback reception*

| Level of feedback | Criteria displayed from the peer feedback activities |
|---|---|
| Feedback on the process level with feedback reception | • expands students' understanding from a different perspective<br>• processes underlying tasks or relating and expanding evidence<br>• transference to more difficult task and improving the self-efficacy<br>• suggestions for alternative solutions<br>• deeper goal and performance awareness in improving the work<br>• need deeper critical thinking and reflections on own learning |

## Excerpt 3

The third excerpt, gives a picture of the *self-regulated level* on own feedback from course 1, where the students worked both individually and collaboratively with cases of teacher leadership that illustrates a situation in which pupils, parents and / or teachers, felt that they had been badly treated. Student 3 summarizes her own peer feedback to five fellow students' cases with *revisions and reflections*.

**Student 3:** *Overall, I think the group have covered a fairly wide range of different leadership problems, though far from all. It has been interesting and instructive to take note of everyone's opinions and at the same time being able to see that we do not have an identical picture of how the school will conduct its leadership. Literature wise, I have based much of my thinking on the school's equality plans on the basis of Children and Pupil Safety Law (course literature) and Discrimination Legislation in Sweden (course literature). It seems to me that more are thinking as I, even if I realize that I have not been as active as many of the other in the source reference to these. [...] The hard questions for me are not so much what is wrong, but how teachers can bring all students together. Where is it wrong? Is it a social problem or is it the individual schools, individual principals or groups of teachers? Do we not open our eyes and see that schools need to work systematically and with prolonged equal plans in order to change attitudes and generate empathic pupils?*

In excerpt 3, identifies the meaning content of the peer feedback on the *self-regulation level* and with some *self-level* (Hattie & Timperley, 2007) when Student 3 makes *revisions and reflections* on her groups various cases that have covered a fairly wide range of different school leadership problems. She has revised and reflect over her feedback to five fellow students before she is summing up the other students´ opinions as a result of the feedback provision and the feedback reception in a metacognitive process. Likewise, she is practicing a *gap closure* in revising the groups' cases and realise that they do not have an identical picture of how the school should conduct its leadership (Reinholz, 2016). Her thoughts and feelings of self-efficacy, i.e. her belief on own ability to perform the assignments successfully about teacher leadership ability, lead to self-assessment of being more active in using more course literature with source references, which shows the capability to create internal feedback and self-assess by seeking help through inquiry questions about what is wrong in school and how teachers can bring all pupils together (Hattie & Timperley, 2007). She is self-monitoring her own understanding and regulation of measures with alternative strategies at a *self-level* that leads to changes in her engagement for how teachers can work systematically with prolonged equal plans, and how they generate empathic students. The *self-level* is influenced by personal evaluations that lead to changes in her self-concept to be effective in increasing her understanding and performance (Hattie & Timperley, 2007).

A summary description of the *self-regulation level* (Hattie & Timperley, 2007) with *revision and reflection* (Reinholz, 2016), added with the *self-level* in the peer feedback in Excerpt 3 is given in Table 3.

*Table 3. Summary description of the self-regulation level with revision and reflection, added with the self-level*

| Level of feedback | Criteria displayed from the peer feedback activities |
|---|---|
| Feedback on the self-regulation level with revision and reflection, added with the self-level | • metacognitive process for self-monitoring and regulation of measures<br>• creating internal feedback, thoughts and feelings of self-efficacy<br>• seeking and dealing with peer feedback information<br>• practicing a gap closure in revising works<br>• closing the assessment cycle with revision and reflection<br>• personal evaluations / self-assessment of understanding and performance |

Throughout the two-phase analysis based on the assessment cycle by Reinholz (2016) and the model of feedback by Hattie and Timperley (2007), it has appeared in the results of the study that it is possible to describe the power and development of the peer feedback processes, not only as an individual ability, but also as an extended, collective competence to collaborate and learn together in the group to generate feedback provision and give constructive feedback reception. A summary of the four levels of feedback in an assessment cycle is illustrated in Table 4.

*Table 4. Summary of the four levels of feedback in an assessment cycle*

| Level of feedback | Criteria displayed from the peer feedback activities |
|---|---|
| Feedback on the task level with task engagement | • how well a task is understood and carried out<br>• based on goals awareness of desired performance<br>• corrective feedback with use of others knowledge<br>• information and reproductions from course literature<br>• reflecting on the quality and developing performance awareness<br>• lack of own critical thinking and reflections on own learning |
| Feedback on the process level with feedback reception | • expands students' understanding from a different perspective<br>• processes underlying tasks or relating and expanding evidence<br>• transference to more difficult task and improving the self-efficacy<br>• suggestions for alternative solutions<br>• deeper goal and performance awareness in improving the work<br>• need deeper critical thinking and reflections on own learning |
| Feedback on the self-regulation level with revision and reflection, added with the self-level | • metacognitive process for self-monitoring and regulation of measures<br>• creating internal feedback, thoughts and feelings of self-efficacy<br>• seeking and dealing with peer feedback information<br>• practicing a gap closure in revising works<br>• closing the assessment cycle with revision and reflection<br>• personal evaluations / self-assessment of understanding and performance |

In this study, the three excerpts are merely constituting descriptions of the four levels of feedback: the task, the processing, the regulatory, and the self-level, as well as the six activities in an assessment cycle when the students use peer feedback as a tool for learning in a formative way (Wiliam, 2011). This does not mean that these particular students´ contributions display all aspects of these feedback levels and activities in an assessment cycle that a group of other students may have produced in a similar situation.

## CONCLUSION

The results of the study, how peer feedback processes can support student-centered learning toward higher-order thinking and critical ability for self-directed, motivated, adaptive, resource-enriched, and technology-embedded smart higher education, show that peer feedback provides one of the most critical and self-directed impacts on students' learning. However, feedback on task-, process- and self-regulated levels are intertwined and interconnected, and makes it problematic to distinguish between them to give a clear answer to each of the three questions – Where am I going? How am I going? Where to next? – that fills the gap between what is understood and what is aimed to be understood (Sadler, 1989; Wiliam, 2011; 2013), rather than limiting students' opportunities to only receive feedback on their performance (Hattie & Timperley, 2007).

Ideally is, when the feedback process moves from the task level, to the process level with necessary advices to increase and regulate the task to deeper motivated goal awareness and more resource-enriched content as a "consequence" of various contributions of feedback with concrete details of how to improve. Specifically, makes technology-embedded feedback online (e-feedback) the interaction process transparent for students and teachers, either face-to-face, F2F on campus, or as written e-feedback, or in oral F2F-webinars / conferencing in a mobile setting at distance (Amhag, 2013b; Spector, 2014; Zhu, Yu & Riezebos, 2016). Thus, acts peer feedback as a mediated artifact or learning tool for the joint activities for the groups of students' higher-order thinking and critical ability, as well as for student-centered learning and development.

Important benefits of implementing peer feedback between students is that the feedback becomes available faster during the course, and that more analysis, strengths and weaknesses, or alternative strategies for improvement are available earlier than the teachers could ever provide alone (van der

Pol, van den Berg & Admiraal, 2008), and are an intermediate step for self-assessment when students evaluate their own work (Dochy, Segers, & Sluijsmans, 1999; Topping, 1998). Feedback at the *task level* is more powerful when it comes to incorrect interpretations of the content, concepts or ideas, not a lack of understanding (Hattie & Timperley, 2007). This feedback leads to the development of more efficient and effective strategies for dynamic reception, processing and reviewing the task. Feedback at the *process level* is more powerful when it involves relationships between performing or relating and extending the task. Feedback at the *self-regulated level* or metacognitive process level is more powerful when it leads to self-monitoring and regulation of measures for further engagement and effort to develop the task, to enhanced self-efficacy, and that the feedback is deserved and earned. Feedback at the *self- or personal level* is rarely effective, but when the feedback draws attention to the self, the risks to the self are minimized by tackling challenging assignments, exerting effort and fear of failure.

The illustrated three excerpt are demonstrating that the effects of immediate and *corrective feedback* are likely to be more powerful for feedback on the *task level* with *task engagement*. Delayed feedback is more powerful for feedback on the *process level* with *feedback reception* that helps the students to learn independently, analyse critique and improve their work (Hattie & Timperley, 2007; Reinholz, 2016). For difficult assignments, it is more important to provide immediate feedback reception that affords concrete analysis of the content for a greater degree of processing, and delayed feedback reception for deeper goal- and performance awareness to improve and increase the assignment and strength of self-efficacy (Bandura, 1977; 1982; Sadler, 1989). Easy assignments do not require this processing, so delayed feedback is both unnecessary and undesirable (Hattie & Timperley, 2007). At the *self-regulation level*, goal- and performance awareness are a major mediator for the power of positive and negative feedback. Positive feedback increases motivation with comments about "want to do" and decreases motivation with comments about "have to do". To fill the gap between what is understood and what is aimed to be understood, this result highlights the importance of the *inner* feedback process (Nicol, Thomson & Breslin, 2014), *external* feedback triggers and adds student-generated feedback that confirms, complements or contradicts the inner feedback.

The assessment cycle and the model of feedback requires firstly, high knowledge of developing dynamic student groups, and their ability to handle the complexity of reviewing critique and deep understandings of the subject. Secondly, to be prepared to give concrete feedback on an assignment or the relationships between ideas, encourage self-regulation and create space and place to provide feedback. Thirdly, get time and place for resource-enriched feedback provision and feedback reception among students (Hattie & Timperley, 2007; Reinholz, 2016).

## REFERENCES

Alvarez, I., Espasa, A., & Guasch, T. (2011). The value of feedback in improving collaborative writing assignments in an online learning environment. *Studies in Higher Education*, *37*(4), 387–400. doi:10.1080/03075079.2010.510182

Amhag, L. (2013b). *Creativity in and between Collaborative Peer Assessment Processes in Higher Distance Education. Creative Education, 4(7A2)*, 94–104. doi:10.4236/ce.2013.47A2011

Amhag, L., Hellström, L., & Stigmar, M. (2019). Teacher Educators' Use of Digital Tools and Needs for Digital Competence in Higher Education. *Journal of Digital Learning in Teacher Education*, *35*(4), 203–220. doi:10.1080/21532974.2019.1646169

Amhag, L., & Jakobsson, A. (2009). Collaborative Learning as a Collective Competence when Students Use the Potential of Meaning in Asynchronous Dialogues. *Computers & Education*, *52*(3), 656–667. doi:10.1016/j.compedu.2008.11.012

Bandura, A. (1977). Self-efficacy: Toward a unifying theory of behavioral change. *Psychological Review*, *84*(2), 191–215. doi:10.1037/0033-295X.84.2.191 PMID:847061

Bandura, A. (1982). Self-efficacy mechanism in human agency. *The American Psychologist*, *37*(2), 122–147. doi:10.1037/0003-066X.37.2.122

Chaqmaqchee, Z. A. (2015). Teacher's attitude into different approach to providing feedback to students in higher education. *Journal of Education and Practice*, *6*(2), 150–162.

De Wever, B., Van Keer, H., Schellens, T., & Valcke, M. (2009). Structuring asynchronous discussion groups: The impact of role assignment and self-assessment on students' levels of knowledge construction through social negotiation. *Journal of Computer Assisted Learning*, *25*(2), 177–188. doi:10.1111/j.1365-2729.2008.00292.x

Dijks, M. A., Brummer, L., & Kostons, D. (2018). The anonymous reviewer: The relationship between perceived expertise and the perceptions of peer feedback in higher education. *Assessment & Evaluation in Higher Education*, *43*(8), 1258–1271. doi:10.1080/02602938.2018.1447645

Dochy, F., Segers, M., & Sluijsmans, D. (1999). The use of self-, peer- and co-assessment in higher education: A review. *Studies in Higher Education*, *24*(3), 331–350. doi:10.1080/03075079912331379935

Dysthe, O. (2007). How a reform affects writing in higher education. *Studies in Higher Education*, *32*(2), 237–253. doi:10.1080/03075070701267285

Dysthe, O., Hertzberg, F., & Løkensgard Hoel, T. (2011). *Skriva för att lära. Skrivande i högre utbildning* [Writing to learn: Writing in Higher Education] (2nd ed.; S. Andersson, Trans.). Lund: Studentlitteratur.

Dysthe, O., Lillejord, S., Vines, A., & Wasson, B. (2010). Productive e-feedback in higher education – Some critical issues. In S. Ludvigsen, A. Lund, I. Rasmussen, & R. Säljö (Eds.), *Learning across sites: New tools infrastructures and practices* (pp. 243–259). Oxford: Pergamon Press.

Evans, C. (2013). Making sense of assessment feedback in higher education. *Review of Educational Research*, *83*(1), 70–120. doi:10.3102/0034654312474350

Forsythe, A., & Johnson, S. (2017). Thanks, but no-thanks for the feedback. *Assessment & Evaluation in Higher Education*, *42*(6), 850–859. doi:10.1080/02602938.2016.1202190

Gielen, M., & De Wever, B. (2015). Structuring peer assessment: Comparing the impact of the degree of structure on peer feedback content. *Computers in Human Behavior*, *52*, 315–325. doi:10.1016/j.chb.2015.06.019

Guasch, T., Espasa, A., Alvarez, I. M., & Kirschner, P. A. (2013). Effects of feedback on collaborative writing in an online learning environment. *Distance Education*, *34*(3), 324–338. doi:10.1080/01587919.2013.835772

Gunawardena, C. N., Lowe, C. A., & Anderson, T. (1997). Analysis of a global online debate and the development of an interaction analysis model for examining social construction of knowledge in computer conferencing. *Journal of Educational Computing Research*, *17*(4), 397–431. doi:10.2190/7MQV-X9UJ-C7Q3-NRAG

Hattie, J. (2009). *Visible learning. A synthesis of over 800 meta-analyses relating to achievement*. New York, NY: Routledge.

Hattie, J., & Timperley, H. (2007). The power of feedback. *Review of Educational Research, 77*(1), 81–112. doi:10.3102/003465430298487

Hwang, G. J. (2014). Definition, framework and research issues of smart learning environments – a context-aware ubiquitous learning perspective. *Smart Learning Environments, 1*(1), 4. doi:10.118640561-014-0004-5

Nicol, D., Thomson, A., & Breslin, C. (2014). Rethinking feedback practices in higher education: A peer review perspective. *Assessment & Evaluation in Higher Education, 39*(1), 102–122. doi:10.1080/02602938.2013.795518

Raes, A., Vanderhoven, E., & Schellens, T. (2015). Increasing anonymity in peer assessment by using classroom response technology within face-to-face higher education. *Studies in Higher Education, 40*(1), 178–193. doi:10.1080/03075079.2013.823930

Reinholz, D. (2016). The assessment cycle: A model for learning through peer assessment. *Assessment & Evaluation in Higher Education, 41*(2), 301–315. doi:10.1080/02602938.2015.1008982

Sadler, D. R. (1989). Formative assessment and the design of instructional systems. *Instructional Science, 18*(2), 119–144. doi:10.1007/BF00117714

Spector, J. M. (2014). Conceptualizing the emerging field of smart learning environments. *Smart Learning Environments, 1*(1), 2.

Tolmie, A., & Boyle, J. (2000). Factors influencing the success of computer mediated communication (CMC) environments in university teaching: A review and case study. *Computers & Education, 34*(2), 119–140. doi:10.1016/S0360-1315(00)00008-7

Topping, K. (1998). Peer assessment between students in colleges and universities. *Review of Educational Research, 68*(3), 249–276. doi:10.3102/00346543068003249

Topping, K. J., Smith, E. F., Swanson, I., & Elliot, A. (2000). Formative peer assessment of academic writing between postgraduate students. *Assessment & Evaluation in Higher Education, 25*(2), 149–169. doi:10.1080/713611428

van der Pol, J., van den Berg, B. A. M., Admiraal, W. F., & Simons, P. R. J. (2008). The nature, reception, and use of online peer feedback in higher education. *Computers & Education, 51*(4), 1804–1817. doi:10.1016/j.compedu.2008.06.001

Wegerif, R. (2006). A dialogic understanding of the relationship between CSCL and teaching thinking skills. *International Journal of Computer-Supported Collaborative Learning*, *1*(1), 1. doi:10.100711412-006-6840-8

Wiliam, D. (2011). What is assessment for learning? *Studies in Educational Evaluation*, *37*(1), 3–14. doi:10.1016/j.stueduc.2011.03.001 PMID:22114905

Wiliam, D. (2013). Assessment: The bridge between teaching and learning. *Voices from the Middle*, *21*(2), 15.

Wong, L.-H., Chai, C. S., Aw, G. P., & King, R. B. (2015). Enculturating seamless language learning through artefact creation and social interaction process. *Interactive Learning Environments*, *23*(2), 130–157. doi:10.1080/10494820.2015.1016534

Zhu, Z. T., Yu, M. H. & Riezebos, P. (2016). A research framework of smart education. *Smart Learning Environments, 3*(1), 4.

Zimmerman, B. J. (2008). Investigation self-regulation and motivation: Historical background, methodological developments, and future prospects. *American Educational Research Journal*, *45*(1), 166–183. doi:10.3102/0002831207312909

# Chapter 6
# Reflection and Self-Assessment in Smart Education


## ABSTRACT

*Higher education is increasingly adopting blended and mobile learning strategies for reflection and self-assessment to better meet the demands and expectations of students' challenges. This chapter highlights different focuses and common terms of reflection and related ideas from theories about reflection and self-assessment, and how these processes can be a tool for student-centered learning in a self-directed and motivated learning environment. Methodologically, selected reviewed articles on reflection and self-assessment show a number of different focuses and common terms of reflection and related ideas from theories. The qualitative excerpts are from a group of six student-written reflections during their school-based practical training courses. Theoretically, the analysis of the students' digital log journals is based on the framework of 5Rs and steps of meaning. In the results, the digital log journals demonstrate that reflective processes are essential in relation to the self, other, and contextual conditions during professional training.*


DOI: 10.4018/978-1-7998-4183-8.ch006

## INTRODUCTION

The goal of academic and professional reflection and self-assessment is to develop both an intellectual and emotional understanding how to be able to move between theories and practice, and critical review these experienced based knowledge, as well as the self-regulated and self-directed learning to achieve the highest level of reflection (Colomer, Pallisera, Fullana, Burriel & Fernández, 2013; Tomkins, 2009). The teaching and learning in smart higher education can with advantageous technology be designed with blended learning activities, i.e. a mix between campus and mobile at distance, which allows the students to practise self-directed and self-regulated learning, take a step back, reflect and self-assess professional practice and theories in a critical way (Broadbent & Poon, 2015; Marin, Jääskelä, Häkkinen, Juntunen, Rasku-Puttonen & Vesisenaho, 2016; Mirriahi, Liaqat, Dawson & Gašević, 2016). The word 'smart' is defined as self-directed, motivated, adaptive, resource-enriched, and technology-embedded and refers to wisdom as bounding together the ability of using and motivating knowledge building, problem solving, critically reflections on professional experiences, collaborating and evaluating different circumstances with resource-enriched, and technology-embedded learning environment.

Frequently, reflection and self-assessment are used in both theoretical and practical courses in higher education professions, but reflective methods are not often used (Fullana, Pallisera, Colomer, Fernández Peña & Pérez-Burriel, 2016; Jordi, 2011; McIntosh, 2010). Reflective methods can be understood as the activity in which students recapture their experience, think about it, consider it over and assess it. However, the common use of the concepts of reflection and self-assessment is problematic, when little or no agreement on the meaning of these concepts exists among teachers or students (Ryan, 2013). The value of reflection as a learning tool is also doubtful and tend not to equip students well for these processes in a learning society (Boud, 2000). Self-assessment studies show a mixed result without clear reasons or conclusions, often with a focus on grade or rating (Boud & Falchikov, 1989; González-Betancor, Bolívar-Cruz & Verano-Tacoronte, 2017). Moreover, the concepts are often unclear and used loosely to embrace a wide range of conceptions and strategies, because of a lack of educational training in reflection and self-assessment methods (Bain, Ballantyne, Mills & Lester, 2002; Hatton & Smith, 1995). Often, it is taken for granted that students know how to think critical and write reflectively on their own way and can realise the value of it. The key process is derived from both the dominant constructivist approach to experiential learning, and the cognitive reflection approach as through which individuals extract knowledge from their concrete experiences (Illeris, 2009). Basic components, such as inductive and deductive inference are involved, but it goes beyond the second-order reflection and evaluation of one's own or another's thinking (Kuhn, 2016).

This chapter highlights different focus and common terms of reflection and related ideas from theories about reflection and self-assessment, and how these processes can be a tool for student-centered learning in a self-directed and motivated learning environment in smart higher education. Researchers emphasize the importance of using reflection and self-assessment of different circumstances and contexts, which new media forms can easily integrate and made possible by resource-enriched and technology-embedded enhanced mobile devices (e.g. Amhag, 2016a; 2016b; 2017; Zhu, Yu & Riezebos, 2016). The following questions are addressed:

- In what way can teachers a) design and b) use different reflection and self-assessment methods and activities in a learning environment with tools that are appropriate for student-centered learning and active participation?
- How do the students experience reflection and self-assessment activities and the tools for their learning?
- In what way can the reflection and self-assessment theories and methods be analysed comparing to the students' performance?

However, there is a fundamental tension between reflection and self-assessment (Sumsion & Fleet, 1996). Reflection is driven by doubt and explorations and focuses on lack of understanding, questioning and investigating deviations. Self-assessment refers to the involvement of learners in making judgements about their own learning and the ability to select and present the best work, emphasizing what one knows and reviewing the results in a convincing way (Boud & Falchikov, 1989). On the other hand, there are some possible interactions between reflection and self-assessment. Students can use their reflections as input for motivated self-assessment after completion of the assignment (Dochy, Segers & Sluijsmans, 1999). Teachers can promote reflection on the works of your own and others, and support reflections of the transition to the next learning assignment.

Thus, reflective learning can be described as a resource-enriched process that leads to reflection on all sources of knowledge that may contribute to understand an incident, issue or problem situation, including the ability to reflect and self-assess in a technology-embedded smart higher education. Therefore, it is important to teach and train the students to act and think professionally, which involves the use of reflection and reflective practice as an informal learning-to-learn tool, as well as the use of self-assessment as a formal metacognitive strategy which include the awareness to monitor, plan, and regulate learning (Boud, 1999; Broadbent & Poon, 2015).

Consequently, reflection and self-assessment represent a kind of `higher order thinking´ to promote critical and creative `meta-reflexivity´ and to exercise the reflexivity to produce this outcome (Archer, 2010; Hatton & Smith, 1995). Inquiry and dialogic argumentation is an important key dimension in critical thinking and has been identified as pathways to argumentative competence (Kuhn, 2016). Reflection and self- assessment allows students to progress to argumentative competence and to act and think critically and professionally. Important is also to make connections with theoretical readings, and practical trainings as a part of the educational agenda, which should be modified and discussed to learn more about the specific course goals and course assignments. Superior knowledge is needed on how university teachers can design different reflection and self-assessment processes and be able to assess what characterizes students' ability to reflect on and self-assess their theoretical and professional development during their education, as well as obtain students' views on the benefits, obstacles and limitations of incorporating reflective learning methodologies in smart higher education.

## THEORIES OF REFLECTION

The concept of reflection is common to a number of learning theories, but they have different meanings and implications (Jordi, 2011). Many researchers have studied the potential of reflective learning with a focus on pedagogical theory and practice by studying students' reflection processes when they are using different active methods. Reflection involves that students are processing their experiences based on broader descriptions, exploring their understandings of what they are doing, why they are doing it and what effects it is giving for them and others (Boud, 1999). The process is associated with questioning, uncertainties, discrepancies and dissatisfactions, which represents a recognition that learning is difficult to gain and to construct its own meanings within a *community of practice* (Wenger, 1998). Like self-assessment, reflection is important for learning and occurs at different levels, whether or not it is encouraged. Informal reflection, such as informal self-assessment, occurs all the time, if not teachers are avoiding these activities among students.

Culturally, there has been an element of debate about reflection in theory and in practice (McIntosh, 2010). Reflection is seen as a "good thing" to be encouraged in both theory and practice, but is most evident in the relationship between students and their teachers. These two ideas are linked to students' need for pedagogical support to help them learn to reflect in depth, but also in a critical and transformative way to support progressive learning. First, a mutual understanding on what is needed in practice. Secondly, the changed perspective of observing on the self, rather than on others. Superficial reflections, e.g. what is right and what is not right has practically no effect on learning or future practice (ibid.).

Dewey's theoretical and practical work focuses on the *process of reflection* that involves an active, persistent and careful consideration of any belief or supposed form of knowledge, thus, this is a starting point for thinking about reflection and self-assessment (Ashwin, Boud, Coate, Hallett et al., 2015). Four important keys of reflection are described in Dewey's work and the subsequent interpretations (Hatton & Smith, 1995).

1. The first is whether reflection is limited to thinking in action, or unfavorably bound in action.
2. The second refers to the time frame and place of reflection, whether it is immediate and short-lived, or more extended and systematic (Schön, 1983).
3. The third refers to whether the reflection itself is problem-centered or not (Schön, 1987).
4. The fourth is about how consciously the reflections consider social values or beliefs in framing and reframing practical problem solutions, a process that has been identified as "critical reflection"."

Dewey (1938/1997) stressed that experience does not come directly from practical activities, but rather through interaction between reflection and activity, since theory and practice belong together. Similarly, experience does not come directly from reflections that lack anchoring in action. Reflective learning can arise from perceived difficulties or conflicts, which encourages them to stop and reflect on the situation to find a solution, and be a catalyst for further investigation. The capacity to reflect depends largely on how, and to what extent, the surroundings stimulate reflection. Through careful reflection on direct experiences, a self-assessment can be formulated, determining whether it is valuable to engage in a particular practice within a particular context.

Schön (1987) was extended Dewey's theory in analysing the actions of many different professional practises. Central in reflection is the `art´ to deal with situations of uncertainly, instability, uniqueness, and value conflict (p. 50). Therefore, a reflective practice involves a dialogue between thinking and doing, and through this process, the student becomes more skilled (Schön, 1983). One way to do this is through *reflection-in-action*, which hangs on the experience of surprise and the ability to think about doing something while doing it (Schön, 1987). This idea is captured in the common expressions 'thinking on your feet' and 'learning by doing', which Dewey (1938/1997, p. 54) is often associated with. Schön (1987) also described the process of *reflection-on-action*, or reflecting before and after teaching, e.g. teaching design, redesign, problem analysis, and identification of potential solutions to problems (Bain, Ballantyne, Mills & Lester, 2002).

According to Townsend in the book review on Schön's "reflective practice" (Schön, 2010), he refers to the relationship between coach and student, who coordinates viewing and imitation, storytelling and listening, and addresses the gaps on each component to the learning process. Learning and coaching produce experiments in professional education and the communication are developing new problems and confusions that become material for mutual reflection between the student and the coach. The model of communication between student and coach challenges the traditional didactic lecture in class and instructional teaching in higher education as processes that cannot make sense in professional education. The profession must be able to solve problems in reality through a process of "reflective practice". Schön is not commenting the problems that can arise in the design and practice of reflective education. The outcomes of a reflective practise can be as varied as the possible progress of any learning process by searching for meaning and a convergence of meaning between the student and the coach. If there are a frozen miscommunication, the reflective practice can produce counter-learning (giving coaches what they want) or over-learning (there is only one way), which is often an outcome of a more traditional academic and professional education.

Within theories of adult education, reflection is predominantly conceptualized as the rational analytical process based on experience-based knowledge. Jordi (2011) argues that a perspective on embodied learning should not prefer the body, rather the mind as a source of knowledge, but also refute reflection as an exclusively cognitive process. Reflection methods can facilitate a learning dialogue between the implicit embodied experiences and conceptual aspects of our consciousness.

## PREVIOUS RESEARCH OF REFLECTION

Research on reflection has a long tradition and covers a larger area than self-assessment, and have been developed in the relationship between reflective learning and subsequent measures and activities, e.g. reflective practice, reflective learning, transformative reflective learning and self-assessment, but particularly on reflective thinking for personal and intellectual progress (Dewey, 1938/1987; Kegan, 2009; Schön, 1997; 1983; 2010). They are describing their idea of reflective learning, and how they have been applied and designed from different theoretical perspectives, for example from critical theory or professional practice and other disciplines (Bain et al., 2002).

Selected articles for the review of previous research were obtained from searches in databases within education and social sciences such as ERIC, Libsearch etc. and from studies cited by these authors of the articles and from previous used peer review articles published in the current field with the keywords: reflection and self-assessment in higher education. The articles describes different theories, traditions and terms that have been used, as well as analytical methods and frameworks. Mainly, they have been used in practical research where different levels of mental processing have been discovered and developed, from reflective learning, transformative reflective learning or knowledge reflection to critical reflective thinking, but also about grades. Habermas (2015) is dividing critiques of reflection into the following three levels:

1. *Technical reflection* is concerned with the competence and efficacy of meaning to realise confident ends, and is not open for criticism or modification.
2. *Practical refl*ection is open for examination of both means and goals, and the assumptions upon which the reflection is based, as well as the actual outcome.
3. *Critical reflection* adds to the previous two types of reflection by making judgements about whether the professional practice is equitable, as a kind of ethical criterion.

The following sections highlights different theories and terms about reflection and self-assessment in higher education based on various framework or methods.

## Reflective Learning

A *reflective learning model* uses Pallisera, Fullana, Palaudarias and Badosa (2012) among 98 social educators with a focus on contributing to their personal and professional development and helping them prepare to face situations of uncertainty and manage the risks in their future profession with autonomy, creativity and professionalism. The model is also a framework for developing strategies that foster anti-discriminatory practices, such as self-knowledge, and how experiences, feelings, emotions, and values affect professional behaviour and guaranteeing users' rights. The students were organized into four groups of 12 or 13 students and each group had their own tutor. As a basis for reflection, the students were working with six activities.

- Activity A consist in reading and analysing a life story taken from materials related to social education work.
- Activity B consists in constructing a family genogram and produce a written narrative reflecting on the effects of the family system on personal development, and specifically on their interest in becoming a social educator.
- Activity C consists in producing a drawing that represents their personal path through life, symbolized of a river with the most significant events, people and/or situations marked on it.
- Activity D consists of graphically depicting their desired future path on a personal, family and work level, and responding to how they would like to see themselves in ten years.
- Activity E consist in prepare an interview script in the group and conduct the interview and then produce a written narrative on what impact the interview had on their view of the profession and the relationship with users and other professionals.
- Activity F consist in viewing and analysing fragments of films and analyse the relationships and situations on empathy, exploring different models of relationship and analysing the difficulties of establishing the educational relationship.

The students' learning was assessed via a portfolio of the six different learning activities. The result shows that the students evaluate the learning activities as positive and they have provided them with additional learning tools to practice and develop their professional duties from a critical perspective. The activities have helped them to understand the relationship between their life experiences and personal actions and to improve their reflection ability to analyse complex situations in a deeper way, as well as the relationship between one's own beliefs and personal experiences and ways of responding and reacting in certain situations.

The theory of *reflective learning* was developed further in relation to self-knowledge, i.e. the relationship between experience and knowledge, as well as self-reflection and self-regulation. In two studies Colomer, Pallisera, Fullana, Burriel and Fernández (2013) and Fullana, Pallisera, Colomer, Fernández Peña and Pérez-Burriel (2016) examined reflective learning methods in four different fields: nursing, psychology, social education, and environmental sciences, that have used different design methods to promote students' reflective learning. In the field of nursing, a reflective journal was used that allowed students to reflect on and learn from their experiences before transforming this learning within the context of real practical experience. In the field of psychology, a reflective portfolio was used for teaching and assessment. In the social education field, activities were based around reflective learning strategies designed to develop personal and professional skills to prepare students for their subsequent work placement. In the environmental science field, students worked on independent study and reflection on learning through activities such as solving case experiments, viewing videos, etc.

Methodologically, the levels of students' self-reflection are quantified by using a Self-Reported Reflective Learning questionnaire. A number of 162 students answered the questionnaire anonymously with closed-ended and open-ended questions, none of these students had not used any reflective methods during previous education levels. The data analysis was carried out in two phases: one investigative descriptive phase and in the second phase the comparison between the four fields: the field of nursing, psychology, social education and environmental science. The result showed that the students consider the implemented reflective methods as positive with either reflective journal, portfolio, strategies preparing future work placement, or activities with case experiments, recorded video instructions etc. The methods have helped them become more aware of their learning process, motivation to learn, encouraged their critical thinking and to self-assess their knowledge abilities. The students identified challenges related primarily to understand the aims of the experience, the degree of personal openness and the system of assessment. They propose both improvements and new strategies for addressing challenges that arise during reflective learning that can serve as a useful and appropriate method for developing both generic skills and adaptations to other professional situations. Especially, allows reflective learning to create their own meanings and they are enhanced by reflective narration like in a reflective journal during practical work situations to support the relationship between theory and practice and understand the professional field (Fullana, et al., 2016).

## Nature of Reflective Thinking

Additional theory of reflection is related to the nature of *reflective thinking* (Hatton & Smith, 1995). In general, reflective thinking addresses to practical problems which allows students to experience doubts and confusion before being working with their assignments or discussions, to reach possible solutions that can lead to deeper critical reflection.

A well-known and frequently cited study by Hatton and Smith (1995) start with a review of literature about reflection focusing on strategies that assist its progress. The nature of reflection in teaching is examined to define specific forms of reflection and to evaluate the strategies of conscious thinking in action to enhance action and to what extent it facilitated specific forms of reflection. The present study involved 34 student teachers at the University of Sydney. The data were triangulated and included the following: a written report (4000 words), two self-evaluations, two 7-minute video tapes with teaching and a 20-minute interview in pairs with structured questions about their strategies they had used, along with responses to a problematic practicum vignette, where they would identify and comment on issues that were considered as important. However, there are a number of obstacles that hinder the attainment of reflective strategies, e.g. concept of teaching as a profession, conditions and encouragement to develop different kinds of reflection, and in particular, to have endurance and strength to conceptualize own teaching. In the result identified four types of writing, three of which were characterised as different kinds of reflection: descriptive writing, descriptive reflection, dialogic reflection and critical reflection.

- *Descriptive writing* only reports events or literature.
- *Descriptive reflection* tries to provide reasons, often based on personal judgment or on own literature reading.

- *Dialogic reflection* is a form of discourse with oneself, an exploration of possible reasons.
- *Critical reflection* involves reasoning for decisions or events that take into account the broader historical, social and / or political contexts.

Hatton and Smith (1995) suggest a powerful strategy for fostering reflective action by using a "critical friend", collaborate, engage and discuss different issues, even confronting each other about practice, implementation, and evaluation. It creates an opportunity to give a voice to one's own thinking and at the same time be heard in a sympathetic way, as well as in a constructive and critical way.

Hora and Smolarek (2018) report the *nature of reflective practice* from an exploratory interview-based study examining the degree to which 21 faculties at three California research universities were engaged in reflective practice with teaching-related data. The study was based on rigorous numeric evidence, a process known as Data-Driven Decision Making (DDDM) which has its roots in management, logistics, and organizational studies where the regular analysis of and response to various forms of performance data was widely viewed as an essential component of organizational efficiency and productivity. The result showed three distinct types of reflection: instrumental, structural-critical, and social critical.

1. *Instrumental reflections* are focusing on technical teaching tasks that are affecting the teaching and learning in the courses, such as textbooks or syllabi issues.
2. *Structural-critical reflections* are focusing on institutional issues that are affecting the teaching and learning where class sizes were critically considered as one of several factors influencing teaching behaviors and students' outcomes.
3. *Social critical reflections* are focusing on the reflective process that are affecting the teaching and learning in a socio-cultural and economic contexts of students' lives, e.g. historically underrepresented populations are doing more poorly in class, than dominant populations.

The three different types of reflection are demonstrating the varied functions and forms that reflection can take. Although, the faculty consistently were engaged in the reflective practice, the outcomes of reflection were severely limited by both individual bias and institutional constraints. In order to better serve the students, more institutional support is needed in facilitating critical examination by providing faculty the necessary space, time, and guidance to engage in critical reflection, as well as the appropriate institutional mechanisms to voice concerns and enact changes.

## Transformative Reflective Learning

Another theory of reflection is related to *transformative reflective learning*. According to Kegan (2009) need transformative learning to be clearly distinguished from other forms of learning, i.e. the form that is undergoing transformation needs to better be understood; if there is no form, there is no transformation. Transformative learning includes to some extent an epistemological change, rather than just a change in the behavior of the repertoire and assume that students' capacity can be promoted by teachers' design of the activities. "Epistemology" refers to our way of knowing. The first process is the meaning forming, which forms a coherent meaning from the outer and the inner. The second process reforms our meaning forming, which is a metaprocess with reflections on the meaning construction. Further transformative learning might involve the development of a capacity for abstract thinking with reflections about the outer and inner meaning forming and reforming of the meaning construction. Kegan describe this process of transformation as follows:

*We do not only form meaning, and we do not only change our meanings; we change the very form by which we are making our meanings. We change our epistemologies. [...] That is, the psychological process of transformations in our knowing (Kegan, 2009, pp. 44-45).*

The central characteristic in transformative learning is the process of reflection that includes the intellectual and affective activities, which leads to exploration of experiences to develop understandings and appreciations (Boud, 1999). The study of Ryan (2013) focused on the process of *transformative reflection*. This definition reflects the belief that reflection can operate at a number of levels to achieve the second element (reimagining). The student must reach the higher, more abstract levels of critical or transformative reflection. When reflective processes move to transformative or intensive levels, they become reflexive processes dependent on action. Ryan is using Bain, Ballantyne, Mills and Lesters (2002) terminology of the five 'R's': reporting, responding, relating, reasoning and reconstructing, conflated to four 'R's' as reporting and responding are often difficult to separate, to illustrate levels of reflection in the study. The students in each class were given examples of the four 'Rs', which illustrated the effective use of the four 'Rs' in their context.

1. Level one, *reporting / responding*, is the most basic level of reflection, where the students should learn to notice and consider aspects of their practice. It may be an opinion or an initial emotional response to a question or event that is relevant to the discipline, profession or learning space and the specific topic being studied.
2. Level two, *relating*, is the level that separates reflection from other genres in terms of their own prior experiences about a related problem or in a similar setting, and how these are relating to the values and priorities of other stakeholders and of a broader society.
3. Level three, *reasoning*, moves the reflection largely from personal response to an intellectually rigorous analysis of the context, issue and possible influencing factors.
4. Level four, *reconstructing*, is the highest level of reflection where the student should present new ideas and critically review best professional practice with explanations of different alternatives with predictions about possible effects in a future-oriented way.

The study is part of a larger project to investigate and analyse reflective practices across university courses in Education, Health, Business, Law and Creative Industries at one Australian university. The larger project includes semi-structured interviews in focus groups with 40 volunteer staff and 40 volunteer students from various university faculties, along with reflective excerpts from 60 participating students. This study includes selected student work samples (N=60) and reflective brainstorming from two staff focus groups (N = 10) to investigate the key problem of what support is needed at each reflection level. The result show that there were gaps in the students' and staffs' reflections, especially the difficulty in connecting two important key elements:

- To gain a sense of experience in relation to the self, others, and contextual conditions.
- Be able to reimagining and/or planning future experiences for personal and social benefit.

The conclusion is that both key elements are needed for true transformative reflection. This definition reflects on the belief that reflection can operate at a number of levels. In order to achieve the second element (reimagining) the content must reach a higher and more abstract level of transformative reflection for learning.

## Knowledge Reflection

Supplementary theory of reflection is related to cognitive theory and is named as *knowledge reflection* with steps in critical thinking. This theory is based on the continuum of experience by Dewey (1938/1997), i.e. a continuum is detailed knowledge where the value of it can be evaluated based on what the knowledge is moving towards (goals) and into (goals), based on Kuhn's (2016) and Kegan's (1994) research.

According to Kuhn (2016) has critical thinking developed - from a measure of the individual's knowledge ability - to efforts characterized by the demands of critical thinking in real life. Key dimensions are inquiry and arguments in a process-based account of critical thinking, based on the social activities and by examining them, rather than a strictly individual competence. The inquiry dimension entails that there must be something to find out and bring out evidence about it. Argument is the essence of critical thinking that takes place in collaboration and has a productive importance for developing both individual and dialogic argumentation skills for several reasons. Basic components are involved, one as an input and the other as an output, based on inductive empiricism or deductive based on theory. The approach is to sort through various materials and determine what information is relevant, investigate and analyse it, possibly complement it and then synthesize this input as an important basis for the next step, and use it as output to argue and motivate a decision (Kuhn, 2016).

1) The first level is *content-based reflection*, where experiences are considered against learning goals with structure, feedback, and opportunity to rewrite. This simple level needs some scaffolding that encourage students to focus on evidence.
2) The second level is *metacognitive reflection,* when "different strategies (thoughts) and in experiencing the excitement (feelings) of achieving a line or side" (Grossman, 2009, p. 17), as to be `novice´ in the teacher

profession or "expert" in the vocational profession. At this level, learners need a lot of support and encouragement to develop this reflective capacity.

3) The third level is *self-authorship" reflection*, when inner states become observed objects, rather than lived subjects, as well as facilitating consciousness "self-authorship". Attaining this level requires a capacity to separate thoughts and feelings from the sensory input that generates the process of reflection and to acknowledge that there is often more than one possible interpretation of experience.
4) The fourth level is *transformative reflection*, a more advanced and deeper level of reflection, in which learners are empowered to become aware of thinking, perceiving, and acting, enabling them to accept increased social responsibility and become self-directed and less dependent on false assumptions. This level is applicable in courses and practical experiences where students are exposed to sufficiently strong conflicts if they have time to examine their assumptions.

However, Giroux (2010) stresses pedagogical practice does not transfer knowledge. Instead, means critical, transformative reflection that the reality can be reworked where the student or professional can take an intellectual stance in dealing with critical issues and practices and have the power to initiate change.

Grossman (2009) is analysing a continuum of levels of reflection based on Kuhn's (2016) research about the development of scientific, critical thinking and Kegan's (2009) object-subject theory of development for inspiring students to be able to reflect in their assignments. Grossman (2009) found that many researchers are using the same term on reflection, but they contained a wide range of meanings. The design of this study included that the students would write a personal experience described with sensual details (what they see, hear, touch, taste and smell), in the next part use direct cited definitions of course concepts and last, make point-by-point comparisons between personal experience and concepts. The assignments were followed up by a tutoring session. Afterwards, students had the opportunity to revise the assignment. The result show that the design can explain how and why it is so difficult for students to reflect and recognize the difference between evidence and conclusions in content-based reflections. The strategy with writing, tutoring and revising was helpful in learning how to do metacognitive "self-authorship" with transformative reflections (Grossman, 2009). In other words, the psychological process of transformations in our knowing (Kegan, 2009, p. 45).

The study of *knowledge reflection* by Enochsson (2017) compares outcomes of student teachers' use of oral classroom discussions and online written forum discussions of course literature, and how each mode facilitates reflective practice. The teachers wanted to develop further the literature discussions by letting the students try out written forms of reflective discussion seminars in which they were encouraged to take an active part and write follow-up comments to each other's comments. Data were collected from a class of 11 participating student teachers. Methodologically, the analysis of the transcripts was categorized as *unreflective, related* or *complex*, based on the two levels of *knowledge reflection* by Clinchy (1996) with separate and connected knowing.

1) *Separate knowing* involves distancing oneself through questioning another person's perspectives.
2) *Connected knowing* tries foremost to understand the other person's perspective.

According to Clinchy (1996), it is important to develop both separate and connected knowing. Connected knowledge is an approach to knowledge creation that involves skills and procedures as rigorous as traditional types of rational thought. These types of knowing or critical thinking can also be seen at three different levels. The first and least developed level is unreflective knowledge; the student can reproduce something from literature or experience. The second level is when the students is relating to the understandings of what is learnt and relate it to experience. The third level is complex; the student can value the knowledge, question and compare it to other phenomena. At a group level, Enochsson found that students' discussions had similarities, but differences existed at the individual level between the oral form and different types of academic writing. To help students in their development towards becoming reflective practitioners and to develop as professionally as possible, digital media with its multimodality can improve their *knowledge reflection* or reflective thinking and academic writing through blended learning, both at in-class and at out-of-class with different activities.

In summary, there is a lot of research and rhetoric about reflection, particular about reflective learning and practice, and much less about the design and consequences of reflective learning and practice. The research of reflection highlights the pedagogical balancing act of supporting different reflective levels or elements, as a way to motivate focused reflection and help students to develop and expand new ways of learning, critical thinking and professional practice. Importantly, university teacher must support every level of reflection. Otherwise, there will be specific, observable gaps in the reflections that students produce.

## PREVIOUS RESEARCH OF SELF-ASSESSMENT

Self-assessment is formative because it helps students make improvements in the specific area, but it can also be summative when students decide that they have learned as much as they want within a particular area and can contribute to grades given to students by teachers (Boud & Falchikov, 1989). The term self-assessment is used to encompass two key elements: a) the identification of criteria or standards to be applied to one's work, and b) making judgements about the extent to which work meets these criteria. One characteristic of self-assessment is that students have a realistic sense of their own strengths and weaknesses and that they can use knowledge of their own achievements to develop them further (Boud, 1999; Schön, 1983; 1987). Self-assessment has also been associated with the development of student autonomy in learning, and especially for self-directed learning. For teachers, there is a fundamental desire for students to take greater responsibility for their own learning through commitment and being able to assess their own competence. There is also a practical need to develop assessment procedures by using students more and teachers less in the activities (Boud & Falchikov, 1989).

Studies on the accuracy of self-assessment show a mixed result without clear reasons, often with a focus on grade or rating. For example are Boud and Falchikov (1989) comparing student-generated grades with teacher-generated grades and found from the review of 48 studies several gaps to draw some conclusions to improve the ability of self-assessment over time or with practice. Of the 48 studies, only six of them address gender differences. Recent review of 155 self-assessments and more than 12.000 peer and professor assessments by González-Betancor, Bolívar-Cruz and Verano-Tacoronte (2017) show that self-assessment accuracy is still low, and is also related to the student's gender. Men are even today rated their knowledge higher than women. Additional review by Dochy, Segers and Sluijsmans (1999) found from 63 peer review articles six main topics of self-assessment:

1. The influence of different abilities; high-performing students tend to underestimate themselves and low-performing students overestimate themselves.

2. The time effect; students tend to rate lower at the beginning of the academic year and higher as the semester progresses, moreover, how the tasks are embedded in the overall context of the subject and into their educational life.
3. The accuracy; students were accurate in grading their essays, but less accurate in assessing deep processing, moreover, less motivating and low-performing students tend to be less clear about their understandings of the criteria.
4. The effect of self-assessment; students who engage in explicit self-assessment will obtain higher test results than those who learn without self-assessment.
5. The methods of self-assessment; different methods are used from a Likert-scale of designed abilities to electronic interactive advice system based on questions and answers about goals, criteria, evidence, discussions, judgments and further actions.
6. The content of self-assessment; are mostly used formatively to foster skills and abilities, students gradually internalise their practice of problem-solving and their ability to self-assess.

The implications for practice of the use of self-assessment in educational practice promote in most cases the learning of skills and abilities that leads to more reflections on their own work, a higher standard of outcomes, responsibility for own learning and increasing their understandings of problem-solving. The topics of self-assessment not only help students to make judgments about their own learning and outcomes, but also allow them to consider the characteristics of competent work and learn how to apply these criteria to their own and others' work (De Wever, Schellens, Valcke & Van Keer, 2006; Kostons, van Gog & Paas, 2010). These self-assessment processes foster reflection on the quality of the students' reflections and the input of others after complementing the task, and to support next learning and development. Furthermore, the processes include creativity as `higher order thinking skills´ to develop awareness of effective contributions and discussions online, and perceive the various qualities that contribute relevant (Archer, 2010). It is argued here that this type of creativity is a central characteristic of mobile and blended learning.

Furthermore, self-assessment is an important characteristic of a professional or an educated and competent person (Boud, 1999). Self-assessment lead to the development of oral presentation skills, experienced learning, confidence in making better presentations and developing their assessment ability (Boud

& Falchikov, 1989). The raise of student's self-esteem is also an outcome of self-assessment (Papanthymou & Darra, 2019). They know what they know with confidence and humility, and in the same way, what they do not know. Therefore, are professionals referring to others or consult other expertise that they themselves lack (Boud, 1999). It is more important in academic and professional practice to be very confident in the knowledge boundaries, than to have partial and uncertain expertise in a broad field. Informal self-assessment occurs all the time and includes involving students in their learning process in order to be able to review and determine what a relevant work is in a given situation (Ibid.). It requires them to consider two important elements in the self-assessment:

a) What goals, requirements and characteristics does the assignment have, e.g. a good essay or competent practice in a particular field.
b) Apply these criteria to their own work in a critical and a reflective way.

Students may be credibly involved in establishing or discussing the criteria in these areas. In Boud's (1999) view, can criteria be removed in the basic processes of learning; they can inhibit the students from joining the *community of practice* to which they aspire (Wenger, 1998). The term sustainable assessment can be defined as assessment that meets the needs of the present without compromising the ability of students to meet their own future learning needs (Boud, 2000). In order for students to become lifelong learners, they need also to be prepared to reflect and self-assess their challenges they face throughout their lives. They shall be able to do this in ways that are appropriate and seek forms of feedback from peers, other practitioners, from literature and other trustful resources. Students who are resource-equipped will be able to contribute to their own learning and that of others and will be lifelong reflections assessors engaging in sustainable assessment.

In competitive contexts, where some professional programs operate, the use of self-assessment should not generate grades. One of the reasons why reflection is often incorrectly applied is because teachers try to find ways to make it compatible with assessment; it is the assessment practice that needs to be changed first. Self-assessment is more effectively placed as a contribution to the teaching and learning process, rather than as a substitute for other assessments (Boud, 1999). However, it is important to realize that the practice of self-assessment does not imply that this engagement is an isolated or individualistic activity. It usually involves peers, use of teachers and other practitioners, based on appropriate literature. If self-assessment is to be used as a formal metacognitive strategy, it may refer to the awareness to monitor, plan, and regulate learning (Broadbent & Poon, 2015), such as reviewing the problem solving, clarity of the work, text flow, and central concepts, etc. and do reflections on these parts and rewrite (Amhag, 2019).

## DESIGN OF REFLECTION AND SELF-ASSESSMENT

The design of reflection and self-assessment activities in different courses is not about how learning practices should occur or not. It is more about how these processes are integrated as part of the formal course curriculum. Courses in higher education are conducted for students of a mature age who have other commitments with family, work and living. Therefore, it is necessary to clearly and explicitly embed reflection and self-assessment practices in the course design if students shall develop the skills they need. Important is, that students should be able to connect practical experiences to theoretical knowledge from course literature or vice versa, supported by resource-enriched and technology-embedded tools and with sufficient time to use them, as well as critical review and discuss the content in relation to the experiences of the work placement that can provide catalysts for further investigation to better achieve the course goals (Bain, Ballantyne, Mills & Lester, 2002; Tomkins, 2009).

The critical incident technique, CIT, revised from Flanagan (1954), is useful when practical implementation of important facts shall be used for a defined and clear situation. The following aspects should be taken into account:

1. measuring typical performance (criteria);
2. knowledge goals and knowledge requirements;
3. training in what the assignment consists of;
4. selection and classification;
5. work design and distinction;
6. operating procedures;
7. construction of resource-enriched, and technology-embedded higher education;
8. motivation and leadership (attitudes);
9. tutoring and support.

Another useful design is when the students are working with a set of activities to enable them to reflect critically on the experiences during their practical training and to evaluate their strengths and weaknesses (Tomkins, 2009). Tomkins study involved 34 students and they were invited to complete the exercises in storytelling in order to map their learning progress and their journey through five stages. From the group, a selection of six students accepted that the study was using extracts from their learning diaries and analyse how it affected their reflective learning, with the ultimate goal of reaching the learning stage where transformative learning could take place. Methodically, uses a map of learning to stages of learning through storytelling, as shown in Table 1.

*Table 1. Links between learning and storytelling (Tomkins, 2009, p. 125)*

| Map of Learning | Stages of learning through storytelling |
|---|---|
| Noticing | Stage 1 Story finding |
| Making sense | Stage 2 Storytelling |
| Making meaning | Stage 3 Story expanding |
| Working with meaning | Stage 4 Story processing |
| Transformative learning | Stage 5 Story reconstructing |

1. The first stage of the process, *noticing*, involved a meaningful critical incident from earlier work experience that made them stop and think about the significance of the incident to them, what they could learn from the identified situation, and how the process of exploring critical event can help improve.
2. The second step, *making sense*, involved further thoughts on their critical incident by writing a short account of a maximum of 50 words about how their situation either had helped them to learn or made them questioning aspects of their working methods.
3. The third step, *making meaning*, involved further exploration of their identified critical incident by providing new and deeper perspectives on the presented situation. They could extend their critical incident to a story of how they had developed their skills and to prepare a presentation.
4. The fourth step, *working with meaning*, involved Schön's (1983) theory of reflection-in-action (during an event) and reflection-on-action (after an event have taken place). To learn from previous actions and previous reflections requires a deep level of reflection and self-assessment.

5. During the final fifth stage, *transformative reflective learning*, evidence was presented as digital stories, a media artefact between narrated audio-text and still images. The key aim of this stage of the project was to encourage students to demonstrate transformative learning in their reflections.

After these five stages, the students were working with peer learning within the group to share their stories of their learning and if or / and how storytelling helped them to engage in transformative reflective learning (Tomkins, 2009). This process provided many useful insights to deal with the emotional challenges of taking a future professional role. Theoretically, the analysis of the students' digital storytelling is based of *reflective learning*. The result shows that some students found the process easier than others did. By using the idea of transformative learning through storytelling to academic staff must be challenging by producing clear evidence of reflective learning from students themselves, and especially in the form of digital storytelling.

## METHOD OF REFLECTION AND SELF-ASSESSMENT

Methodically, selected articles are used for the review of searches in databases in education and social sciences from Libsearch that allow searching at almost all library databases, such as Web of Knowledge, ERIC, Scopus and Google Scholar, as well as from studies cited by these authors of the articles and from previous used peer review articles published in the current field with the keywords: reflection and self-assessment and higher education. As a result of this review of selected articles, a number of different focus and common terms of reflection and related ideas from theories by associated authors are summarised in Table 2.

For each theme, the focus of reflection followed by the most common term used in that tradition of reflection are listed, and the name or names of the researchers associated with them. Each of them represents a tradition or ideological approach with related ideas from theories and has slightly different designs for the application in practice. It should be noted, that the focus and common terms and related ideas from theories are overlapping between them.

The qualitative empirical data involve a group of 51 vocational student teachers (Amhag, 2020). From this group follows closely six students (2 women, 4 men), who were selected because they were using the same blended learning activities. Each student had an e-portfolio with different tools in

*Table 2. Focus and common terms of reflection and related ideas from theories by associated authors*

| Focus | Common term | Associated authors |
|---|---|---|
| Learning | Reflection | Dewey, Ashwin, etc. |
| Professional practice | Reflective practice | Schön, Boud, Bain et al. etc. |
| Knowledge | Metacognition | Clinchy, Colomer et al., Grossman, Kuhn etc. |
| Social & transformative | Critical reflection | Flanagan, Habermas, Hatton & Smith, Kegan, Ryan etc. |
| Identity & community of practice | Reflexivity | Wenger, Archer, etc. |

the online learning management system, LMS. The e-portfolio had folders where the students could upload different course documents, literature and instructions, as well as an own folder to download their lesson plans with pictures and videos. There was also a folder where they could upload their written reflections and self-assessments after each course for the tripartite conversation between the teacher educator and the supervisor. The data consist of digital log journals with written reflections and self-assessments from the six students' professional development after each five four-week periods of school based teacher training courses, total over a 20-week period. The written reflections and self-assessments in their digital log journals include a critical incident about a situation, incident, or issue, which were uploaded in their LMS. Representative excerpts were selected from this group. Before the study, these six students signed an agreement to participate and returned it via e-mail. At the end of the study, they were again asked to provide their agreement to participate via e-mail.

## ANALYSIS OF REFLECTION AND SELF-ASSESSMENT

Theoretically, is the digital log journals with a critical incident of a situation, incident or problem from school based teacher training courses a kind of a process method that offers transformative reflective learning to reach the higher, more abstract levels of critical or transformative reflection, i.e. from the outer and the inner coherent meaning, and as a metaprocess with reflections on the meaning construction (Kegan, 2009).

The analysis is based on the framework of 5Rs by Bain, Ballantyne, Mills and Lester (2002) which is developed among teachers and students in higher education to improve *reflective thinking* in their written journals during the course. The purpose of the framework of 5R was for teachers to enable the students to achieve two important goals:

a) Supporting students' understanding of what is involved in serious reflection.
b) To increase their ability to self-assess the content of their writings.

Bain et al. (2002, p. 13) were using five main levels of reflection: *reporting, responses, relationships, reasoning* and *reconstruction*, which are the 5Rs. Every level has distinct criteria to assist student teachers to develop their writing and reflective thinking. Individual skills are ranked from these four reflection types and for each participant, which characterize the students' reflection capability by analysing these levels of abilities and challenges the students demonstrate and are addressed and self-assessed. The five reflection types characterize the students' reflection capability by analysing these levels of abilities and challenges they demonstrate in their log journals. For each participant, the five levels of reflection are ranked according to the rubric, and the results contain representative excerpts of the progressions. The five levels of reflection are described with criteria according to the rubric in Table 3.

- Level 1: the least developed content with minimal descriptions.
- Level 2: adding broader content descriptions to level 1.
- Level 3: adding sufficient details and own conclusions to level 1 and 2.
- Level 4: adding new understandings applied to a personal approach or theory from course literature to level 1, 2 and 3.

The findings in the students' digital log journals are oriented on the two learning goals of the school based teacher training courses: 1) analysis and reflectivity of the student role and professional development in connection with the theoretical studies; 2) self-assessment of their professional development with a view to future occupation. The researchers were analysing and characterising students' progressing toward these goals by using the 5Rs framework and criteria (Bain et al., 2002). Afterwards the analysis was complemented with the result of the reviewed articles and related ideas from theories by the associated authors, summarised in Table 2 that can further ensure the validity and the reliability of the added results. After the excerpts, the findings are summarized and analysed further from the reviewed articles.

In summary, we can observe in excerpt 1 from semester 1 in practical training, that the student displays the most basic level of reflection, with

*Table 3. The 5Rs framework with criteria for each level, revised from Bain, Ballantyne, Mills and Lester (2002, p. 13)*

| 5Rs framework | Level 1 | Level 2 | Level 3 | Level 4 |
|---|---|---|---|---|
| **Reporting**<br>Descriptive account of what happened or of the situation, incident, or issue. | Minimal description of the situation, incident, or issue. | Broad description with limited significant details. | Sufficient details, allowing learners to draw their own conclusions. | |
| **Responding**<br>Emotional or personal response to the situation, incident, or issue. | Focuses on significant aspects with related feelings. | Reasoned judgement of a situation, incident, or issue. | Adds to levels 1 and 2 by questioning or identifying a problem. | |
| **Relating**<br>Relate or make a connection between current personal or theoretical understandings of the situation, incident, or issue. | Own strength, weakness, personal learning, professional matters, or future practice. | Adds to level 1 a superficial or limited discussion of the connection to theory. | Adds to levels 1 and 2 expanded insight, discussions, or understandings of the connection between theory and practice. | |
| **Reasoning**<br>Highlight in detail or show why the situation, incident, or issue occurred with exploration, questioning, or explanation. | At least one relevant factor analysed in detail with regard to its importance, impact, or questions for future practice. | Adds to level 1 Alternative explanations and / or interrelationships / factors. | Adds to levels 1 and 2 insights from different perspectives. | |
| **Reconstruction**<br>Drawing conclusions and developing a future action plan based upon a reasoned understanding of the situation, incident, or issue. | The discussion leads to a conclusion or a plan for future action. | Adds to level 1 a consideration of the reason. | Adds to levels 1 and 2 the possible impacts of different circumstances. | Adds to levels 1-3 new understandings applied to a personal approach or theory of teaching. |

reporting and relating aspects that reflect an initial emotional response and a superficial basis. The student progresses to the highest level of reflection at the end of semester 4, with reasoning and reconstructive aspects of reflection on different situations, both practically and theoretically. However, it is crucial that the student shows a clear progression already evident in semester 2, through level 2 responding reflection about teaching design for pupils' learning outcomes, as well as reasoning reflection at level 3, with insights from different viewpoints. The student is presenting a critical incident with deeper insights and perspective, which can lead to higher levels of reflection (Archer, 2010). After semester 3, the reflections are falling back to rather superficial level 2 relating reflection, with incomplete and merely descriptive theoretical connections. Furthermore, the context of teaching and learning

*Table 4.* **Student 1** *is from Treatment and Care program and has worked as a nurse for many years*

| From the log journal | Application of the 5Rs scale |
|---|---|
| **Critical incident semester 1**<br>I have read a lot about different theories and think it would be great if I can make the theories my own, but I realize that it can take a long time until I feel them inside me. I have been able to "feel them in the air" during my training and would like to practice that way. This class of secondary school pupils, the teacher has no good relationships. The class can be characterized as disharmonious. Five of the eight pupils have an immigrant background and have very little knowledge of the Swedish language. Because of this situation, the atmosphere in the class becomes more infected, it becomes difficult for the teacher to handle the teaching.<br>**Conclusions of self-assessment**<br>That conflict which arises can be solved in different ways depending on what it is. My claim is to listen to all without imparting any of my own values into the problem. I must be there for the pupils. | In these sentences, the student is *reporting* (level 1) about different theories and wishes to make them her own. The description of the conflict between pupils exhibits less exploration or questioning; only referring to their immigrant background.<br>The further conclusion is *relating* (level 1) the situation to personal learning, and some future practice. However, there are no connections from theories or the teaching plan. |
| **Critical incident semester 2**<br>My self-confidence has been balancing between succeeding and failing as a teacher, and it can only get better when I have got through various difficult trials. I have tried during this period to contribute to a joyful and efficient classroom together with the pupils in year 3. I have invested a lot of work in designing lesson plans according to the learning goals that go hand in hand with research on different teaching methods and learning.<br>**Conclusions of self-assessment**<br>I believe strongly that a teacher gains a great deal from:<br>1. Plan the next topic lesson with pupil-based topics, then they are responsible for their learning, which can stimulate motivation.<br>2. The pupils are tasked to be prepared from their own questions for the next lesson.<br>3. As the teacher better understands what the pupil can and wonder about, the opportunity is given to plan and preparing future lessons.<br>4. Always provide feedback with emphasis on progress made and provide suggestions for new goals. | Here the student is *responding* (level 2) by judging the classroom as joyful and efficient and focusing on the pupils by designing teaching for pupils' learning outcomes.<br>The further conclusion is *reasoning* (level 3) about what the student believes about teaching, with insights from different perspectives on pupil-based topics, as well as questioning for better understandings of pupils' learning. However, there is a lack of any theories or questioning on vocational didactics. |
| **Critical incident semester 3**<br>During my teaching practice this period, I have experienced that teachers find that there is quite a lot involved in the teacher mission, and that it is difficult to know what to prioritize when resources are insufficient, while the pupil groups are increasingly different in knowledge and size. My view is also that there is much involved in the objectives, and that nobody really knows how much or what matters most.<br>**Conclusions of self-assessment**<br>I feel that I can describe and relate to theories of knowledge, learning, and development, as well as relate them to the national curriculum. As a teacher, I want to work on the basis of a scientific approach. I am used to working and teaching in a scientific way as a nurse. In course literature describes professional knowledge including a vocational language with associated vocational theoretical concepts, and that professional knowledge is based on scientific reasons of varying degrees. | Here the student is *relating* (level 2) to the teaching objectives by drawing a superficial relationship between teaching resources and size of pupil groups and what matters most, but without any theoretical connection.<br>The further conclusion is *relating* (level 2) to the student's own feelings on scientific learning, with one limited connection to literature about scientific reasons of varying degrees. |
| **Critical incident semester 4**<br>As a student teacher, I experienced a gradual development during VTEP, but there has also been a rollercoaster of frustrations, reflections, and solutions about my own teaching, role, and mission as teacher. My theoretical abilities have been developed, but mostly in practice in the meetings with pupils, teachers, and parents. I have received many tools from my vocational teacher training that stimulate my career development in a positive direction.<br>**Conclusions of self-assessment**<br>I've thought a lot about the teacher's mission to promote pupils' knowledge, but also to educate them for the society. According to Vygotsky, pupils are learning and developing with others through their own choice in a socializing community (course literature). We live at a time when the school is characterized by economic demands on profitability, international knowledge measurements, and efficiency requirements. The teacher's mission is to promote the development of knowledge, but it is much more than that, and it is described in the literature as a dual mission (course literature). | Finally, the student is *relating* (level 3) to the theoretical and practical development as a rollercoaster between teaching, role, and mission as teacher, with expanded insight about different tools that stimulate the career in a positive way.<br>The further conclusion is a *reconstruction* (level 4) with possible impacts of promoting pupils learning and socializing at a time with economic demands and international dimensions, applied to theory of teaching. |

regarding special education was not taken into account for the ongoing translation of knowledge from theory to practice (Boud, 1999). This excerpt can be categorised as d*escriptive reflection* when the student tries to provide reasons, often based on personal judgment or on own literature reading (Hatton & Smith, 1995). The excerpt is linked to practical and theoretical knowledge, as well as a certain understanding of the connection between the self and others in a social context that shows an initial ability to reason through dialogic reflective considerations (Bain et al., 2002; McIntosh, 2010). From the perspective of Tomkins (2009), the student is on the third step, *making meaning,* which involve further exploration of the identified critical incident by providing new perspectives on the presented situation and extending it to a story of how she has developed her skills during the practical training to a written presentation with practical and theoretical knowledge.

In summary, excerpt 2 displays basic reflection on level 1 with relating, responding, and reporting aspects after all four semesters. The relating and responding levels show a kind of internal conversation in the reflective process, with some relationships based on personal and collegial interactions regarding pupils' learning and theoretical understandings in reading, but without any expanded insight on the discussions. In reasoning, which this student only used in semester 1, learners move from a largely personal response to an intellectually relevant reflection, as here about the importance of meeting the pupils at their knowledge level and engaging and motivating them. However, the student lacks rigorous analysis of the context or theoretical connection (Archer, 2010; Ryan, 2013). After the change of practice during semester 3, the student describes only limited perceptions about more focused pupils at a national program, without any practical comparison, contrast, or analysis of significant differences from the vocational introduction class. This excerpt can be categorised as d*escriptive reflection* when the student tries to provide reasons, based on personal judgment (Hatton & Smith, 1995). The essence is about the importance of collegial learning and professional experiences in teaching, as well as how to document and plan lessons to increase goal achievement for the pupils. From the perspective of Tomkins (2009), the student is mostly on the first stage, *noticing*, and lesser on the second stage *making sense*, that involve thoughts on the critical incident from the practical training that made him to stop and think about the significance of the incident by writing a short log journal.

In summary, excerpt 3 demonstrates, after semester 1, the most basic level of reflection, with reporting and relating aspects, about the need of insights into different methods and theories to fully understand them and to develop

*Table 5.* **Student 2** *is from a Vehicles and Transport program in vocational education and has worked as an informal vocational teacher for five years, after several years as a car mechanic*

| From the log journal | Application of the 5Rs scale |
|---|---|
| **Critical incident semester 1**<br>I feel that I have had a rather long practice already, since I have worked at the school for five years, first as a resource for three years, then with my own class. But since I started VTEP, I've become more observant of things that happen based on what we read and learned at the lectures.<br>**Conclusions of self-assessment**<br>It is important that we meet the pupils in their knowledge and not take for granted that they can do certain things. I have also begun to think about how to better motivate my pupils to be on time and be more involved in what is happening in the classroom and at school. | In these sentences, the student is *relating* (level 1) between personal learning at lessons and theoretical understandings in reading.<br>The further conclusion exhibits *reasoning* (level 1) about the importance of meeting the pupils at their level of knowledge and better motivating them, but without any theories. |
| **Critical incident semester 2**<br>After each day, I and my colleagues discuss and analyse the day's lessons. I feel I can better document and plan my teaching to increase goal achievement for the pupils. I have also become more comfortable with the fact that my previous professional experiences are very helpful in teaching.<br>**Conclusions of self-assessment**<br>My ability to meet the pupils in their knowledge and sense of mind has improved when I feel me more engaged with the pupils. Then they listen and respect my teaching in practice more. I have now extra understandings about documentation of the pupils' knowledge, both in school and during their workplace-based learning. | Here the student is *relating* (level 1) to the collective study about pupils' learning and professional experiences in teaching.<br>Likewise, the further conclusion relates information about the student's own strength of engaging the pupils' knowledge. However, the text still lacks any theories or questioning on vocational didactics. |
| **Critical incident semester 3**<br>During this semester I have practiced in a class in the National Vehicle Program. It's always useful to change to a new group of pupils and get some experience- based learning about how my colleagues work and plan their courses. The biggest difference for me is that it is easier to plan for a more focused group, than in vocational introduction. However, there are also pupils who have difficulty in different subjects or are unmotivated, especially theoretically.<br>**Conclusions of self-assessment**<br>What I miss when I'm only in a class for a short period is how much easier it is to teach pupils where I know them and have built mutual trust. During this semester, I have understood how much I'm already working on special education for my pupils in vocational introduction. | Here the student is *reporting* (level 1) the change of practice leading to an insight about teaching at a national vocational program, where the pupils are more focused, but also have some difficulties.<br>The further conclusion is *responding* (level 1) to the importance of relationships with pupils and their need for special support. The text still lacks theories. |
| **Critical incident semester 4**<br>This last semester, I have been thinking a lot about how I can develop vocational introduction for the pupils' workplace-based learning. The biggest problem I see is that we have to fight for our pupils at school; despite the fact that the introduction program is the biggest program at school, we are often set aside for the national programs.<br>**Conclusions of self-assessment**<br>In my role as a teacher, I feel that I am constantly developing more confidence in my teaching career and that I become safer in different classroom situations. At the same time, I feel that there is always a progression in the work we do in the teacher team. Previously, we have worked with assessment for learning, and now we are working with constructive alignment. In these common meetings, we learn from each other and test new methods in the classroom. This means that, the more knowledge I get, the more I am active in the teacher team's discussions. | Finally, the student is *relating* (level 1) to the difference between resources. Workplace-based learning needs to be developed, but there is a lack of support from school.<br>The further conclusion is *relating* (level 1) to the relationship between personal and collegial learning about assessment for learning and constructive alignment. This promotes the quality of the vocational program. However, there is a lack of theory. |

*Table 6.* **Student 3** *is from a Restaurant and Food program and has worked as a head cook for many years*

| From the log journal | Application of the 5Rs scale |
|---|---|
| **Critical incident semester 1**<br>After the first semester, I realize that there is so much more than just learning. I need to get a deeper insight into different methods and theories of learning to fully understand what I can do. My lesson planning feels good, but I have to develop and adapt my lessons also to the individual pupils I'm teaching, not only the whole class.<br>**Conclusions of self-assessment**<br>Theoretically, I want to understand why things are happening and how research would be useful. Also to constantly update my subject-specific knowledge. The practical part feels quite ok when I've used "hands-on learning" throughout my life. However, I feel that I would like to observe theoretical lessons to learn even more how different theories are combined, but also to get insight in how other teachers I work with behave and handle learning according to different didactic methods. | In these sentences, the student is *reporting* (level 1) about the need of insights into different methods and theories to fully understand them and to develop individualized teaching.<br>The further conclusion is *relating* (level 1) on the relationship between vocational knowledge and theories and how they can be integrated into teaching, as well as how colleagues are teaching. However, there is a lack of theories or examples. |
| **Critical incident semester 2**<br>My absolute first reflection on this semester is that I have so much left to learn. What I have focused on is to listen and take in more of everything that happens around me in classroom situations. I am interested in the theories of Socrates and Dewey, and I want to teach pupils through meaningful discussions and to learn while they are doing tasks. Learning shall come naturally by their curiosity, but catching and holding their interest is not easy.<br>**Conclusions of self-assessment**<br>I really feel that I am in need of learning to be able to concretize what I expect from the pupils and what I want them to achieve. My language use as a teacher needs also to be improved, I realize after reading the literature we had this semester, in using my vocational language. The absolute biggest and most important thing I reflected on was, after our tripartite conversation, I implemented the things I was criticized for and afterward had the best lesson ever. If the a-ha experiences will continue that way, this profession will be my best choice ever. | Here the student is *relating* (level 2) learning in classroom situations and theoretical understandings to Socrates' idea of meaningful discussions and Dewey's idea of learning by doing, albeit in a limited way.<br>The further conclusion is *responding* (level 2) to the meaning of the use of vocational language in practice after reading the literature. Additionally, the student responds to the importance of a tripartite conversation to get feedback on what can be developed and in what way. |
| **Critical incident semester 3**<br>Reflections from this semester include, in particular, how much and how different I as a teacher must work to reach all pupils. It's not just to be a teacher and making use of clear and relevant material. I have been in many different meetings regarding a pupil and have worked out different ways to get this pupil to achieve the grade E [approved], as this is extremely important for his future (course literature). The responsibility of the pupil is negligible, according to course literature the pupils should take responsibility.<br>**Conclusions of self-assessment**<br>During the tripartite conversation, I primarily assume that I will try to use the knowledge I have, but spend more time to understand the connection between the theories we are reading. I think more about different difficulties pupils can have and how they can turn out. I have to adapt my teaching in different ways. | Here the student is *relating* (level 2) to working in different ways to encourage pupils to take responsibility for their studies and achieve approved grades, with superficial connections to some literature.<br>The further conclusion is *responding* (level 2) to the importance of the tripartite conversation with the university teacher and the supervisor at school for support in teaching. |
| **Critical incident semester 4**<br>When I now summarize the practice I have done over two years, the first thing I think about is the nervousness I had when I started VTEP. That I would go from novice to professional felt so incredibly far away. Creating a good relationship to the pupils, and to the teacher team, and not least to myself in my new role as vocational teacher are incredibly important (course literature). Developing strategies to reach out to all pupils in the way they want to be treated and to go from pure facts to understanding what they really want to learn, is one of the keys for success (course literature).<br>**Conclusions of self-assessment**<br>The fact that I, as a student teacher, am taking care of thoughts, education, and research in the field of education, I consider is a survival instinct. Teaching goes in circles, and what I think I need additional knowledge in is primarily to use assessment in a formative way for pupils' learning (course literature). As a teacher, I shall provide feedback in a way that the pupils understand, so they can achieve their full potential (course literature). I must also critically review what I do, for example, through auscultations to reach further development as teacher (course literature). | Finally, the student is *reasoning* (level 3) about two insights, first the development from novice to professional connected to the importance of relationship to all pupils, the teacher team, and oneself based on literature, and second the didactic strategies as keys for success.<br>The further conclusion is a *reconstruction* (level 4) with new teaching understandings and a personal approach to use formative assessment for learning, as well as a critical review of teaching theory for further development as teacher. |

collective and individual teaching. By the end of semester 4, the student has reached the highest level of reflection, with reasoning and reconstructive insights at levels 3 and 4. This is an example of metacognitive reflection, where the student connects thoughts to the use of different strategies, such as formative assessment and critical review of one's own practice (Grossman, 2009). Likewise, the importance of help and support during the tripartite conversation between the teacher educator and the supervisor as coacher (Schön, 2010), which can provide challenging encouragement to develop reflective capacity for further development as teacher. This excerpt can be categorised as d*escriptive reflection* as a form of discourse with oneself, and exploration of possible reasons, as well as some *critical reflection* when there is some reasoning for decisions of own practice (Hatton & Smith, 1995). From the perspective of Tomkins (2009), the student is on the fourth stage, *working with meaning*, which involve both theory of *reflection-in-action* during the practical training and *reflection-on-action* after the practical training (Schön, 1983). To learn from previous actions and previous reflections requires a deep level of reflection and self-assessment.

## CONCLUSION

The results of the study on six students digital log journals, in what way reflections and self-assessment can support student-centered learning toward higher-order thinking and critical ability for self-directed and motivated smart higher education who is adaptive, resource-enriched, and technology-embedded, show that it is important that students have the ability to be active agents who mediate and challenge their subjective experiences, e.g. feelings and descriptions of practical and theoretical knowledge and teaching practises (Archer, 2010). Likewise, the students' objective circumstances, e.g. course and assessment requirements to act in certain ways during the school based vocational teacher training courses at a partner school or within the students' own teaching position as informal teachers. These process of reflection can help learners developing new ways of critical thinking through written and oral reflections and conclusions of self-assessment (Bain et al., 2002; Flanagan, 1954).

Most significantly, the analysis of the digital log journals show that the reflections supported the students' *reflection-on-action* after various elements of *reflection-in-action*, which occurs while an action is being undertaken through written reflections and self-assessments (Schön, 1987).

The assistance of professionals as coaches (teacher educator and supervisor) with written material for reciprocal reflection between the student and the coaches is needed about different problem solving (Townsend, 2010), as in this study on a critical incident about a situation, incident, or issue. This is also one means for distinguishing between the learners' roles as `experts` in their vocational profession from their status as `novices´ in the teacher profession (Grossman, 2009).

More specifically, the excerpts show content-based reflections, where experiences are measured against practical and theoretical knowledge. Through written digital log journals with self-assessed conclusions, the students were able to reflect on what way they learned from different situations, incidents, or issues (Grossman, 2009). Highlighted are the areas of professional didactic theories, pedagogical leadership, and formative assessment. Essentially, the process for gathering certain important facts concerning a clear problem-solving and afterwards critically reflect and self-assess them (Flanagan, 1954). However, it is crucial to approach these processes with explicit scaffolding by teachers and supervisors as coachers. In the present excerpts, scaffolding occurred through the tripartite conversation between the student and supervisor that encouraged the student to focus on theoretical and practical evidence in a well-communicated text, as well as to determine if something has real value to put into practice in a particular context (Bain et al., 2002; Dewey, 1938/1997; Hatton & Smith, 1995; Ryan, 2013). To avoid a frozen miscommunication with counter-learning or over-learning, as with the traditional didactic lecture in the classroom and the instructional teaching, the model of communication between student and coach must be extended with the design of "reflective practice" (Schön, 2010) with challenging blended learning activities.

Moreover, the excerpts demonstrate that students progressed to ´higher order thinking´ levels of reflection when different strategies and experiences of enthusiasm allowed them to distinguish between "novice" in teaching and "expert" in the profession (Grossman, 2009). Through careful and critical reflection on direct experiences, conclusions of self-assessment can be formulated (Dewey, 1938/1997). However, both separate and connected knowing are important to develop reflective thinking, both at an individual and a group level, students need different kinds of resource-enriched blended support to improve their reflective thinking (Enochsson, 2017). Students search for much help from teachers and fellow students, as well as challenging encouragement to develop this reflective capacity to connect practical and theoretical knowledge (Ryan, 2013). Awareness of the value of the written contributions and experience exchanges in the digital log journals emerged during the five four week periods with practical training (Meyer, 2003; Richardson & Ice, 2010; Schellens & Valcke, 2005; Wegerif, 2007).

Furthermore, the excerpts illustrate that "self-authorship" reflection helps students to separate thoughts and feelings from empathetic input (e.g. on the teacher mission, relationships or pupils' responsibility, and motivation for learning). Through self-authorship, students generate deeper reflections and awareness of that there is often more than one possible interpretation of different experiences (Grossman, 2009). Some of the excerpts demonstrate transformative reflective learning, which is a deeper level of reflection that develops by involving and evaluating awareness of critical thinking and learning, the value of careful perceiving, and reflective acting, supported by the digital log journals in a technology-embedded environment. In this transformative reflective learning, students learn how to progress through increased theoretical and practical ability and critical higher-order thinking, and they become less dependent on false assumptions and statements (Archer, 2010; Grossman, 2009; Kuhn, 2016). However, the pedagogical practice does not translate knowledge of itself; without developing students' intellectual stance in dealing with critical issues and practices, and where the students has the authority to initiate changes (Giroux, 2010).

From the perspective of Tomkins (2009), the students working with digital log journals enable them to reflect critically on the experiences during their practical training courses and to evaluate their strengths and weaknesses by steps in *noticing, making sense*, and *making meaning*, as well as *working with meaning*. These activities involve further exploration of the identified critical incident by providing new perspectives on the presented situation and extending them in their reflections in the digital log journals and conclusions of self-assessment. To learn from previous actions and previous reflections requires a deep level of reflection and self-assessment. In the conclusions of self-assessment, students gradually internalize their practice with various problem solutions and their ability to reflect and self-assess develops (Dochy, Segers and Sluijsmans, 1999). Therefore, the process of reflection and self-assessment on experiences is important in relation to self, others, and contextual conditions of the development in practical training courses, as well the students' knowledge progression to plan and anticipate future experiences for personal and professional learning (Dewey 1938/1997; Ryan, 2013).

## REFERENCES

Amhag, L. (2016a). Mobile technologies for student centered learning in a distance higher education program. In *Wearable Technology and Mobile Innovations for Next-Generation Education,* (pp. 184-199). IGI Global. https://www.igi-global.com/book/wearable-technology-mobile-innovations-next/142108

Amhag, L. (2016b). Mobile technologies for student centered learning in a distance higher education program. *Blended Learning: Concepts, Methodologies, Tools, and Applications*, *4*, 802–817. doi:10.4018/978-1-5225-0069-8.ch010

Amhag, L. (2017). Mobile-Assisted Seamless Learning Activities in Higher Distance Education. *International Journal of Higher Education*, *6*(3), 2017. doi:10.5430/ijhe.v6n3p70

Amhag, L. (2020). Student Reflections and Self-Assessments in Vocational Training Supported by a Mobile Learning Hub. *International Journal of Mobile and Blended Learning*, *12*(1), 1–16. doi:10.4018/IJMBL.2020010101

Archer, M. (2010). Routine, Reflexivity, and Realism. *Sociological Theory*, *28*(3), 272–303. doi:10.1111/j.1467-9558.2010.01375.x

Ashwin, P., Boud, D., Coate, K., & Hallett, F. (2015). *Reflective Teaching in Higher Education*. New York: Bloomsbury Academic.

Bain, J.D., Ballantyne, R., Mills, C. & Lester, N.C. (2002). *Reflecting on practice: Student teachers' perspectives*. Flaxton: Post Pressed.

Boud, D. (1999). Avoiding the traps: Seeking good practice in the use of self-assessment and reflection in professional courses. *Social Work Education*, *18*(2), 121–132. doi:10.1080/02615479911220131

Boud, D. (2000). Sustainable assessment: Rethinking assessment for the learning society. *Studies in Continuing Education*, *22*(2), 151–167. doi:10.1080/713695728

Boud, D., & Falchikov, N. (1989). Quantitative studies of student self-assessment in higher education: A critical analysis of findings. *Higher Education*, *18*(5), 529–549. doi:10.1007/BF00138746

Broadbent, J., & Poon, W. L. (2015). Self-Regulated Learning Strategies & Academic Achievement in Online Higher Education Learning Environments: A Systematic Review. *The Internet and Higher Education*, *27*, 1–13. doi:10.1016/j.iheduc.2015.04.007

Clinchy, B. M. V. (1996). Connected and separate knowing. In N. R. Goldberger, J. M. Tarule, B. M. Clinchy, & M. F. Belenky (Eds.), *Knowledge, difference and power: Essays inspired by Women's ways of knowing* (pp. 205–247). New York: Basic Books.

Colomer, J., Pallisera, M., Fullana, J., Burriel, M. P., & Fernández, R. (2013). Reflective learning in higher education: A comparative analysis. *Procedia: Social and Behavioral Sciences*, *93*, 364–370. doi:10.1016/j.sbspro.2013.09.204

De Wever, B., Van Keer, H., Schellens, T., & Valcke, M. (2009). Structuring asynchronous discussion groups: The impact of role assignment and self-assessment on students' levels of knowledge construction through social negotiation. *Journal of Computer Assisted Learning*, *25*(2), 177–188. doi:10.1111/j.1365-2729.2008.00292.x

Dewey, J. (1997). *Experience and Education*. New York: Touchstone. (Original work published 1938)

Dochy, F., Segers, M., & Sluijsmans, D. (1999). The use of self-, peer- and co-assessment in higher education: A review. *Studies in Higher Education*, *24*(3), 331–350. doi:10.1080/03075079912331379935

Enochsson, A. B. (2017). Reflective discussions in teacher training: A comparison between online and offline discussions of course literature in a class of pre-service teachers. *Education and Information Technologies*, *§§§*, 1–17. doi:10.100710639-017-9602-5

Flanagan, J. (1954). The critical incident technique. *Psychological Bulletin*, *51*(4), 327–358. doi:10.1037/h0061470 PMID:13177800

Fullana, J., Pallisera, M., Colomer, J., Fernández Peña, R., & Pérez-Burriel, M. (2016). Reflective learning in higher education: A qualitative study on students' perceptions. *Studies in Higher Education*, *41*(6), 1008–1022. doi: 10.1080/03075079.2014.950563

González-Betancor, S. M., Bolívar-Cruz, A., & Verano-Tacoronte, D. (2017). Self-assessment accuracy in higher education: The influence of gender and performance of University Students. *Active Learning in Higher Education*, *§§§*, 1469787417735604.

Grossman, R. (2009). Structures for Facilitating Student Reflection. *College Teaching*, *57*(1), 15–22. doi:10.3200/CTCH.57.1.15-22

Habermas, J. (2015). *Knowledge and human interests*. John Wiley & Sons.

Hatton, N., & Smith, D. (1995). Reflection in teacher education: Towards definition and implementation. *Teaching and Teacher Education*, *11*(1), 33–49. doi:10.1016/0742-051X(94)00012-U

Hora, M. T., & Smolarek, B. B. (2018). Examining faculty reflective practice: A call for critical awareness and institutional support. *The Journal of Higher Education*, *89*(4), 553–581. doi:10.1080/00221546.2018.1437663

Illeris, K. (2009). A comprehensive understanding of human learning. In K. Illeris (Ed.), *Contemporary theories of learning: learning theorists... in their own words* (pp. 7–20). Routledge. doi:10.4324/9780203870426

Jordi, R. (2011). Reframing the concept of reflection: Consciousness, experiential learning, and reflective learning practices. *Adult Education Quarterly*, *61*(2), 181–197. doi:10.1177/0741713610380439

Kegan, R. (2009). What "form" transforms? A constructive-developmental approach to transformative learning. In K. Illeris (Ed.), *Contemporary theories of learning: learning theorists... in their own words* (pp. 35–52). Routledge.

Kostons, D., van Gog, T., & Paas, F. (2010). Self-assessment and task selection in learner-controlled instruction: Differences between effective and ineffective learners. *Computers & Education*, *54*(4), 932–940. doi:10.1016/j.compedu.2009.09.025

Kuhn, D. (2016). A role for reasoning in a dialogic approach to critical thinking. *Topoi*, *37*(1), 121–128. doi:10.100711245-016-9373-4

Marin, V. I., Jääskelä, P., Häkkinen, P., Juntunen, M., Rasku-Puttonen, H., & Vesisenaho, M. (2016). Seamless Learning Environments in Higher Education with Mobile Devices and Examples. *International Journal of Mobile and Blended Learning*, *8*(1), 51–68. doi:10.4018/IJMBL.2016010104

McIntosh, P. (2010). *Action research and reflective practice*. London: Routledge. doi:10.4324/9780203860113

Mirriahi, N., Liaqat, D., Dawson, S., & Gašević, D. (2016). Uncovering student learning profiles with a video annotation tool: Reflective learning with and without instructional norms. *Educational Technology Research and Development*, *64*(6), 1083–1106. doi:10.100711423-016-9449-2

Pallisera, M., Fullana, J., Palaudarias, J. M., & Badosa, M. (2012). Personal and professional development (or use of self) in social educator training. An experience based on reflective learning. *Social Work Education*. doi:10.1080/02615479.2012.701278

Papanthymou, A., & Darra, M. (2019). The Contribution of Learner Self-Assessment for Improvement of Learning and Teaching Process: A Review. *Journal of Education and Learning*, *8*(1), 48–64. doi:10.5539/jel.v8n1p48

Richardson, J. C., & Ice, P. (2010). Investigating students´ level of critical thinking across instructional strategies in online discussions. *Internet and Higher Education*, *13*(1-2), 52–59. doi:10.1016/j.iheduc.2009.10.009

Ryan, M. (2013). The pedagogical balancing act: Teaching reflection in higher education. *Teaching in Higher Education*, *18*(2), 144–155. doi:10.1080/13562517.2012.694104

Schön, D. (1983). *The reflective practitioner. How professionals think in action*. New York: Basic Books.

Schön, D. (1987). Educating the Reflective Practitioner. Jossey-Bass Publishers.

Schön, D. A. (2010). Educating the reflective practitioner: Toward a new design for teaching and learning in the professions. Book review by Townsend, R. *Australian Journal of Adult Learning*, *50*(2), 448.

Sumsion, J., & Fleet, A. (1996). Reflection: Can we assess it? Should we assess it? *Assessment & Evaluation in Higher Education*, *21*(2), 121–130. doi:10.1080/0260293960210202

Tomkins, A. (2009). "It was a great day when…": An exploratory case study of reflective learning through storytelling. *Journal of Hospitality, Leisure, Sport and Tourism Education*, *8*(2), 123–131. doi:10.3794/johlste.82.198

Topping, K. (1998). Peer assessment between students in colleges and universities. *Review of Educational Research, 68*(3), 249–276. doi:10.3102/00346543068003249

Wiliam, D. (2011). What is assessment for learning? *Studies in Educational Evaluation, 37*(1), 3–14. doi:10.1016/j.stueduc.2011.03.001 PMID:22114905

Wiliam, D. (2013). Assessment: The bridge between teaching and learning. *Voices from the Middle, 21*(2), 15.

Zhu, Z. T., Yu, M. H. & Riezebos, P. (2016). A research framework of smart education. *Smart Learning Environments, 3*(1), 4.

# Chapter 7
# Virtual Learning in Smart Education


## ABSTRACT

*This chapter expands the knowledge about virtual learning in smart higher education, and how these processes can be a tool for motivated and student-centered learning in a resource-enriched virtual learning environment with technology-embedded tools. Methodologically, selected articles are reviewed to expand the knowledge about virtual learning in smart higher education and with an example analysis of an open question (N=57) among teacher educators (N=105) about what kind of education they need for using a virtual learning environment with different tools. Theoretically, the analysis of the answers is based on the TPACK model and Gees five learning principles. The findings highlight that higher education and academic researchers have much to learn about teaching and learning in a virtual learning environment and in virtual reality that can enhance student-centered learning and reveal the pedagogical surplus value in their own teaching and learning context through the use of technology for an educational purpose.*


## BACKGROUND

Digitization have gone through a several paradigms shift where structures, processes and behaviours are fundamentally changed, as well in education as in the society, thereby changing even the teaching (Koschmann, 1996; Wegerif, 2007). Due to the rapid changes, they are changeable and pervasive

DOI: 10.4018/978-1-7998-4183-8.ch007

because they are used in many different ways in everyday life (Koehler, Mishra & Cain, 2013). However, the potential implications of these emerging technologies have tremendous potential for teacher educators, classroom teachers, and students (Dieker, Hynes, Hughes & Smith, 2008). Virtual learning environments, VLE are providing lecture materials encourage and facilitate interactions and additional course content, which allows students to build and develop their own learning space (Kennedy & Dunn, 2018). However, education that uses widespread technology, such as a smartphone, tablet or laptop, is considered to be primarily used for informal learning and lifelong learning, especially for young adult students (Herrador-Alcaide, Hernández-Solís & Galván, 2019).

This article expands the knowledge about virtual learning in smart higher education, and how these processes can be a tool for motivated and student-centered learning in a resource-enriched learning environment with technology-embedded tools. The word 'smart' is an acronym for self-directed, motivated, adaptive, resource-enriched, and technology-embedded, and refers to wisdom as bounding together the ability of using and motivating self-directed learning, knowledge building, problem solving, critically reflections, collaborating and evaluating different circumstances in a resource-enriched virtual learning environment with technology-embedded tools (Hwang, 2014; Zhu, Yu & Riezebos, 2016). The following questions are addressed:

- In what way can teachers a) design and b) use different virtual learning activities and tools that are appropriate for student-centered learning and active participation?
- How do the students experience the virtual environment and tools for their learning?
- In what way can the virtual learning and tools be analyzed comparing to the students' performance?

Virtual reality, VR can be defined as a computer-generated simulation of a three-dimensional image or virtual learning environment, VLE with which a person can interact with different tools. VLE is a gateway to a variety of resource-enriched and technology-embedded tools, such as lecture material, lecture recordings and / or images, online face-to-face webinars, F2F, online quizzes, chat, blogs, discussion forums, and other online resources (Kennedy & Dunn, 2018). VR is based on three basic principles: a) Immersion/engagement, b) Interaction/collaboration, and c) User involvement/participation within the computer-embedded simulation technology and the narrative to making learning more motivating and engaging (Ott & Freina, 2015). Two different types of VR can be identified: non-immersive and immersive. Non-immersive VR is a computer-embedded environment that can simulate places in the real or imagined world. Immersive VR, named IVR provides the notion of being physically present in the non-physical world that increase the feeling of presence through VR images, sounds or other stimuli. VR and IVR have mostly been used in adult education for special situations e.g. cognitive disabilities or needs of special support (Ott & Freina, 2015). Simulations occur also in different styles, such as a) live simulations that occur in natural environments with humans and / or with equipment suitable for the environment (e.g. role-playing), b) virtual simulations that occur with humans and / or with equipment in a computer-controlled environment in which the human is involved in a loop (e.g. flight simulator), and c) constructive simulations that do not involve humans, but rather are driven by nature-based sequencing of correct events (Dieker, Hynes, Hughes & Smith, 2008).

The main motivation to use VR, IVR or VLE in education is that they make it possible to experience situations that are either inaccessible in time or space or problematic, dangerous or unethical (Ott & Freina, 2015). The affordances of VR, IVR or VLE make these technologically mediated environments suited to facilitating the ability engage in creative problem-solving and to communicate effectively across cultures through authentic learning activities (Gregory & Wood, 2018). An affordance can be defined as the perceived and actual properties of the technology that determine how that technology can be used for learning. The potential of virtual immersive learning environments can engage students in authentic learning activities. These skills include problem-solving, the ability to work with others, communication and appreciation of, and respect for diversity. The assessment of the students on the online virtual learning activity and in-class conversations between tutors and students confirmed that learning in a virtual platform supports knowledge sharing between students and enhances creative thinking and problem-solving (Ott & Freina, 2015).

For university students, VR can be used to practice various hands-on situations or treatments of virtual patients, e.g. within medical care and health care, most commonly clinical reasoning, bioethics, clinical decision-making, leadership, and history taking (Pantziaras, Fors & Ekblad, 2015). Likewise, within special education for pupils with different disabilities or where there are ethical dilemmas in using pupils in real-life for educational purposes, for example in language, writing and reading investigations. Observe, that VR does not exclude pupils from reading printed texts or developing skills in collecting information, understanding material or processing information (Dieker, Hynes, Hughes & Smith, 2008). But the art of reading printed text is not the only way to read and understand material, much like handwriting is not the only way to express ideas. Even pupils who cannot process or simply write the written word should feel successful through digital tools. Instead, a VR simulation of a recorded language, writing and reading survey can be reviewed and discussed by a group of students. IVR gives an idea of being physically present in the non-physical world which increases the feeling of presence through VR images, sounds or other stimuli (Ott & Freina, 2015).

Moreover, the computer-embedded simulation technology is becoming increasingly user-friendly and economically accessible. A regular computer screen can have a three-dimensional environment when recorded simulations are displayed on the screen. VR glasses, so called Head Mounted Displays, HMD, are most often used with headphones to coordinate between main movements and how the image moves in the three-dimensional environment. There is also a special AR technology (Lanier, 2017), with so-called AR glasses, for example can they help the elderly and disabled to train their balance. AR stands for augmented reality, or augmented reality. The technology works by increasing the perception of current reality, unlike VR which replaces the real world with a simulated one. VR and AR are different types of immersive technologies, also called "spatial computing" or the cryptic collection term XR. Sometimes "Mixed Reality" is also used as an umbrella term for the entire immersive spectrum.

However, several boundaries exist in higher education, such as lack of pedagogical abilities among university teachers and training in digital competence (Amhag, Hellström & Stigmar, 2019; Hwang, 2014; Kearney, Schuck, Burden & Aubusson, 2012; Zhu, Yu & Riezebos, 2016). A high level of digital competence requires an exemplary digital practice, characterized by good technical infrastructure, teachers with high technological-pedagogical knowledge, continuous professional development and a well-functioning technology-embedded mediated communication and administration (Amhag, 2016a; 2016b; Olofsson, Fransson & Lindberg, 2019). Therefore, there is a need of to expand the knowledge about virtual learning in smart higher education, and how these processes can be a tool for motivated and student-centered learning in a resource-enriched learning environment with technology-embedded tools.

## PREVIOUS RESEARCH OF VIRTUAL LEARNING

The review from searches in different databases in education and social sciences such as ERIC, Libsearch etc. and from studies cited by these authors of the articles, show that virtual reality, VR is a relatively broad concept and is often used in the areas of education, special education and motivation (Ott & Freina, 2015). VR offers a way to approach, practice and reflect on learning based on the combine of audiovisual and kinesthetic learning (Leite, Svinicki & Shi, 2010) often delivered via a virtual learning environment, VLE which is a resource-enriched learning environment with technology-embedded tools for using with digital devices, such as laptop, tablet or smart phone (Amhag, 2016a; 2016b). Virtual Patients (VPs) have also been technologically developed and can take many forms and provide highly effective ways of addressing well-structured educational patient encounters, and opportunities for students to practice in safe and responsive VLE (Ellaway, Poulton, Fors, McGee & Albright, 2008).

### Virtual Reality and Learning

Students' interest, motivation, attention and commitment to learning are considered as a potential instrument for future academic success both digitally and in the classroom (Ott & Tavella, 2009; Robertson & Howells, 2008). A large number of research studies have examined how behaviors of learning can be influenced, promoted or changed from two different starting points: on the one hand, from psychological and sociological grounds about students' different attitudes to learning tasks and that focusing on students' interests is a valuable motivational strategy (Covington, 2000). On the other hand, why and how different educational tasks and digital tools have impact on student engagement (Robertson & Howells, 2008). Successful students use both aspects of metacognition, the cognitive ability and the self-regulating mechanisms to monitor their own understanding (Black et al., 2006). Emphasis in higher education should be placed on practices that have the potential to promote autonomy in learning, which is a common research result at all levels and reflects the importance of working with teachers' attitudes and practices. While teachers are designing student skills, the principle of student autonomy must be to give them opportunities for strategic thinking and reflection on their own learning.

A review of articles on the advantages and potentials of the use of immersive IVR in education by Ott and Freina (2015) is from searches in databases: Web of Knowledge, Google Scholar, and Scopus during the years 2013 to 2015 (54 in 2013, 37 in 2014 and 2 published in 2015). A large number of the 93 articles from 10 countries have been written in the United States and in the United Kingdom and a majority of them (60%) in the Computer Science area, and more than 22% were somehow related to medical issues. The results show that IVR can play a significant role in research activities, giving the possibility to visualize and simulate events that are not perceivable in real life. In medical research, IVR allows not only the visualization, but also the possibility to move through tissues and organs. The main motivation for using IVR in various occupational programs is that it provides the opportunity to experiment with different situations that cannot be physically reached. For example, is it possible to experiment with different historical periods, explore the solar system by freely moving around planets and practicing dangerous situations, e.g. training firefighters in live firefighting situations, ambulance operations in the event of serious accidents, and ethical problems such as in serious operations and advanced surgery (ibid.).

The educational potential of VR and computer games in education is often discussed in the society and in schools, compared to researchers who claim that the game actions give students a 'mental training' that develops a number of cognitive skills due to the embedded structure of the activities. The students face both long-term and short-term decisions and they must plan different strategies and problem solving that involve monitoring complex tasks (Robertson & Howells, 2008). Free choice of learning environments affects how students learn and interact in multiple environments, show the study by Dieker, Hynes, Hughes and Smith (2008). Their focus was on the potential technological advances and how it affected pupils' literacy and their functional and social skills, but also how these new tools can affect the future of teacher preparation, along with how mixed reality environments have potential consequences for teachers, pupils, schools, families and society. One of the issues is that pupils with disabilities in general struggle with their actual learning of social skills. In more traditional ways they are working with peers, video showing, or direct social skills instruction. Despite the usefulness for teachers and from research to support each of these approaches within a virtual learning environment, VLE, the pupils either lack the technology context in school or must learn new skills among intolerant peers. The authors recommend either an online tool, to an immersive environment as options for all pupils, but specifically for pupils with disabilities to learn skills using digital tools.

Bousfield (2017) examines the behavior of novice teachers and expert teachers and their preparation for a simulated inclusive VLE with a virtual student with autism. During phase one, best practices were selected by experienced experts in the field of teachers who teach pupils with autism spectrum disorders, ASD in inclusive secondary environments. During phase two, a framework of 11 high leverage simulation methods (HLSP) was identified that expert teachers should use while teaching in a simulated secondary inclusive environment. The qualitative data included observing and interviewing 10 teachers, five beginners and five experts. The analysis of the observations and reflections showed 4 HLSP among experts and 5 HLSP among beginners. Further HLSP was seen through the teachers' reflections. The results show that expert teachers could talk about and demonstrate skills to minimize behaviors and deliberately ignore unwanted behavior from all pupils, but their previous experience did not affect their teaching in the student avatar simulator for the disabled. The beginning teachers could use more group work as a way to include universal design for learning, UDL where they exchange knowledge and experience both in the classroom and online for their lessons.

The pre-service special teacher education program needs extensive and advanced opportunities to prepare pedagogically teaching before entering the classroom. Peterson-Ahmad (2018) is observing when this is offered by practicing pedagogical strategies in a virtual simulation environment as a way to improve the teaching and practice of various pedagogical aspects when new teachers come into their first classroom for inclusive general education or special education. The exploratory case study investigated the extent to which virtual simulations combined with instructional coaching influenced how pre-service teachers learned to provide opportunities to respond, OTR to avatar pupils through repeated teaching in a four-session lesson. The participants consisted of eight undergraduate special education teachers in pre-education studies who participated in a first teacher certification program. Each participant performed four virtual simulations over a five-week period. Participant self-reflections were analyzed and following themes emerged: 1) positive comments (17.43%); 2) negative comments (3.66%); 3) things to change for the next session (21.81%), and; 4) feelings about providing OTR (17.74%). The result indicated that training in a virtual simulation environment with opportunities to respond, OTR during the same lesson proved to be effective in learning the basic aspects of teaching, and could also be a model for teachers in other preparation courses.

Another study with special teacher education students from Finland (N=94) and Sweden (N=59) by Takala and Wickman (2019) is about collaborative case-based virtual learning to bridge between theoretical and practical studies to develop the students critical and creative thinking and to make meaning out of their experiences. The case was consisted of videos of an imaginary school, and proceeded in the form of a narrative. In small groups the students were practicing challenging situations and critical thinking. Afterwards they responded to a questionnaire with six open-ended questions and six closed questions. They evaluated the virtual activity positively as a new, inspiring method and as an alternative to traditional lectures in higher education. Only a few critical comments were received, such as that there was too little time for deep discussion. Interactions and new professional skills, such as co-teaching or discussions with parents were other topics these students would like to study in a similar way. Special teacher profession need solid knowledge, but also transversal abilities, specifically, soft skills such as excellent social interaction and communication skills, as well as to work together with teachers, for example on how pupils can best be supported in an inclusive school. Therefore, there is a need of carefully aligned reflective activities such as virtual case-based learning, involving critical thinking, noticing, analysing and taking action to link together theory and practice and to contribute to meaningful knowledge and skill development among students in higher education.

Virtual patients, VPs are Ellaway, Poulton, Fors, McGee and Albright (2008) using and the steps that have been taken to support researchers to use a VP-strategy more sustainably and adaptably through commonly agreed data standards and core specifications. Virtual patients are usually presented as pre-existing cases that the student is working through, usually on their own, but they can also be collaborative or cases they build up themselves. Virtual patient activities can be about solving a problem such as a diagnosis or treatment, learning a clinical process and thinking, or accessing and learning from a knowledge base in a clinical context. VP activities that can be used by university educators, teachers and students, are as follows:

- *Feedback and reporting* refer to formative feedback when the student is working on scenarios with a virtual patient and at the end of each activity write a summary feedback report.

- *User agency and autonomy* refer to the predetermined virtual patient activity and the level of detail and type of alternatives available to explore alternative approaches or pathways.
- *Validity and faithfulness* refers to the fact that the virtual patient scenario is a valid and coherent real representation to ensure that students' immersion and commitment are maintained.
- *Pacing and cognitive load* refer to the virtual patient scenario to ensure that the students learns by controlling how much is required to manage and / or remember as they progress through the scenario (ibid., p. 171).

Along with a common technical data standard, a virtual patient provides usability through a number of community-based activities. These have been broadened to include all sets of resources owned or accessed jointly by a community. A virtual patient protection is created, adapted, shared, reused and can thus be a bank with virtual patient cases held by the group or the university.

The pedagogical effect of a virtual patient is evaluating by Pantziaras, Fors and Ekblad (2015) about the confidence to provide clinical care for traumatized refugee patients. The authors had developed an educational tool based on virtual patient methodology that describes the case "Mrs. K", a traumatized refugee woman with symptoms of post-traumatic stress disorder in a teenage patient, PTSD and depression. A group of physicians (N = 32) evaluated before and after the educational tool using a validated confidential questionnaire about their confidence in various aspects of providing clinical care for this patient group. The physicians showed a statistically significant improvement in overall confidence, as well as in four more specific areas of clinical care, and in identifying and evaluating trauma-related diagnoses and disabilities. The conclusion is that the Virtual Patient, VP-system can lead to physicians improving confidence in providing transcultural clinical care for traumatized refugee patients.

## Virtual Learning Environment

Digitization has undergone a number of paradigm shifts over some decades where structures, processes and behaviours have changed from the ground, both in research, in education and in the society (Koschmann, 1996; Wegerif, 2007). In the first paradigm shift, which was given the term Computer Aided Instruction, CAI, the teacher should effectively deliver and control learning via one-way communication (Koschmann, 1996). The second paradigm,

Intelligent Tutoring Systems, ITS focused more on an interactive, transferable form, where the computer program poses problems and provides feedback to the student. Interest in the individual knowledge construction, first arose under the third paradigm, Logo-as-Latin. Under the fourth paradigm, Computer Supported Collaborative Learning, CSCL, the interest was focused on collaborative learning based on the understanding of language, culture and various aspects of the social environment, but also on the importance of the context and collaboration for learning and development (ibid.).

Wegerif (2007) has distinguish three research paradigms that have traditionally been theorized in educational research: 1) *Objectivism*, where the computer / computer program was assumed to be an educational machine that should transfer knowledge, in the case of better teaching material, minor problems arose; 2) *Constructivism*, where the computer should act as a "memory tool" because the achievements were available in learning environment after the students' publication and could be examined based on the knowledge they had; 3) *Sociocultural theory*, where the computer was understood as a mediating resource for collaborative learning. Wegerif proposed a fourth paradigm, "computer as support for dialogic space", and emphasizes that the Internet is not so much a "tool of tools" (p. 181), but it brings a cacophony of voices that provide innumerable opportunities for dialogic collaboration from multiple subject perspectives.

The use of technology-enhanced learning, TEL has increased in higher education – from a centralized technology-push strategy where the learning content is only used by a predefined group of students (Chatti, Agustiawan, Jarke & Specht, 2010) – to be delivered via a virtual learning environment, VLE as a gateway to a variety of resource-enriched and technology-embedded tools, such as lecture material, lecture recordings and / or images, online face-to-face webinars, F2F, online quizzes, chat, blogs, discussion forums, and other online resources, i.e. interactive white-board (Amhag, 2016a; 2016b; 2017; 2020). To determine best practices that meet the students' needs, the study of Kennedy and Dunn (2018) have reviewed previous studies on TEL via VLE and how they can be improved for the future. The self-developed sample of students comprised a total of 487 participants who answered a questionnaire with two open questions: What are the benefits of technology-enhanced learning for you? In what ways could the delivery of technology-enhanced learning via VLE be improved? The most common answers on the first question are related to easy access to information and resources that are relevant to the course in one place, such as direct access to distance resources and thus can spend their time engaging with the core material and their learning. Students also warned that the easy accessibility of lecture recordings may hamper participation in the lectures themselves. Inside of class, students felt that TEL / VLE changed the lectures positively by using innovative methods, such as the use of Twitter feeds and interactive quizzes. It allows them to recap information that they have either missed, or found difficult to understand initially which allow students to do learning at their 'own pace'. The online lecture slides were mostly valued when they were uploaded in advance that enabled them to print them out and to use them as a framework for making notes during the lectures. The most common answers on the second question were simply that the students wanted more virtual practices in a more dynamic way and for greater engagement, both within lectures and outside of them, such as online lecture recordings, discussion forums for important questions, resources addressed on the bulletin board for wider readings that explain theories and research. They found five specific recommendations for teachers using technology-enhanced virtual learning environments:

- The TEL / VLE content should be uniform between the modules, both what is offered and how it should be used.
- TEL should be used more often to improve communication between students and with the teacher.
- VLE content should be more focused and relevant with more explanatory content, such as links to videos from external sources explaining concepts.
- TEL should be used as a way have peer activities that could be facilitated both within lectures and outside of them and to create more interactions and social engagement between teacher and students.

Furthermore, a resource-enriched VLE in higher education can have advantages over traditional face-to-face teaching in a classroom, show the study by Herrador-Alcaide, Hernández-Solís & Galván (2019). Every student can connect from anywhere and at any time to receive online instructions and training, which results in greater specialization and the possibility of having virtual contact with teachers and peers via the use of e-tools, such as digital whiteboards, chats, web-conferences or web-videos. The work and life balance is better when the students' can control their study times and can learn without physical or space restrictions, since all they need is technology embedded and resource-enriched in the course. The analyses of students' perceptions of their satisfaction levels of a resource-enriched

VLE were made partly on the basis of their generic skills and partly on their perception of VLE. The results show that the students experienced a high level of satisfaction (score 4 on a Likert scale from 1 to 5, where 5 is the highest score). The self-perception of their generic skills also received an average of 4 points, while the perception of their attitude towards VLE was slightly lower. The ability to organize their own work stands out as the best skill. The lowest relationship occurs between the ability to work in a group and written communication skills. The results extend the knowledge of satisfaction with a resource-enriched VLE, especially in subjects that require a high level of analytical and mathematical competence.

## Virtual Tools

Jensen and Konradsen (2018) are updating the knowledge about the use of VR glasses, called head-mounted displays, HMDs in education and training by a comprehensive search of 21 peer-reviewed research documenting experimental or quasi-experimental studies. The result identified that HMDs are useful for skills achievement as *cognitive skills* related to remembering and understanding spatial and visual information and knowledge (six studies); *psychomotor skills* related to head-movement, such as visual scanning or observational skills within a training simulator in which the student repeatedly goes through the actions being trained until a level of proficiency has been reached (five studies); and *affective skills* related to controlling emotional response to stressful or difficult situations where the student interact with a virtual agent systems that can be used for training interpersonal, communicative and other affective skills (five studies). Outside these situations had the HMDs no advantage compared to less immersive technologies or traditional instruction. In some cases, they were counterproductive because of widespread cybersickness, technological challenges, or because the immersive experience distracted from the learning task. The motive for using HMDs in education is that it can expose students to challenging educational situations and repeatedly allow them to practice new skills in an environment that enables correction and non-hazardous failure. VR technology is primarily suitable for educational approaches such as constructivism, active learning or simulation-based learning.

## DESIGN OF VIRTUAL LEARNING

A model can provide support for the design and decision when and how a virtual learning environment, VLE or virtual reality, VR should be used in a course in higher education. The teacher must decide when and where to use it. Figure 1 illustrates a revised version of a 10-step model by Pantelidis (2009, p. 68) that provides the following guidelines for using VLE or VR in higher education:

*Figure 1. Revised version of a 10-step model by Pantelidis (2009, p. 68) for the use of VLE or VR in higher education*

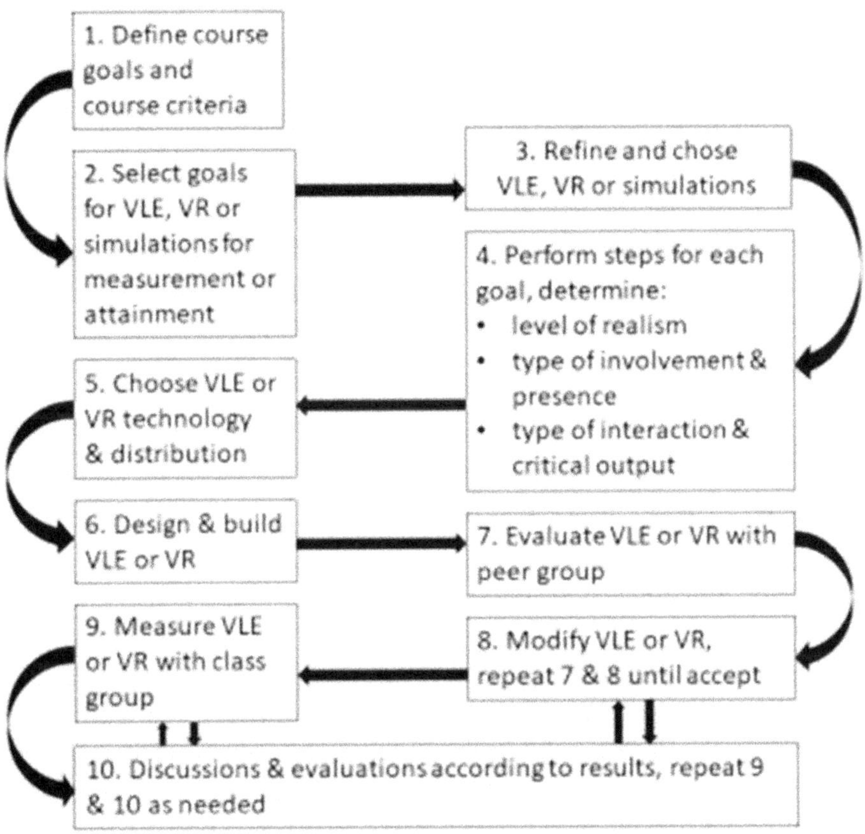

The 10-step model of Pantelidis (2009, p. 68) takes into account the research on the reasons for the use and the benefits of using VLE and VR or simulations, based on course goals and course criteria before deciding on the performs steps, design, technology and distribution. The model is wide enough to be able to adapt to future changes in VLE and VR technology.

## METHOD OF USING A VIRTUAL LEARNING ENVIRONMENT

Methodically, selected articles are used for the review of searches in databases in education and social sciences from Libsearch that allow searching at almost all library databases, such as Web of Knowledge, ERIC, Scopus and Google Scholar, as well as from studies cited by these authors of the articles published in the field of keywords: virtual learning or virtual learning environment or virtual reality in higher education.

The qualitative empirical data, as an example of an analysis of VLE, comprises 105 teacher educators from two universities in Sweden (Amhag, Hellström, & Stigmar, 2019) with an open question with answers (N=57) about what kind of education they need for using a virtual learning environment with different tools, such as lecture material, lecture recordings, online face-to-face webinars, F2F, chat, discussion forums, and other online resources i.e. interactive white-board (Amhag, 2016a; 2016b; 2017; 2020).

## ANALYSIS OF USING A VIRTUAL LEARNING ENVIRONMENT

Theoretically, the analysis of the open-ended question (N=57) is based on the TPACK model by Koehler, Mishra and Cain (2013) with a focus on the technological, pedagogical and content knowledge of the teacher educators need of education to use a virtual learning environment, VLE with different tools (Amhag, Hellström, & Stigmar, 2019), such as lecture material, lecture recordings, online face-to-face webinars, F2F, chat, discussion forums, and other online resources (Amhag, 2016a; 2016b; 2017; 2020). TPACK is supplemented by Gees (2017) five learning principles as a basis for the analysis with a focus on media and visual skills that can clarify the outcome and ensure the validity and the reliability of the added results.

The TPACK model consists of three knowledge domains (see Figure 2): pedagogical knowledge, PK, technological knowledge, TK and content knowledge, CK, and, importantly, the interaction between these domains. The greater the three domains coincide, the better the prerequisite for effective teaching with digital tools (Koehler, Mishra & Cain, 2013). The area where the domains of technological knowledge and pedagogical knowledge interact explains how teachers can use technology for an educational purpose, while the area where the domains of technological knowledge and content knowledge interact explains how teachers can integrate technology into a particular subject content. Lastly, the area where pedagogical knowledge and content

*Figure 2. TPACK-model by Koehler et al. (2013, p. 15)*

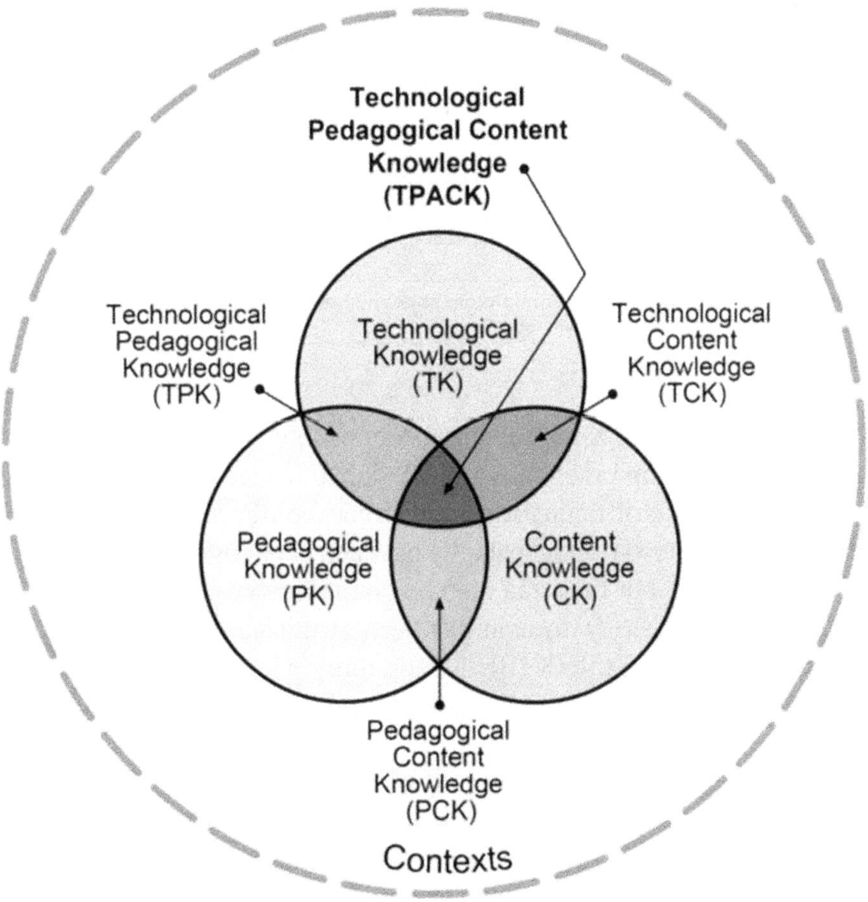

knowledge interact explains how teachers can use taught content together with subject didactic knowledge in the students' teaching practice.

The theoretical framework of TPACK is focusing on how technology knowledge is integrated into pedagogical knowledge and content knowledge and becomes a holistic view of the entire knowledge base that teachers need to master in order to effectively apply technology in teaching and learning (Willermark, 2018). Koehler et al. (2013) argue that there is no single digital technological solution that solves every teaching and learning situation. Nevertheless, it is essential that teachers learn how pedagogical, technological and content knowledge can interact and compensate for the problems that the students are facing in school. In table 1 gives a summary of the interaction between the knowledge domains: Technological, Pedagogical, and Content Knowledge in the TPACK Model.

*Table 1. Summary of the interaction between the knowledge domains: Technological, Pedagogical, and Content Knowledge in the TPACK Model (Koehler et al., 2013)*

| **Technological, pedagogical, and content knowledge, TPACK** (Koehler et al., 2013) |
|---|
| **Pedagogical knowledge, PK**. Pedagogical knowledge and content knowledge interact when teachers can us taught content together with subject didactic knowledge in the students' teaching practice. |
| **Content knowledge, CK**. Technical knowledge and content knowledge interact when teachers can use technology in a particular subject content. |
| **Technological knowledge, TK**. Technical knowledge and pedagogical knowledge interact when teachers can integrate technology into an educational purpose. |

However, the TPACK-model has been widely disseminated, but also criticized for not being practically useful, due to inaccurate and insufficient definitions. TPACK is difficult to distinguish between the different overlapping three domains of knowledge, especially between pedagogical knowledge and content knowledge, but they can also be contradictory (Ruthven, 2014). In particular, the technology domain has been criticized for being vague and too extensive (Willermark, 2018). A literature review of 55 peer-reviewed journal articles by Voogt, Fisser, Pareja Roblin, Tondeur and van Braak (2012) about the theoretical basis and the practical use of TPACK showed different understandings about TPACK, especially on technological knowledge. Teacher knowledge and beliefs about pedagogy and technology were intertwined and determined whether a teacher decided to teach using technology. Only the use of technology is not enough, it is about how it is used and coincide with the other two domains. Another systematic review by Wu (2013) on the TPACK research from 2002 to 2011 show that the number of TPACK studies has significantly increased with various research methods.

Further systematic literature review of 107 peer-reviewed journal articles concerning the use of TPACK in empirical studies published from 2011 to 2016 by Willermark (2018) show a variety of approaches and instruments to examine teacher TPACK, but the ways TPACK is operationalized as a measuring instrument are often implicit and make comparison of results difficult. A promising strategy for the development of TPACK is active involvement in (re)design and enactment of technology-enhanced lessons. For example, show a study by Mouza Karchmer-Klein, Nandakumar, Ozden and Hu (2013) that participants experienced significant improvements in all TPACK domains when they applied their teaching and knowledge in practice with technology.

One strategy is to supplement TPACK for the analysis of VLE or VR with media and visual skills online and in the classroom through Gees (2007) five learning principles for clarifying the outcome. The learning principles include the following:

- *Semiotic principle* refers to understanding interrelations within and across multiple sign systems as text, video, photo, picture or simulation / replication.
- *Identity principle* refers to using role-play to better understand real and virtual concepts of identity / identities.
- *Achievement principle* refers to providing inherent rewards for learners of all levels of skill, customized to each learner's level, effort, and growing mastery, and signaling the learner's ongoing achievements.
- *Practice principle* refers to providing ample opportunities for practice in ways that engage and empower the learner.
- *Discover principle* refers to maintaining a learner-centered focus, with opportunities for the learner to experiment and make discoveries on their own.

Gee (2007) stresses the interreflective function of language that is not limited to information communication. It has a much wider mission because the language, partially supports social actions and identities, and partially forms belonging within cultures, social groups and institutions. The mission of the language is closely intertwined and are produced, reproduced and transformed by human action. He claims that schools, workplaces, families and academic researchers have much to learn about learning through VLE and VR and respectable video games that enhance learning in which students are active, critical, and reflective producers of knowledge, as a kind of "embodied" learning, i.e. the holistic blending of mind and body embedded in a material, social, and cultural world. The user allows to be producers when they are engaging in this four-part cycle: probe, hypothesize, reprobe, and rethink, and afterwards reflect on how these actions expands their learning.

Gees (2007) five-part cycle can also be complemented by Dewey's (1997) description of the five phases or aspects of reflective thinking in experience and education:

1. *Suggestion* refers to the actions to get one or more ideas for possible solutions. Thinking is an action directed at oneself and that examines its aims and conditions, resources, tools, difficulties and obstacles.
2. *Intellectualization* refers to the difficulty or confusion formed into a problem to be solved, or a question that requires an answer. The problem and the solution arise simultaneously.
3. *The hypothesis* refers to guiding idea initiatives and direct observations and other operations in the collection of actual material into an assumption, which becomes not only a possibility, but a tested and perhaps measurable probability.
4. *Reasoning* refers to mental development of the idea or assumption, a suggested solution that can be long-sought or wild speculation. As a whole, they are reshaped to evolve into conclusions in different directions.
5. *The testing of a hypothesis through action* refers to experimental confirmation or verification of the assumed idea.

The five phases do not follow any set pattern. Equally important in reflective thinking is the reference to the past. The ability to structure knowledge is largely due to the student reviewing past facts and ideas and relate them to each other on the basis of a new base, namely on the basis of the conclusion reached by the student.

## Example of Analyse

The findings of the answers (N=57) to the open-ended question about the teacher educators need of education to use a virtual learning environment with different tools (Amhag, Hellström, & Stigmar, 2019), such as lecture material, lecture recordings, online face-to-face webinars, F2F, chat, discussion forums, and other online resources i.e. interactive white-board (Amhag, 2016a; 2016b; 2017; 2020), firstly display that more than one-quarter of the teacher educators (26.3%) have need of continuing didactic VLE-training with an emphasis on their work and use of *content knowledge, CK* with digital tools and what works in digital teaching (Koehler et al., 2013):

- Continuing training in how I can use all the components that the learning tools we use can offer.
- How can the tools be used; how can tasks be created, smartboards or other tools in the classroom for using in teaching?
- Continuing education with the aim of building on what works in teaching/learning, not necessarily recreated and innovative.
- Such training that provides concrete examples of how other teacher educators work with digital teaching.

According to Gees's (2007) five learning principles, it is obvious that teacher educators have to understand the *semiotic principle* that there is a connection within and between several sign systems, such as between text, video, photo, image or simulation of a learning situation e.g. through role play, to better understand real and virtual concepts of *principle of identities*.

Secondly, almost one fifth of the teacher educators (17.5%) convey that they also need *technological knowledge, TK* to interact with a particular *content knowledge, CK* (Koehler et al., 2013). For this reason, support is needed in concrete and practical use of a virtual learning environment with different technology and tools:

- The biggest obstacle in using digital tools is the technology. Making it work without problems is stressful!
- Wishing that we had more courses that technically concretize and practically show how web-based education can be developed and used in higher education. I have mostly learned everything myself.
- To have time to get to know the programs a bit more (always lacking time to learn new teaching methods) and to get more support for using new computer programs in teaching.
- Practical workshops and concrete examples of applications.

These answers demonstrate that the teacher educators also need to know which specific technology is best suited for addressing subject-matter learning and by *practice principles* in ways that engage, motivate and empower the students (Gee, 2007), e.g. by creating features and applications, or even make changes of technology.

Third, a surprising result is that only a few teacher educators (3.6%) highpoint the need for pedagogical knowledge, PK to improve their competence that can provide educational benefits with learning in a virtual learning environment and digital teaching (Koehler et al., 2013):

- Continuing to focus on the pedagogical benefits of learning rather than on the technology itself (especially for the students, but also the teachers).
- The type of continuing education where experienced and pedagogically competent teacher educators participate in the design of teaching.
- Didactic support directly in core activities, preferably for the teacher team.
- An education based on pedagogical/didactical working methods and discussions how digitization can promote students' learning.

These answers highlight problems with teacher educators' *pedagogical knowledge, PK* and the interaction with *content knowledge, CK* for their subject didactic knowledge in the teaching practice (Koehler et al., 2013). These teacher educators have not fully *discovered the principles* to maintaining a learner-centered focus, with opportunities for the learner to experiment and make discoveries on their own (Gee, 2007). Likewise, not fully identified the pedagogical surplus value in their own teaching and learning context in a virtual learning environment with different tools. A focus on technological knowledge itself is not enough; pedagogical/didactical content knowledge and teaching is needed.

In summary, show the analysis of the teacher educators answers, based on TPACK interrelated dimensions of technological-, pedagogical- and content knowledge (Koehler et al., 2013), as well as Gees (2007) five learning principles, that it is important to discover the interrelation with the use of technology in an educational purpose with a particular subject content. Noteworthy is that teacher educators have a great need for different digital support and continuing education on how to use a virtual learning environment with different tools:

- A varied - information-based as well as practical with guidance because I experience that my skills are very low.

- You need everything regularly, a little refill for repetition and new inspiration.
- Practical concrete advice: do like this, have good support available all the time, and always greater access to digital tools.
- Workshops and supervision in my own digital teaching, based on my prerequisites, in suitable locations and with appropriate equipment.

## CONCLUSION

The main conclusions that may be relevant and applicable for virtual learning in smart education worldwide are the following:

- The selected articles in education and social sciences expands the knowledge about virtual learning in smart higher education, and how these processes can be a tool for motivated and student-centered learning in a resource-enriched virtual learning environment with technology-embedded tools.
- Higher education and academic researchers have much to learn about teaching and learning in a virtual learning environment, VLE and in virtual reality, VR that can enhance student-centered learning in which the students are active, critical, and reflective producers of knowledge, as a kind of "embodied" learning, i.e. the holistic blending of mind and body embedded in a material, social, and cultural world (Gee, 2007).
- It is important for university teachers to discover the pedagogical surplus value in their own teaching and learning context through the use of technology in an educational purpose with a particular subject content in a virtual learning environment with different tools.

## REFERENCES

Amhag, L. (2016a). Mobile technologies for student centered learning in a distance higher education program. In *Wearable Technology and Mobile Innovations for Next-Generation Education,* (pp. 184-199). IGI Global. https://www.igi-global.com/book/wearable-technology-mobile-innovations-next/142108

Amhag, L. (2016b). Mobile technologies for student centered learning in a distance higher education program. *Blended Learning: Concepts, Methodologies, Tools, and Applications*, *4*, 802–817. doi:10.4018/978-1-5225-0069-8.ch010

Amhag, L. (2017). Mobile-Assisted Seamless Learning Activities in Higher Distance Education. *International Journal of Higher Education*, *6*(3), 2017. doi:10.5430/ijhe.v6n3p70

Amhag, L. (2020). Student Reflections and Self-Assessments in Vocational Training Supported by a Mobile Learning Hub. *International Journal of Mobile and Blended Learning*, *12*(1), 1–16. doi:10.4018/IJMBL.2020010101

Amhag, L., Hellström, L., & Stigmar, M. (2019). Teacher Educators' Use of Digital Tools and Needs for Digital Competence in Higher Education. *Journal of Digital Learning in Teacher Education*, *35*(4), 203–220. doi:10.1080/21532974.2019.1646169

Black, P., McCormick, R., James, M., & Pedder, D. (2006). Learning how to learn and assessment for learning: A theoretical inquiry. *Research Papers in Education*, *21*(2), 119–132. doi:10.1080/02671520600615612

Bousfield, T. (2017). *An Examination of Novice and Expert Teachers' Pedagogy in a Mixed-Reality Simulated Inclusive Secondary Classroom Including a Student Avatar with Autism Spectrum Disorder*. Electronic Theses and Dissertations. 5559. https://stars.library.ucf.edu/etd/5559

Chatti, M. A., Agustiawan, M. R., Jarke, M., & Specht, M. (2010). Toward a personal learning environment framework. *International Journal of Virtual and Personal Learning Environments*, *1*(4), 66–85. doi:10.4018/jvple.2010100105

Covington, M. V. (2000). Intrinsic versus extrinsic motivation in schools: A reconciliation. *Current Directions in Psychological Science*, *9*(1), 22–25. doi:10.1111/1467-8721.00052

Dewey, J. (1997). *Experience and education*. Simon & Schuster.

Dieker, L., Hynes, M., Hughes, C., & Smith, E. (2008). Implications of mixed reality and simulation technologies on special education and teacher preparation. *Focus on Exceptional Children*, *40*(6), 1. doi:10.17161/foec.v40i6.6877

Ellaway, R., Poulton, T., Fors, U., McGee, J. B., & Albright, S. (2008). Building a virtual patient commons. *Medical Teacher*, *30*(2), 170–174. doi:10.1080/01421590701874074 PMID:18464142

Gee, J. P. (2007). *What Video Games Have to Teach us About Learning and Literacy*. New York, NY: Palgrave Macmillan.

Gregory, S., & Wood, D. (2018). *Authentic Virtual World Education*. Springer. doi:10.1007/978-981-10-6382-4

Herrador-Alcaide, T. C., Hernández-Solís, M., & Galván, R. S. (2019). Feelings of satisfaction in mature students of financial accounting in a virtual learning environment: An experience of measurement in higher education. *International Journal of Educational Technology in Higher Education*, *16*(1), 20. doi:10.118641239-019-0148-z

Hwang, G. J. (2014). Definition, framework and research issues of smart learning environments – a context-aware ubiquitous learning perspective. *Smart Learning Environments*, *1*(1), 4. doi:10.118640561-014-0004-5

Jensen, L., & Konradsen, F. (2018). A review of the use of virtual reality head-mounted displays in education and training. *Education and Information Technologies*, *23*(4), 1515–1529. doi:10.100710639-017-9676-0

Kearney, M., Schuck, S., Burden, K., & Aubusson, P. (2012). Viewing mobile learning from a pedagogical perspective. *Research in Learning Technology*, *20*(1), n1. doi:10.3402/rlt.v20i0.14406

Kennedy, M., & Dunn, T. J. (2018). *Improving the use of technology enhanced learning environments in higher education in the UK: A qualitative visualisation of students' views*. Contemporary Educational Technology.

Koehler, M. J., Mishra, P., & Cain, W. (2013). What is technological pedagogical content knowledge (TPACK)? *Journal of Education*, *193*(3), 13–19. doi:10.1177/002205741319300303

Koschmann, T. (1996). Paradigm shifts and instructional technology: An introduction. *CSCL: Theory and Practice of an Emerging Paradigm, 12*(4), 18-19.

Lanier, J. (2017). *Dawn of the new everything: Encounters with reality and virtual reality*. Henry Holt and Company. https://www.immersivt.se/ar-glasogon-en-oversikt/

Leite, W. L., Svinicki, M., & Shi, Y. (2010). Attempted validation of the scores of the VARK: Learning styles inventory with multitrait–multimethod confirmatory factor analysis models. *Educational and Psychological Measurement*, *70*(2), 323–339. doi:10.1177/0013164409344507

Mouza, C., Karchmer-Klein, R., Nandakumar, R., Ozden, S. Y., & Hu, L. (2014). Investigating the impact of an integrated approach to the development of preservice teachers' technological pedagogical content knowledge (TPACK). *Computers & Education*, *71*, 206–221. doi:10.1016/j.compedu.2013.09.020

Olofsson, A. D., Fransson, G., & Lindberg, J. O. (2019). A study of the use of digital technology and its conditions with a view to understanding what 'adequate digital competence' may mean in a national policy initiative. *Educational Studies*, 1–17. doi:10.1080/03055698.2019.1651694

Ott, M., & Freina, L. (2015). A Literature Review on Immersive Virtual Reality in Education: State Of The Art and Perspectives. *The 11th International Scientific Conference eLearning and Software for Education.*

Ott, M., & Tavella, M. (2009). A contribution to the understanding of what makes young students genuinely engaged in computer-based learning tasks. *Procedia: Social and Behavioral Sciences*, *1*(1), 184–188. doi:10.1016/j.sbspro.2009.01.034

Pantelidis, V. S. (2009). Reasons to use virtual reality in education and training courses and a model to determine when to use virtual reality. *Themes in Science and Technology Education,* 59-70. https://files.eric.ed.gov/fulltext/EJ1131313.pdf

Pantziaras, I., Fors, U., & Ekblad, S. (2015). Innovative Training with Virtual Patients in Transcultural Psychiatry: The Impact on Resident Psychiatrists' Confidence. *Diss. PLoS ONE, 10*(3), e0119754-e0119754. doi:10.1371/journal.pone.0119754

Peterson-Ahmad, M. (2018). Enhancing Pre-Service Special Educator Preparation through Combined Use of Virtual Simulation and Instructional Coaching. *Education in Science*, *8*(1), 10. doi:10.3390/educsci8010010

Robertson, J., & Howells, C. (2008). Computer game design: Opportunities for successful learning. *Computers & Education*, *50*(2), 559–578. doi:10.1016/j.compedu.2007.09.020

Ruthven, K. (2014). *Framework for analysing the expertise that underpins successful integration of digital technologies into everyday teaching practice. In Mathematics Teacher in the Digital Era: An International Perspective on Technology Focused Professional Development* (pp. 373–393). Retrieved from http://www.eblib.com

Takala, M., & Wickman, K. (2019). Collaborative Case-Based Virtual Learning in Higher Education: Consultation Case in Special Education. *Journal of Digital Learning in Teacher Education, 35*(4), 236–248. doi:10.1080/21532974.2019.1646171

Voogt, J., Fisser, P., Pareja Roblin, N., Tondeur, J., & van Braak, J. (2013). Technological pedagogical content knowledge–a review of the literature. *Journal of Computer Assisted Learning, 29*(2), 109–121. doi:10.1111/j.1365-2729.2012.00487.x

Wegerif, R. (2007). *Dialogic education and technology: Expanding the space of learning* (Vol. 7). Springer Science & Business Media. doi:10.1007/978-0-387-71142-3

Willermark, S. (2018). Technological pedagogical and content knowledge: A review of empirical studies published from 2011 to 2016. *Journal of Educational Computing Research, 56*(3), 315–343. doi:10.1177/0735633117713114

Wu, Y. T. (2013). Research trends in technological pedagogical content knowledge (TPACK) research: A review of empirical studies published in selected journals from 2002 to 2011. *British Journal of Educational Technology, 44*(3), E73–E76. doi:10.1111/j.1467-8535.2012.01349.x

Zhu, Z. T., Yu, M. H. & Riezebos, P. (2016). A research framework of smart education. *Smart Learning Environments, 3*(1), 4.

# About the Author

**Lisbeth Amhag**, Associate Professor, PhD in Education/e-Learning at the Faculty of Learning and Society, Malmö University, Sweden. Since 2002, Lisbeth has been teaching students in Teacher Education 90 ECTS at distance and campus; as course leader and examiner/assessor at ground and advanced levels; and as mentor for students in didactic training. Has published several national and international articles about on-line learning and assessment and is active in the further development of distance education and mobile learning activities. Lisbeth received Malmö University Teaching Award 2010. Previously, Lisbeth worked as a television journalist, media teacher and as web editor.

# Index

## M



## O



## P



## R



## S



## T



## V

www.ingramcontent.com/pod-product-compliance
Lightning Source LLC
LaVergne TN
LVHW081322300926
849161LV00008B/1847
* 9 7 8 1 7 9 9 8 4 1 8 3 8 *